STUDIA THEOLOGICA 2
UNISA 1984

GOD'S CREATIVE ACTIVITY THROUGH THE LAW

A constructive statement toward a theology of social transformation

S.S. MAIMELA

UNIVERSITY OF SOUTH AFRICA
PRETORIA 1984

ISBN 0 86981 299 8

Printed by
Gutenberg Book Printers
Pretoria West

Published by the
University of South Africa

For Mabel, Gracious and Lebogang
My faithful companions

Preface

In the face of increasing repression and oppression by fascist, racist, and totalitarian regimes in our time in the name of law and order, it can no longer be taken for granted that what the conception of law is is understood by those who happen to rule in various countries. Indeed, confusion rather than clarity on the issues of law and order seems to be evident and, consequently, some regimes use the law as a political weapon against their opponents who are often held as "political prisoners". Other regimes use law as a reactionary means to preserve the *status quo* merely out of preference for stability even if the existing order does not serve useful human needs. Others still use the law as a means for the transformation of social environment and distribution of services. Because of these conflicting and often contradictory notions of law — *unless the conceptions of law and order are to mean anything, and whatever the powers that be say they mean, thereby rendering them vacuous* — the question of what the law is and means as well as what ends it serves, must be opened anew and answered positively.

To be sure, there has always been disagreement on what law is and how best it must be used to structure social relationships, seeing that tyranny is the oldest enemy of humankind. But the cirisis of law in our time is more serious because of the sophistication of methods of oppression as well as the rapidity by which governing authorities are installed and changed either through military coups or through the democratic processes. And because even worst, dictators can decree and claim that what they do is in the "national interest" and therefore in accordance with law and order, or peace, the task to give a theological accounting on the emergence of social institutions and how they might be understood to serve God's holy loving will for the promotion of general welfare for humankind, has never been more urgent for churches and theologians.

Theologians may not have all the answers, but neither can they afford to remain mute and without a word for political arena where the law is constructed and exercised because, whether it is admitted or not, political actions — involving the people of God as they do — necessarily have theological dimensions unless it is assumed that God is indifferent to what happens among humans and to what they do to one another. Indeed, if God's people do not ultimately belong to the ruling authorities in such a way that they might do what they please and choose with them, then a question of what it is that humans do when they engage themselves politically to design laws or mechanisms that regulate their sociocultural and economic interrelationships, must be given a theological answer. For, unless a positive answer is given theologically, it will be irresponsible for churches and theologians to urge every person to "render obedience to the governing authorities; for there is no authority except from God, and those in authority are divinely ordained" (Rom. 13:1).

The churches and theologians have made and continue to make mistakes in their understanding of the political sphere. More often than not the realm of the law and order, peace and justice are taken for granted when it is assumed that these realities exist "out there", and that the duty of governments is merely to preserve them rather than to create them. Consequently, theologians see no need to establish criteria by which *de facto* law and order could be sharply distinguished from distortions. It is not sufficiently appreciated that the realm of creation and political practice and, therefore the realm of the law whose proper administration is the *raison d'être* of existence of states, are also the realm of promise. Therefore, every and each human institution cannot be assumed to be the servant of God's creative will of love and as such can claim that it is ordained by the Creator until it truly serves divine love and justice. Indeed, each human social structure must be regarded with suspicion until it satisfies definite criteria, that is, of truly serving God's love and justice. This must necessarily be the case because, the fact that human institutions can be instruments in the service of divine purposes must remain a statement of hope, promise and expectation until such time that they are not only divine instruments *de jure,* but their creation become realized when they become *de facto* institutions that serve God's loving will and justice for the benefit of humans.

The challenge before the church and theologians is both to give a theological account of the emergence of human structures, and to provide a functional criteria by which these institutions can be judged either positively or negatively with reference to their ability and adequacy as instruments that truly serve divine purposes. Until this is done, it would be useless for churches to talk about the preaching of the divine law to the earthly social relations, especially when the relevance of this divine law to socio-political structures is not and cannot be demonstrated theologically. The upshot of what is contended here is this: as long as the connection between the divine law of love and human instrumentality cannot be taken for granted in view of the fact that laws are often abused, and as long as there is a gulf between a theory with reference to divine law and practice in political action, theology has the duty to establish the circumstances under which the legitimacy and legality of human structures can be upheld as divine instruments in service of divine love.

In the present essay, I have attempted to address some of these concerns. Not only have I redefined what the law is, but I have also tried to demonstrate theologically the connection between the divine and the human creativity through the law. In fact it does more than that, for it tries to demonstrate that the realm of law and order and thus of justice are promises that await to be created, and that their creation is a victory that must be won in order for them to be brought to realization even in their imperfect forms. In this way, it was possible to provide constructive and critical criteria by which what is demonic can be distinguished from the good. The essay attempts to situate the notion of the divine law within an all-embracing context of God's ongoing creativity and thereby grounds law theologically in the dynamics of the divine creative *logos.* The law is defined as the agent of divine creative will of love, and because it is the instrument of the creative *logos* it is constitutive of all finite reality; for it was through the utterance of the divine command that creatures came to be and were given their reality. Also, as the means of divine creativity, the divine command is the mode by which the Creator is present and related to the creatures and, consequently, it is the means by which humans become involved in the dynamics of ongoing creativity and thus becoming co-creators with God in the production of the world and history.

Because the essay arose out of a painful awareness that current notions of law are inadequate responses to the problem of oppression and demonic structures in our time, the study not only provides a fundamental grounding of the law theologically, but also lays a foundation for the construction of a theology of social and cultural transformation, a theology solely needed if Christians are to have better self-understanding as "foot-soldiers" in their role as initiative agents of creative change for the humanization of social structures. For it is when the law is understood positively as a means by which we become involved as God's instruments in the dynamics of ongoing creative process in the world that a better theological accounting for the emergence of human institutions, that may become servants of divine holy will of love, might be given.

Without the help of many people this study would not have been undertaken and completed. Unfortunately, it is not possible to acknowledge the help of everyone but only those who have directly contributed to the outcome of my labors. I wish to express a special thanks to Professor Kaufman, of Harvard Divinity School, who as my advisor fathered my theological growth by forcing me to think again and again through his critical comments and encouragement. Professor George Rupp, the Dean of Harvard Divinity School, was very helpful in the early development and writing of this work at Harvard University, where the project originated. Professor Ian Siggins, as a Luther scholar, gave me invaluable suggestions. The Reverend, Dean H.N. Seloane, my spiritual father, has been a faithful companion and to his continued encouragement I am eternally indebted. Last but not least, I wish to express my hearty gratitude to my wife, Mabel, and our children, Gracious and Lebogang, who through their love, warmth, and support created a homely climate conducive to serious theological reflection.

Simon S. Maimela
University of South Africa
Easter, 1981

Contents

Introduction

The following study attempts to present a theological understanding of the divine law and its uses in the world. Even though it opens with an exposition, which is followed by a critique of a debate between two theologians on law and gospel, this study rightly stands on the side of construction rather than exposition as such.

To be more precise, the objective of the study is to construct, outline, develop, and offer an alternative theological understanding of the conception of law, one which is, in our opinion, much more adequate, comprehensive, dynamic, and positive, and one which will emphasize God's creative activity through the use of law as the Creator involves human beings in the dynamics of continuous creative process. Therefore, it is an additional work in a field which is crowded with thousands of pages of articles, books and dissertations. It was with some reluctance that we undertook to add another work to this area, but we were consoled by the fact that it was a necessary investment of our energy.

The study fulfills a real need, because the current state of discussions on law is very much unsatisfactory; it leaves most believers confused or unsure as to whether there is anything positive and creative about God's use of law. An impression is given, partly due to omission or overemphasis, and partly due to inadequate grounding of law in the creative will of God, that law functions always in the negative; that it is something which threatens human peace; that it makes troublesome demands which cannot be fulfilled and, thus, preys on human weakness; that it subordinates humanity to unreasonable demands of an authoritarian God. Our contention is that the divine law, when it is correctly understood, is positive, creative, and inspires rather than suffocates human creativity; it need not function in the negative because, in its use, God never demands servile obedience to unreasonable demands that cannot be met. Rather, God intends to involve our mature humanhood in the dynamics of divine creative activity, so that we may become willing participants in an historical creative process in which natural and social environments are being transformed as structures arise in order to promote healthy human relationships, nourish life, and serve God's creative will of love.

It is our contention that it is in the above sense of involvement in the dynamics of divine creative activity that prophets called for obedience to God's law, but the content of that obedience was always specified with reference to social justice and righteousness. For God never uses the law so that it should be obeyed for its own sake, nor does the Creator require obedience for obedience's sake. On the contrary, the utterance of the command and its use by God aim no further than the ordering and structuring of the world and human community so that life and health of all creatures may be enhanced. Our thesis is that the divine command, in so far as it is no less the word of the Creator than the gospel, is characterized by a divine willingness to give life as well as God's goodness and love.

However, the fact that the negative understanding of the function of law lingers on, and that believers are often unsure as to whether there is any way that they can speak about the goodness of activities which comes through the use of the divine law – activities which can be judged as good and positive here and now for their lives – are indications that theology has not always understood law positively nor adequately in its cosmic creative aspects. Indeed, theological treatises not only reveal that there are major flaws in the conceptions of divine law, and that there has been conscious or unconscious suppression of certain elements that clearly indicate that law functions positively when it is understood in the light of God's creative activity, but also point to a need for reconstructions of our theological conceptions of the law – if the negative attitudes toward it are to be overcome.

More than in any other area, theologians have not, in our opinion, performed at their best. They have not been as responsible in their conceptions of the law, nor have they clearly spelled out its status and positive function in relation to God's creative dynamics, as they have done in the conceptions of the gospel in its relation to God's redemptive dynamics and healing acts of love through Jesus Christ. That is, the relationship between the gospel and redemption is crystal clear and here most problems have been pretty much solved. Consequently, no believer is left unsure, uncertain, or confused about the positive function of the use of the gospel by the Creator. But this cannot be said with regard to God's use of law. Indeed, the relationship between its employment and God's dynamics of continuing creativity is and remains unclear, confused, and unsettled for most believers. The result has been a reinforcement of negative stereotypes about law; that its use by God is necessarily negative and therefore uncreative; and that its use is never for the good and well-being of the human community.

Indeed, one is left with the impression that theological talk about the law aims at leaving no chance for a positive view of the law, that it does not lead believers to the conclusion that the use of the law leads to life for the community here and now rather than to idolatry (its worship) or to the conclusion that its content is nothing else but God's will of love which is essentially creative, but rather to something else that is neither creative nor divine will of love.

To illustrate the conceptions of divine law which often lead to the conclusion that its use by God functions mainly in the negative and in an uncreative manner, two typical representatives of two basic approaches to the understanding of the law in Protestant theology have been selected for study, analysis, and critical evaluation; these steps constitute Part one and Part two.

One of these theologians is Werner Elert, who is both a Lutheran and a representative of the traditional order where the law is understood to precede the gospel and a representative of the theology of "orders of creation," one which grounds its conceptions of the law in the doctrine of creation and in God's ruling activity in the world. Elert uses his sources in the most imaginative, insightful, and illuminating manner. Because he is exceptionally original, Elert gives us the best as well as the worst elements of the Lutheran theology and of the theology of "orders of creation."

The other theologian is Karl Barth. He stands at the opposite end of the traditional order of the law-gospel dialectic and tries to reverse this order so that theology should now begin with gospel rather than with the law. No one can represent Karl Barth better than he himself could, and thus he will be the spokesman for this new theological point of departure, anchored in the Christology. I believe a majority of Protestant theologians stand to the middle, in between, or to the extreme right or left of the positions of either Barth or Elert. Consequently, even though Barth and Elert have been selected as the main focus of this study, the positions which will be taken in support of, or in opposition to, these two theologians will also have some bearing on the positions of many other theologians. This relevance will be established as we move from the critique to the constructive part of this study. Thus, this study has broader implications beyond its immediate data of focus.

As it should become clear in the critique and the constructive statement, some of the conceptions which have reinforced the negative understanding or stereotypes about the function of the law are: The use of law is often contrasted with the gospel. The law is construed as the enemy who accuses or makes demands humans cannot fulfill. The gospel, however, grants forgiveness and comfort freely. The law becomes the slavemaster from whom the gospel rescues us. This means that theological understanding of law is often based on the fact of sin from which we must be saved. Thus, the use of law is often correlated with the fall; and its use is viewed as retributive because the sinner must be punished. Or because the sinner has misused God's gift of law, the divine law of freedom comes in to liberate from self-incurred enslavement to a misused law which results from the sinner's attempt to use the law to judge between good and evil. Also, the use of the law is often correlated with a fallen creation which now must be protected against the threat of chaos. God uses the law to conserve the creature and protect it from destruction. Law becomes *remedium peccati.*

Barth, to be sure, modifies the retributive function of the law when he suggests that God kills through it only to make alive, and that God's commands are permissions, releases, and freedom to act beyond inherited human morality for the goal of sanctification. But, again, the context is one of sin from which law rescues and permits. Further, the heavy hand of a human subordination to the Deity which is characteristic of Barth's understanding of the Christian life means that the law is viewed as functioning negatively, to rein us in and to contain human irresponsibility. The most serious problem is one of the tendency to lodge conceptions of law within the narrow and one-sided categories of justification of human beings before God at the expense of social righteousness of one human being before others. Judged against such an eternal moral principle (absolute) before God, the law functions always in the negative because human actions can never be regarded as adequate, good, and fulfilling its demands. Also, equally serious is a theological attempt to anchor conceptions of the law on the doctrine of creation, especially when such a conception of creation is static, one which understands creation as a complete and finished event.

The same is true when law is anchored on, or correlated with, redemption of humanity in Christ (through the gospel). Often the result is that salvation becomes the only arena in which God is understood as presently active. Creation and the use of the law become merely a prologue to the salvific act, and their realities are often swallowed up by the gospel. Hence, law functions almost like the gospel; God through it elects, frees, and invites for fellowship. The distinctiveness of creation or law is lost and obscured by their "Big Brother," namely the gospel. These examples should suffice and serve to sharpen the reader's anticipation of the kinds of problems that are to be dealt with in detail later on.

Over against such static conceptions of creation — a creation that is complete and in which law functions to preserve it — there is no room for continuous activity of the law in the positive sense of continuing creation in the present. It functions negatively to preserve the creature for the sake of salvation. Against this it will be contended that it is a mistake to try to ground law in anything but the dynamic, continuous creative will of God, because failing to do so will lead neither to a correct understanding nor to an adequate expression of the positive, creative, and dynamic aspects of God's use of law. Also, it shall be contended that positive and creative functions of the divine law can be given their adequate expression only when enough attention is paid to the social or political uses of law in the human community and in the cosmic dimensions of God's creative activity. Only in this way will the correct understanding of the command not be swallowed up by, nor be forced into, a narrow definition of the law as a consequence of some preconceived framework in which justification before God, rather than human beings, is the only decisive thing.

It is our thesis that any emphasis on human obedience to the divine law to which we must submit — and yet one which is incapable of being fulfilled — is misleading. Such an understanding of the law needs to be radically corrected by stressing the participatory theme wherein God's use of the command is understood to involve human beings in the divine dynamics of creativity, so that their actions may lead to responsible, creative works for the human community.

The emphasis on the participatory theme rather than on servile obedience to some authoritarian law is taken up in Part three. There we utilize Luther's theology, which stand as the bone of contention between Barth and Elert. This was not the only reason. The main reason was that we found resources in Luther that helped us both to develop the participatory theme (which is lacking in Barth and Elert) and to overcome the negative emphases on law which are inherent in the "obedient motif." Also, we found Luther's theology particularly helpful in the development and construction of a much more comprehensive, adequate understanding of the law that is both dynamic and positive – where the totality of the divine process of creativity through the command is taken up. When the law and its uses are understood against the context of the all-embracing creativity of God, it becomes possible to see that a restriction of the meaning of the law to religious justification before God is just but a part of its whole activity, because God also employs the command outside of the human sphere or conscience.

On this cosmic scale, the use of the law is pretty much concerned with the penultimate, relative, and limited good as well as the love that a finite creature can show to another. Luther's resources are used as a bridge; an exposition of his theology here is not intended in its totality. Once the bridge is built, we do appeal to other pertinent sources in our outlining of the third alternative understanding of the law, one which promises to overcome both the polarization of conceptions of the law inherent in the views of Barth and Elert, and also to broaden our understanding of law in such a way that the positive, creative, and dynamic aspects of its function are given rightful expression. At the same time,this alternative conception of the law takes unto itself useful insights from these two theologians.

Part three presents a systematic and constructive statement in which various parts are outlined and held together in a pattern of layers of description and argumentation. Because we try to explore and analyze various parts that normally belong together – as we distinguish between them for the sake of clarity – the subject-matter lends itself to an inevitable overlap at which the reader is asked not to take offense.

The substance of the discussion in the constructive part runs thus: God's command should be understood as embracing the totality of the divine creative process in which the world and history are being made.

That is, the command is that creative *logos* that expresses a quality in the being of the Creator, a quality that is both a power and an activity which brings into existence things that are not by means of the uttered word (command, fiat). Also, the command involves finite agents who become partners in the production of the world and history, a production which has been going on and still continues until creation reaches its completion in the coming Kingdom in which dwelleth justice, righteousness and God's love.

Our constructive statement is offered with the full realization that some of its parts may require refinement of prose, conceptualization, style of presentation, and even recasting, in order that our reflections here be given the clarity of expression they deserve. Our hope is that the weakness of stylistic refinement will not obscure the contribution being made there toward an ongoing discussion about what the divine law means. Indeed, it remains our hope that the alternative proposal toward a theological understanding of the law, which this study offers, has a future insofar as it tries to ground the theological conception of law sufficiently in the dynamics of the divine creative will of love, thereby giving our understanding of the law and its use by God a fundamental theological grounding.

Therefore, this constructive study is submitted in the humble but confident hope that it will go a long way towards clarifying the relationship between God's command and the dynamics of divine creative activity, which began with the inception of history and will continue until the completion of creation at the end of history. If it can clarify this relationship in such a way as to remove any uncertainty and doubt from the minds of believers that the law functions positively and creatively within the context of God's creative activity, this study will have achieved its modest objective. For it is our firm conviction that it is important to believers that, to the extent that the relationship between the gospel and the redemptive dynamics of God's healing love is explicitly clear, so must be the relationship between the dynamics of God's creative will and the function of the command (law). For in the use of the command, the Creator does not express anything that is contrary to the divine will, a will which is characterized by God's creative love and a willingness to give.

PART ONE

The law in the theological debate between Barth and Elert

Chapter one

Law and gospel in the light of Christology

> It is St. Paul's opinion that in Christendom a certain difference be learned and comprehended both by preachers and Christians between the law and faith, or between the command and the Gospel..... For this is the highest art in Christendom which we should know, and when one does not know this you cannot be absolutely certain of who is a Christian in the presence of a heathen or a Jew. For everything rests absolutely upon this difference.[1]

Luther, following the Pauline discovery that there are two means through which salvation can be attained, here contends that it is of crucial importance that law and gospel be distinguished in Christian preaching. Therefore, the distinction as well as the relation between them once again became central issues during the Reformation. In a sense, theology has continued to grapple with these two issues up to the present, and the distinction and relation between law and gospel have not been fully resolved.

However, since Luther made this declaration, the debate in theology has shifted somewhat, and the issue about the distinction can no longer be stated in black and white contrasts. Indeed, in the nineteenth century as well as in the twentieth century, many other problems arose, and theologians became less persuaded that "everything rests absolutely upon this difference." Today we are living in a period in which meanings about the concepts of law and gospel have become problematic, to say the least. Therefore, there is no agreement among theologians about what these concepts really mean.

1.1 THE CONCEPT OF LAW : A THEOLOGICAL PROBLEM

To be sure, theologians are aware that the material content of what the gospel is believed to consist of often differs from one theologian to another as, for instance, between a conservative evangelical theology and a radical liberation theology. But it is above all the conception of the law which has become the most thorny and difficult for theology to deal with, because its meaning has changed radically since the time of the Reformation.[2]

For this reason, while Luther could polemicize against those who wanted to impose Mosaic law on sixteenth century Europe on the presupposition that his readers knew what the law was (for it is written on everyone's heart),[3] and does not bother to explain in detail what he means by it except to state what it does to the conscience, the assumptions with which he made his claims cannot be affirmed without further ado because the concept of law itself has become a theological problem and unclear to most people. Many factors have contributed to the problems theology is faced with in its discourse about law.

An important factor (among many others) is the rise of modern positivistic theory of law, which prepared the way for an enthronement of totalitarian states which manipulate laws for the interest of those who happen to be in power.[4] Prior to the triumph of positivism, however, the law was often understood as a means of meting out justice rather than as a tool of the ruler, because there was always the possibility of appealing to God, the source of law, and therefore of justice and morality. This does not mean to imply that there were no cases of arbitrary use of power, but as long as a metaphysical basis of justice was a common point of departure between the citizens and the rulers, who were simply carrying out a divine mandate the possibility of declaring existing laws illegal and unjust in the name of a higher justice remained. But with the collapse of the metaphysical basis of laws, justice, and morality – or even categories of wrong and right in the political process, because what matters is what the majority say the law is – it becomes difficult to find another basis, source, and criterion by which what is validly legal can be distinguished from what is illegal. The result is to resort to the existing will of those who control power and author laws until the victims overturn the party in power, thereby becoming lawgivers themselves.[5]

However, legal positivism proved defenseless in the face of "lawlessness of law" from which most people have suffered painfully in the twentieth century. We are all acutely aware that states commit atrocities and brutalities against their citizens because laws have become servants of states or ruling parties rather than servants of justice. Under the cloak of positivistic legal theory, states do not go beyond "justice" of the actual law in statute books because a question of unjust laws no longer arises. Justice is determined by what the law (in state books) says, rather than requiring that law be what justice aims at.

It is not altogether surprising that in legal positivism the question becomes: "What does the law say?" (as conceptualized by the state in statutes), and not what "ought the law to say?" in view of justice which must be served. For the same reason, positivism has penetrated the courts and judges are held captive even to "lawless governments" because they see their duty as that of interpreting what the powers that be say law and the will of the state are.

Because our century has suffered from what some of the theologians cited above call the "crisis of law" (because of its enslavement to the powers that be), there are many questions theologians in the twentieth century found themselves facing, such as: What is the proper theological response to legal positivism? Are Christian ethics and natural law supplementary or opposed to each other? Is the Christian interpretation of law to be derived from Christology (Barth)? Or is law to be grounded in the first article of the creed and, therefore, in the theology of "orders of creation" (Elert)? It is against this background of the problem of "lawlessness of law" and of "crisis of law," arising (for the most part) out of positivistic legal theory, that the debate of Barth and Elert has to be understood; for each of them tries as best as he can to give a proper theological response to this difficult problem about law.

1.2 THE GOSPEL IS THE BASIS AND GROUND OF LAW

Karl Barth, in his essay entitled "Gospel and Law,"[6] to the surprise of many Lutherans, proposed a radical re-orientation of theology when he suggested that the law-gospel dialectic be reversed. This means that now theology must begin with God's revelation in Christ and, therefore, with the gospel rather than with the law. Since the timing of the publication of his essay is not without significance, a brief outline of the events at this time may be helpful.

First, at the time of the publication of his essay, Barth had already made decisive theological shifts in his thinking. Von Balthasar holds the view that as early as 1927 Barth had come to the conclusion that theology must no longer begin with "homo religiosus" but with the miracle of God's gracious self-disclosure in Jesus Christ.[7] This meant that Barth could no longer live with a theology that focused attention not on the gospel but on statements concerning Christian awareness, depriving believers of a reliable norm. Hence, when he re-wrote his *Church Dogmatics* in 1932, Barth criticized the earlier existential-philosophical point of departure he had used in *Die christliche Dogmatik* (1927).[8]

Now, instead of starting with the analysis of the phenomenological and existential mode of believers, Barth argued that it was only in the light of the grace and therefore of Christology that humans saw the impossible nature of their existence. It was, therefore, to be expected that he would give an angry retort to Brunner's suggestion that God could be known through natural revelation apart from Jesus Christ.[9] Barth could only affirm uncompromisingly, even at the risk of arrogance, that the true God and the Father of Jesus Christ could not be known otherwise than as this God disclosed the divine self to humanity. This Christocentric starting-point had much to do with Barth's attempted reversal of the traditional order where law was construed as preceding the gospel.

Second, Barth was deeply distressed by the bankruptcy of Lutheran ethics, whose exponents saw no conflict between Christian ethics and the war policies of Wilhelm II.[10] The situation was made even worse when, during Hitler's regime, some Lutheran theologians tried to use Luther's idea of the two kingdoms – based on the traditional formulations in which the law precedes the gospel – to subordinate the concept of divine law to national ethos, or *Volksnomoi.*[11] Barth warned about a mortal danger to the Church herself as a result of the support the *Deutsche Christen* party gave to Nazi practices. Not only was God's law compromised by a Nazism that wanted to dress itself in Christian trappings while doing violence to religious truths to serve its ideological interests, but also this ideology sought recognition from the Church as a new divine revelation.

It was against this background that Barth took active leadership in the formation of the "Confessing Church" in order to oppose Nazism and the aberrations of the *Deutsche Christen* party. Thus, in the very year in which Barth proposed that theology should begin with God's revelation in Jesus Christ, he was also playing a dominant role in the formulation of the famous "Barmen Theological Declaration."[12] In both documents – "Gospel and Law" (1934) and "Barmen Declaration" (1934) – the same Christocentric spirit is at work. Barth declared that Jesus Christ was the one word of God and denounced as false any teaching that left the impression that there were areas of life that did not belong to Christ but to another Lord.

Therefore, Barth's attempted reversal of the traditional order, viz., Law-Gospel, is the result of a general theological program, and of an attempt to affirm the Lordship of Jesus Christ in both Church and State, and to understand all Christian doctrines in the light of Christology because in Christ we have to do with "the eternal beginning of all ways and works of God."[13] We now proceed to unpack just how Barth went about implementing this theological reorientation. Because the theological shift preceded the political implications of his views, it is proper that we should first of all take up his Christological point of departure.

1.3 THE LAW IS A NECESSARY FORM OF THE GOSPEL

Barth's main thesis is that Jesus Christ is the basis, the foundation, the ground, the form, the content and the goal of God's claims, or law,[14] for in Him God has declared His most decisive and Absolute Word of truth. This means that in order to understand what God has done, what is wanted from us, and what God wants to do with us, we must begin with the concrete event in which God's will is disclosed. By beginning with this event of God's self-disclosure, Barth assures us, we shall be anchoring our understanding of God's law on that which is indubitably certain rather than on abstractions.[15] Further, he insists that we correctly define and understand the meaning of God's law only when we speak of its content, which is the gospel of God's grace.[16] And this grace of God is what is designated by the name of Jesus, one whom we cannot hurry past because it is in Him that the divine content of the divine claim, or the substance of God's law, is addressed to us.[17]

On the basis of this thesis, Barth launches an attack on the traditional formulations of the issues. He charges that the traditional order is dangerous because it discusses law without considering first what its legitimate content is, namely grace. This is because it thrives on separations of the law from the gospel and fails to see what holds the two together. Indeed, it is so content with separations that it never moves beyond the duality and the apparent conflict between law and gospel. The result is that the law appears to have a different content from that of the gospel, and the impression is created that the divine law is a separate, alien, and independent reality alongside of, and in competition with, the gospel.

What is more, the traditional order of the law-gospel dialectic not only courts the danger of the law being presumed to be untouched by the gospel and its content of grace, but it also leads theologians to tend to talk about the law in abstractions. Indeed,the traditional order is full of generalities and ambiguities of every kind,[18] especially when theologians imagine that God's law is an empty positivity which they must give content to;[19] or when they think that God's law is ever uttered *in abstractio* rather than in concrete forms;[20] or when they confuse the command with imagined and self-constructed concepts of law and norms of behavior, which can be reducible into natural laws, propositional rules of conduct, or *sensus communis moralis,* and which, as such, is directly identified with God's law.[21]

These abstractions, Barth concludes, are misguided because they are predicated upon a mistaken belief that God's will, and thus His law, is manifest to us in all things that come from the hand of the Creator. In reality, this is not the case. In their failure to root the theological understanding in the event of God's self-revelation, traditional conceptions of law are no different from human theories and interpretations which are not expressions of divine law, the content of which is not identical either with natural law, abstract reason, or *Volksnomoi* (people's laws which people happily invent and give content and control to).[22]

All these views are illegitimate because they have not allowed themselves to be shattered and judged by a radical confrontation with the real law of God, the content of which is always grace. And because God's true law cannot be adequately understood when the traditional order is followed, Barth exhorts us never to go that way. He writes:

> If the Law is also *God's Word,* if it is further *grace* that God's Word is spoken aloud and becomes audible, and if grace means nothing else than *Jesus Christ,* then it is not only uncertain and dangerous but perverse to want to understand the Law of God on the basis of any other thing, of any other event which is different from the event in which the will of God, tearing in two the veil of our theories and interpretations, is visible as grace in both form and content.[23]

Barth does not say that gospel and law should not be distinguished. He does concede that it is proper to see them as different, and argues that to think they are identical is contrary to biblical witness because neither is law gospel nor gospel law. But the need to distinguish them should not be a pretext to separate them in such a way that an impression is created that the law we speak about is not a law which is completely enclosed in the gospel. To separate them in this manner contradicts the witness of the scripture which attests that Jesus Christ is indubitably the grace of God who is both the form and content of the law. Consequently, it is a serious error to construe law differently from biblical testimony as if it were "a second entity next to and outside of the Gospel,"[24] and as if the law we are talking about were not the one which has been fulfilled in all its great or small, external and internal parts[25] by Jesus Christ, who is the indubitable "evident grace of God" as well as the content of law.

Indeed, to separate law in such a way that it is understood apart from its criterion, ground, basis, form and content – Jesus Christ – is to fail to see that God's law is neither antithetical to the gospel nor is it something which "precedes or only follows it."[26] Rather, beyond all separations or distinctions, beyond all duality and contradictory voices which we often hear from the gospel and the law, there is a higher word of the Father which is greater than this duality.[27] And because the Word of the Father is one Word of truth and light in whom there is no "variation or alteration of light and darkness," this Word preserves the unity of gospel and law. In the presence of this one Word, which is the sovereign grace of God, all duality is silenced. Therefore, because the content of this Word of the Father is grace "under all circumstances," even when God speaks to us in judgment and death, what it says must properly and ultimately be grace and nothing else.[28]

Any word which may differ, or proclaim anything that is contradictory to God's grace must be rejected.[29] Indeed, even the law in its apparent distinction from the gospel must be included in the unity of God's Word of grace and be understood relative to this content of grace. And just because the gospel has grace as its content, one which includes the content of law, Barth concludes, the gospel (which is the same thing as Jesus Christ, or God's grace in Him) has priority over the law, and the latter must be construed always as relative to the former.[30] Therefore, Barth further contends "anyone who wishes correctly to approach our subject must speak first of the content of the Gospel, of God's *grace.*"[31]

The claims Barth is making in his attack on the traditional order of the law-gospel dialectic are subtle and often insightful. Indeed, he seems to be saying that there is one valid manner in which the Christian God's law can be truly and rightly understood. This God is not a general God but a particular and concrete God. He has to be understood in the context of divine goodness and gracious works that have been concretely done to us. In these works, God acted concretely, and the divine will was given concretely. Because there is a particular and concrete place where such a concrete will and law are given, theologians have no liberty to by-pass this concrete event. This means that the correct place to seek God's will, and therefore His command, is where the Christian God has revealed the divine self indubitably and unequivocally.

It is, as we know, this place where the event occurred and nowhere else that our talk about God begins to move from the generalities and abstractions of human laws to the concrete and true divine law. Only when we begin with grace, or with "what happened in Bethlehem, at Capernaum and Tiberius, in Gethsemane and on Golgotha, and in the garden of Joseph of Arimathea,..[32] and therefore with the veritable event in which God uttered His One Eternal word, that we truly can learn what God wants from us.

In the light of Christology, Barth reminds us, it becomes clear that the grace of God was resolved in heaven but in time became actualized and declared here on earth. As this happened, namely, as God graciously gave the fullness of His deity and love to us in Christ, it became clear that He was laying claims on us. It is as God gives us Jesus Christ that His sovereign, commanding grace also proclaims and establishes His authority over "man."[33] The grace which is thus being actualized restores man and reconciles him to the Creator; it is "infinite divine favour to man, as decided from all eternity, which is actualized in this way," thereby determining man to acknowledge in obedience God's sovereignty over him.[34] Consequently, Barth contends that "divine claims" never stand alone *in abstractio* "either as that which precedes the occurrence and proclamation of the grace of God, and is therefore primary," but are "always the form, or shape, or garment of grace."[35]

This means that divine law is, in effect, nothing more than "a repetition of the reality of grace and the promise of grace," by drawing our attention to the fact that God is gracious to us and also wants to be respected, loved and feared.[36] And because the divine claim is addressed to us by the gospel itself, "Law is completely enclosed in the Gospel," and provides a form, or veil to the claims of the gospel which are addressed to us. For the same reason, Barth holds that the gospel is never found alone in an unveiled form because:

> Jesus Christ Himself as the Gospel, revealed, proclaimed, offered to man and affecting him, is always clothed in the Law, hidden in the manger and swaddling clothes of the commandments, His divine commanding. We cannot believe or have Him except in this form. It is in this form, and only in this form, that He is powerful and true.[37]

In his essay of 1934, the unity of gospel and law was expressed, as it was later repeated elsewhere,[38] within the context of the covenant. Barth contends that because the law must follow the promise, its unity with the gospel must be understood as analogous to the tablets of the Decalogue from Sinai, which "were in the ark of the covenant."[39] Expressed differently, the distinction between gospel and law must be expressed in such a way that their unity remains, so that law is understood as *"hidden and enclosed* in it as in the ark of the covenant,"[40] while the gospel must be construed as "always *in the Law* as that which is manifested, proclaimed," thereby claiming man through the garments of commands.[41]

In addition, this unity was expressed as one of form and content of one and the same Word of God. It was out of the concern to preserve their unity as well as an attempt to understand the gospel-law dialectic in the light of Christology that Barth came up with his novel and startling definition of law:

> Thus, we can certainly make the general and comprehensive statement that the Law is nothing else than the necessary *form of the Gospel,* whose content is grace.[42]

In Barth's theology, law is highly particularized because, as we have already pointed out, grace is identical with Jesus Christ who is the one Eternal Word of God and therefore His grace, which was resolved in eternity but actualized in time. Jesus Christ is the only grace of God and its form, and therefore He is both Gospel and Law. Consequently, He is the criterion, the canon over all laws. And any law that does not come from Him, attest to Him, and has any other content must be disregarded because a word or law "with a really different content would as such ..... not be a word of the triune God."[43]

However, by identifying the command of God with "the person of Jesus Christ," who, as such, is "the ground and content but also the form of the divine claim,"[44] Barth has lifted God's law from the immanental plane to the transcendental sphere. The result of this move is that he is able to provide a specific criterion by which God's law can be distinguished,which promises to overcome the problems that the traditional law-gospel dialectic tends to pose. Barth also wants to make it abundantly clear that the command of God cannot be regarded as continuous with each and every historical law without further qualifications. We shall return to this point later.

1.4 THE LAW OF GOD DOES NOT BIND BUT SETS FREE

A second important thesis of Barth, which follows from his formal definition of law, is this: The command of God whose content is grace, is the law of freedom – it grants permissions and sets free. His position, once again, is diametrically opposed to the traditional formulation which contends that law accuses us in order to drive us to the gospel and, therefore, to Christ.

As he develops this thesis, Barth reminds us again and again that the God who claims us in Christ is the one who is already for us. This means that divine claims have to be understood in the light of the covenant which is actualized in Christ. The Christian God is one who is eternally good, one who wants to confer this goodness upon us so that we may participate in it. God's law is given because God does not want us to be left to ourselves and to dominations by foreign lords under whom we have placed ourselves.[45] It is therefore the command of a loving God, one who comes to rescue and liberate us. It is the advice and directive of a friend, God, who is totally for our salvation and for our good.[46] It invites to a fellowship with our Creator; it is intended to actualize our sanctification because it is given so that it may be translated into actions in our lives.[47] For unless the proclaimed grace of God is translated into the life of the believer "even the most serious talk about the will and command of God is only idle chatter."[48] It is as the proclaimed grace shapes lives of Christians that their determination for an existence in a covenant relationship with God is brought about.

However, as it is addressed to us, the divine claim, even in its assaults on us, cannot contradict God's eternal resolve to love and to have us for Himself. It remains a law of life rather than of death. It remains God's renewed offer to have us and be for us, an offer which we have repelled in our disobedience. And because it testifies to the grace of God, and presupposes that God is already for us, it is never an imperative which says to us: "You should!" Rather, it is an indicative which says: "You shall be!"

From this, Barth concludes that the meaning of all the Ten Commandments is this: You, who have other gods, who make pictures of God, who profane God's name, who kill, who are disobedient to parents, who steal, etc., etc., *shall believe,* you *shall love* and fear God, and this is God's law.[49] Because it is God's grace which is being proclaimed in these divine claims, it is to this grace and nothing else that we must respond. For "by it and by it alone we are challenged. To it and to it alone we are responsible."[50]

Further, Barth contends that God's law is not only an invitation, advice, and a directive to live in conformity with this form of the gospel but also grants permission. It wants us to be free, genuinely free for God, to do what we can do willingly. Therefore, God's command never appeals to human weakness nor to human fears; it does not intimidate us. It instills courage. It quickens and refreshes because, as the law of God's grace, it proclaims life and liberty. Consequently anyone who stands under God's law and is not refreshed and quickened is not obedient but lives according to his personal determination. Such a person has "succumbed to the temptation to eat of the tree of the knowledge of good and evil, which is forbidden him for his own good."[51] And this is precisely the case because God's law of man's sanctification has the teleological power to eventuate what it promises: the restoration of man to divine likeness and thus to fellowship with God.

Moreover, this sanctification or determination of man for a covenant fellowship has been actualized through Christ who, on our behalf, has fulfilled the demands of the law and whose life counts also as ours. Since Christ intercedes for us daily, "there is no longer any excuse for human weakness."[52] Nor is there any reason why we cannot make use of the real permission at our disposal so that we may be free. Indeed, there is no reason why we cannot allow God's command to separate us from all forms of domination including our own desires and lusts. In this way, we would be letting the command of God's grace engage us "so that we may begin at last to live in real freedom and joy," and "act on our own decision — our very own, the one which corresponds to our determination."[53] For God's command wants to *set us on our feet,* and it is against us only inasmuch as we are against ourselves.[54]

By contrast, Barth argues that the nature of other commands differs sharply from God's command because they "hold fast," because they are a binding and fettering. They consist of powers and dominions and authorities that restrict the freedom of man. They are not releases of liberation, nor do they grant freedom. Rather, their essence is one of total "refusal of all possible permissions. This is what distinguishes the sphere of these commands very sharply from that of the command of God."[55] This is precisely the case because the real command of God's grace ultimately liberates, even though "it always has *in concreto* the form of one of the other commands, even though it says: 'Thou shalt' and 'Thou shalt not,' even though it stands before man, warning, disturbing, restraining, binding and committing."[56]

The law of God and all other laws do the same; yet it is not really the same because the command of God is not only of a "true and best friend," but also "will always set us free along a definite line," regardless of the garment or guise in which it meets us.[57] It assaults us radically, to be sure, but this is because it does not follow that God should be soft with us when He turns to us through His gracious claims. Rather, He remains absolutely hard as a sovereign God from whom man has no escape. Indeed, to "know His grace is to know this sovereign ty," and to "accept His grace can only be to acknowledge this sovereignty, and therefore the duty of obedience to Him, or, briefly, to become obedient to Him."[58]

In the course of the above differentiations between God's law which sets free and liberates and other laws which bind and forbid, Barth alludes to an important problem. He concedes that alongside God's law there are other laws, and other uses of laws other than the sanctification of man. He refers to commands such as natural or historical objects which often call our attention, observation, consideration, investigation or understanding for their own sake. There are mathematical axioms and logic as presuppositions for understanding the world that have the form of commands. Also human knowledge can assume the role of an intellectual command.[59]

There are commands which are related to decisions of human will, such as compelling necessities of life from food and drink, warmth and sleep, to those of seeing that our life always has the qualitites of dignity and honour. There are commands of foresight and discretion forced upon us by education or custom. There are commands of someone who may be in authority, etc. Barth sums up his observations by saying that "man and race, in every possible grouping and historical circumstance, stand under a plethora of commands."[60]

However, Barth insists that these commands are different from God's command, and that it is wrong to confuse the two kinds of commands. The reason is simply this: the "plethora of commands" in essence binds while the command of God sets free and permits. The question which immediately arises, however, is this: How are these "other commands" related to the divine command? Barth's answer to this question is highly dialectical : God's command must be differentiated from all "other commands, *not just relatively but absolutely,* with the distinction of heaven and earth,"[61] even though the divine command also comes to us through these other commands.

Barth puts this eloquently, when he writes:

> It is indeed the case that — without prejudice to its particular form — the claim of God's command *always* wears the garment of another claim of this kind.[62]

He further adds that objects around us that assume the form of commands, necessities of life even in their primitive forms that appear to be more than a reflection of human will or authority, can be the garment of the command of God.[63] In a sense, they participate in divine authority and dignity.

It is obvious that Barth, while he is unwilling to identify the divine command directly with this "plethora of commands," does concede that at given times God may claim us "wearing the garment of another" seemingly human command. He tries very hard to reassure us that faith is capable of distinguishing which of these commands is truly God's. For the believer knows the true content of God's command, namely, the grace or the gospel. Moreover, even in the guise of another command, it *always* grants a definite freedom, as we have pointed out earlier. And because it can be distinguished by its content and function, Barth contends that any command that may come to us appealing to our fears must be rejected, especially if what it demands

> ..... is not the crying of children to the father whom they have at last found again, if the appeal is not to our innocence, if we are not stirred to action as those who are righteous, as those whom God is for and therefore nobody and nothing can be against.[64]

He concludes that our submission to all other commands, even if made in the name of God, can only be provisional and not binding. However, once it becomes clear that they are commands of another voice — rather than that of God who has redeemed us in Christ — then we must declare them "wrong," for "it is only with a violated conscience that we can submit to them."[65]

Barth is absolutely certain that, apart from faith, the law is a harmful thing; it can only be misused and will ultimately kill us or tear us in two parts.[66] Faith alone can distinguish God's true law from all other laws which are fettering and kill, rather than give life. Faith is also necessary because it alone can maintain the simultaneity of obligation and permission which are inherent in God's law of liberty. Also, Barth argues that, even though this law of double-edged conjunction can be apprehended only through the "eye" of faith, it does not follow that God's law can be reduced to ethical propositions or systems. For every definition of the divine command, which is both a demand and a permission (i.e., law in the form of the gospel) leads inevitably to legalism or lawlessness – no matter how we try to construct and conceptualize it. We shall discuss this in detail later.

1.5 GOD AS THE LORD OVER THE LAW IN BOTH CHURCH AND STATE

Armed with a redefined conception of law – a true law of God and thus of life and liberty, one which is the form of the gospel whose content is grace – Barth responded to the political climate of his time during which conceptions of law were in a serious "crisis" because of lawlessness, a problem which has already been alluded to in our opening remarks.

Once the traditional order of the law-gospel dialectic had been completely turned upside down, Barth was in a position to affirm the Lordship of Christ both in the Church and in the people outside her walls. He bases his thesis on a number of observations, some of which are: Since there is no second revelation outside God's indubitable and unequivocal self-disclosure in Jesus Christ, it follows that, if we are truly to speak about God's law and not human law, we cannot avoid talking about *the only divine law there is,* namely, the one which is already enclosed in the gospel, which comes from and points to Jesus Christ.

For any law which does not attest to Him, and which really has a different content than God's grace, cannot be the Word of the triune God. Moreover, since there are no people to whom God does not give His command – for Christ does not idle outside the walls of the Church but does His work, and since there is no humanity outside the lordship and humanity of Christ[67] – it follows that there can never be a law (in the state) that is the sacrosanct source of God's revelation parallel to, in competition with, or independent of Jesus Christ who is the One eternal Word of God, and who is not only the form and the content of the proclaimed grace of the Creator but also the criterion and norm of all laws.

Consequently, because God's law is available nowhere except as the law which is enclosed and proclaimed by the gospel, Barth is persuaded that the Church has the mission to bear witness to this law in her confrontation with the civil community. Indeed, the Church must uphold and live out this divine directive in her life, but also she must bear witness to it and remind the state that the law which all men must obey is the one which is revealed in Jesus Christ, and that the state cannot have free reign in the realm of law. For the real Lord over the law is Christ Himself both in the Church and in the civil community.

In witnessing to the divine law, the Church will be fulfilling her prophetic function "against all presumption and disorder, against all irreverence and lawlessness of men."[68] In another place, Barth states his case more pointedly, when he writes:

> The Church would not be the Church if, in her very existence, but also in her teaching and keeping of the Law of God, *its commands,* its *questions,* and its *admonitions,* and its *accusations* would not become visible and apprehensible also for the world, for state and society — even if they do not receive precisely the message concerning the grace of the triune God.[69]

It was observed above that Barth, very early in the Church struggle against the nazified *Deutsche Christen* party, was very worried by the perversion to which law was subjected. As a result, he became unwilling to speak about God's true law and human laws in the same breath. This also explains his almost angry rhetorical observations in which he complains that human autocracy takes possession of God's law under the deception of sin; that we deform and distort God's law by exposing it to all kinds of falsifications; that we confuse God's law with our pretended obedience to human fabricated laws, such as natural law, practical reason, or people's law *(Volksnomoi).*[70]

Barth adds that as long as God's law is misused, deformed, and confused with our human laws, the result can lead only to "the arbitrary use of Law of might *(Faustrecht)* which the present German government has openly proclaimed — with ever increasing unscrupulousness — making Germany the land of fear and terror."[71] All this, according to Barth, is a consequence of human forgetfulness that God is the Lord over His true law, and that everything else is a misuse and sinfulness.

In the face of the "lawlessness" and "misuse of law" in Hitler Germany, and in the face of open support given Hitler by the *Deutsche Christen* movement, Barth had to investigate the historical causes for this "crisis of the conceptions of law." He located the origins of this crisis of law, and therefore of Christian ethics, in Luther's distinction between the law and the gospel, a distinction which, in time, led to the separation of the kingdom of this world from the Kingdom of God. It is true that the Luther whom Barth had in mind was the Luther who was expounded by some Lutheran theologians of the 1930s.

These theologians, under the influence of a theology of "orders of creation" *(Schöpfungsordnungen)*, preached a theological ethics that was completely uninformed and untouched by the gospel. For this ethics "moved in the direction of idealistic philosophy, natural theology, and an autonomous primal revelation of God in creation." The result was that it preached a "pseudo-Lutheran view of orders of creation (for example, in the state), which made them a 'law unto themselves.' "[72]

However, during the heat of debates and controversies, Barth made no distinction between Luther and a "pseudo-Lutheran" theology which took an active part in twisting and distorting the notions of law, distortions which it defended as Luther's own theology. In order to counteract these distortions, Barth had to strike at the source of this Lutheranism, for he saw a kind of historical continuity between his contemporaries and Luther himself. Absolutely convinced that the current distortions under Hitler were traceable to Luther, Barth commented:

> Let me just sketch the causes and the real significance of this fact as I understand them ..... The German people suffer from the heritage of a paganism that is mystical and that is in consequence unrestrained, unwise and illusory ..... They suffer from the heritage of the greatest Christian of Germany, from Martin Luther's *error on the relation between Law and Gospel, between the temporal and the spiritual order and power.* This error has established, confirmed and idealized the natural paganism of the German people ..... Hitlerism is the present evil dream of the German pagan who first became christianized in a Lutheran form.[73]

Barth repeated his accusation of Luther in his letter of 1940 to the Dutch Protestants charging that Lutheranism was responsible for German paganism because of its separation of creation and law from their ground, basis, content and goal : the grace of God in Christ or the gospel. As a result, German pagans used Lutheran doctrines of the authority of the state to justify a Christian support for nazist socialism, and in the process, ordinary Christians felt obliged to submit to the powers that be, in spite of distortions to which God's law had been subjected by those powers.[74]

It is beyond the scope of this study to enter the debate as to whether Barth's harsh criticism of Luther arose from a correct understanding of Luther's teachings themselves or from a simple confusion of Lutheran aberrations by the *Deutsche Christen* movement for which Luther cannot be held directly responsible. What is of importance in this criticism is that Barth brought to the surface some of the crucial problems that have plagued Lutheran doctrines; and his criticisms must be accepted, in the context of the period in which they were uttered, as a welcome correction to obvious weaknesses of his contemporary Lutheran scholars. The issues he raised deserve attention, even if one does not agree with his diagnosis.

Barth's contention seems to be that over and above the question of a right understanding of the true law of God, the question of a correct Christian understanding of the government or the state, which administers laws, is equally important. For the state and the administration of law are inseparable and imply each other, whether these laws are distorted or correctly administered by the powers that be.

Therefore, the purification of the conception of the state became another important element in Barth's theological attempt to overturn the Lutheran understanding of law and state — both of which must now be fully grounded in God's revelation of His eternal will in Jesus Christ. What makes this twofold purification a compelling necessity rests on Barth's understanding that there is a single will and therefore one law of God, the administration of which is the *raison d'être* of states. But, in order for proper administration of this will and law to be possible, the right understanding of the state itself is the first order of priority.

Barth begins his discussion of the state from the Christological perspective by regretting the fact that up to his time theology had failed to proclaim the Lordship of Christ over the law both in the Church and in the state or civil community. He contends that, because the Church had failed to proclaim this Lordship, she could not speak with authority, and she had to restrict herself to a false piety in the face of modern "lawlessness" of godless secularized states. He finds it particularly unsettling that Reformation theology itself had dismally failed to ground its teaching about human law and political authority in Christology.

Instead, these teachings were grounded in a "particular *ordinatio* of divine providence, necessary on account of unconquered sin."[75] He suggests that this was a serious error that contributed unwittingly to the present problem, namely, the unChristian conceptions of both law and state as well as their proper roles. Rather than connecting their understanding of the doctrines of justification and sanctification of the sinner by God in Christ (doctrines they wholeheartedly championed) with human justice and, consequently, allowing God's justification to be the *sole source and norm or criterion* of human justice, the Reformers allowed the Church and state to stand juxtaposed with a dangerous tendency toward separating them.[76] This juxtaposition gave the impression that the Christian was governed by the gospel, on the one hand, and the law, on the other.

As we have already observed, the culprit, in Barth's opinion, is Luther who, by insisting on distinctions between the law and the gospel, between the secular and the spiritual realms, only prepared the way for an eventual exclusion of the state from the sphere of the Lordship of Christ. This, according to Barth, is because Luther and other reformers made the magistrates rather than God the exclusive lords over the law, while the Church limited herself to the role of persuading people to submit subserviently to the magistrates.

Barth humorously charges both Luther and Calvin at this point with a dismal failure to ground law adequately in Christology, when he writes:

> Their thoughts about the Electoral Prince of Saxony or the Council of Zürich or Geneva would have been clearly disturbed, had they concentrated intensively upon the person of Pilate. But did the Reformers see clearly at this point? ..... Might they not perhaps have found here a better foundation for what they wished to say on this matter? Here, at any rate, we must try to fill up the gap which they have left.[77]

Barth comments with a feeling of regret that the Reformers failed us, when they failed to see the gravity of the confrontation between Jesus and Pilate and the "demonic" power of this age to which the Church stands diametrically opposed as a homeless pilgrim.

However, because he has seen this clearly, when the gospel precedes the law, he finds himself compelled to give us a radical Christological grounding to political ethics. Not only does Barth derive the law and state from Christology (God's veritable self-disclosure), he also tries to unite the functions of the state and the Christological work, when he writes:

> ..... that power, the State as such, belongs originally and ultimately to Jesus Christ; that in its comparatively independent substance, in its

> dignity, its function, and its purpose, *it should serve* the Person and the Work of *Jesus Christ and therefore the justification of the sinner.*[78]

Barth justifies his assertions here by reminding us of the message that Jesus' confrontation with Pilate (Jn. 18:36) has for us. It is a parable for us regarding the manner in which the Church and state must be understood in their relationship. In this encounter, there is everything the gospel allows us to say about the state, that is, the state often fails to uphold God's law. And this means that the state can become a "demonic" and irresponsible "dragon" that tramples over justice. Nonetheless, Jesus Christ did not withdraw his recognition that the state and its power come from the hand of God, by dying at the hands of Pilate "not in accordance with the state law, but in spite of this law, in accordance with a different law and in flagrant defiance of justice."[79] And just because Pilate failed to take himself seriously as the state representative, justice was miscarried. But this does not nullify the fact that his power came from above. For the state can be compelled to do good and render service.

Therefore, it is not altogether surprising that, even where Pilate failed to uphold the law, and therefore justice, he still became

> ..... the involuntary agent of and herald of divine justification; while at the same time he makes it clear that real human justice, a real exposure of the true face of the state, would inevitably have meant the recognition of the right to proclaim justification, the Kingdom of Christ which is not of this world, freely and deliberately.[80]

Barth sees in this encounter the crucial moment in history, for here the relationship between the order of earthly justice of the state and the order of justification of the sinner in the Kingdom of God became clearly established. Consequently, he not only believes that his grounding of the law in the gospel is justified but also argues that the administration of the state, and therefore of law in the civil community, cannot be said to have "nothing to do with the order of justification." For in this administration of the state, it does not mean to imply that we are "moving in the first article and not the second article of the creed. No. Pontius Pilate now belongs not only to the creed but to its second article in particular!"[81] and therefore to the gospel, which is the grace of God.

Having grounded the law and the state in Christology, Barth is in a position to reject any correlation between state, or law, and the Fall, or sin.[82] For God's true law belongs first and foremost to the Kingdom of God. Thus, the state cannot be a product of sin but is an order of divine grace within which we do not meet a strange and general Creator but rather the Father of Jesus Christ who is the Lord over the law, both in the Church and in the state. When the state is corrupt, it must be reminded that this is not its original purpose, so that it might be forced to render service to the glory of Jesus Christ, its Lord. For the "angelic" powers of the state "have been created in the Son of God as the image of the invisible God," and thus "they do not belong to themselves but stand at the disposal of Jesus Christ. To them, too, His work is relevant."[83]

Furthermore, this Christological relationship between Church and state is expounded by Barth through the use of metaphors of two concentric circles.[84] Christ is Lord over the law both in the Christian community, which forms the inner and smaller circle, and in the civil community, which forms the outer and larger circle. Their common centre is the Kingdom of God which is now being proclaimed by the Church. In their mutual interrelationship and confrontation, the problem of law and the "crisis of law" should be raised and answered within the sphere of the Church.[85]

Because laws of the state are worldly, in the sense that they do not reckon with the basic law of the Christian community, and therefore of the Kingdom of God, the preaching of the justification of the Kingdom by the Church must, by implication, help to establish a true system of law, the true state here and now.[86] This is particularly important because the state and its law can become demonic by virtue of their ignorance of the true law of the Kingdom, Jesus Christ.

However, Barth cautions that the Church should not endow herself with predicates of the heavenly state in her confrontation with the secular state and its laws. But an equation between the two communities is also out of the question. The Church must not impose her law on the state (outer circle) even though she is ordered by the superior law of Jesus Christ.[87] What she should do is witness to this law of the Kingdom. And because the two communities have a common center, the state is capable of analogy, i.e. reflecting Christian truth and reality. Since this imaging does not arise spontaneously, the state (outer circle) should be constantly reminded of this higher law of God which is known and proclaimed by the Church. When it is reminded that its power is not an intrinsic but a transmitted authority, the secular community might subordinate itself to God's law.[88]

Also, Barth reminds us that the Church is a preliminary form of the future of humanity in which salvation, accomplished in Christ, exists. The upshot of this is that the Church stands in the midst of the larger community (state) to remind humans of the future.[89] Concretely, this means that the Church has a political mission or vocation and must tackle social problems. Because her life is exemplary, the first concern of the Church is to serve humanity rather than a particular ideology.

Since God's justification gives men the basis for human justice, the Christian community must stand for the rule of law and, therefore, of justice. The Church will have to take sides with the poor, the sick and oppressed because Christ, too, came for the sick and the lost. Christians will fight for human liberty because their life is based on one baptism, is lived under one Lord and one Spirit. Because God gives many gifts, Christians will work for a separation of political powers into the legislature, the executive, and the judicial branches. And because God discloses Himself, Christians should oppose all secret politics and diplomacy.[90]

Most of the analogies Barth draws between the Christian community and the outer community, such as justice, responsibility, separation of powers, and open diplomacy, betray his bias towards democracy. He is aware of this and argues that it is no accident that democracy developed under the influence of Christianity. He justifies this derivation of democratic government from the gospel on the basis of his exegesis of the "deepest and most central content of the New Testament,"[91] and he therefore rules out the possibility that any kind of government, except democracy, is compatible with the gospel.[92]

Barth is deeply aware that Christians do not have ready-made answers for social or political ills in the outer community (state). But he does not believe that this is a persuasive justification for any "unevangelical conservatism" that distorts God's good news into a "pseudo-gospel," when Christians become "dumb dogs" in their submission to "ruling powers" or become "afraid to tackle the social evils with which they are confronted."[93] Consequently, he urges Christians to act responsibly and will the governments they pray for. In this way, they will be going beyond merely paying taxes and servile obedience.[94]

Above and beyond the willing of states, however, the Church and her law must itself be exemplary, a "pattern for the formation and administration of human law generally, and therefore of the law of other political, economic, cultural and other human societies."[95] In order to do this, the Church must both bear witness to the superior and living law of the living Jesus Christ and be constantly obedient to Him. For it is in listening to Jesus Christ that the Church can discover what the will or the law of God is. In her relation to those who do not have this eternal law and its knowledge, the Church must show that their *worldly law,* which the civil community regards as binding, has ceased to be the last word. For it cannot enjoy unlimited authority and force.[96]

The Church must proclaim that other possibilities exist – not merely in heaven but also on earth, not only one day but already now – than those which the civil community thinks it must confine itself to in the formation and administration of its laws. While the Church cannot directly portray Jesus Christ, who is the living Law and Lord of the whole world (including the state), she can remind the world that this law of the Kingdom is already set up on earth. For already there is on earth an order which is based upon the radical transformation of the human situation, an order that tries to manifest this transformation to the world. The Church, as the manifestation of this transformed human existence, must demonstrate that any *ius humanum* drawn up in ignorance of Jesus Christ is necessarily defective and provisional law that needs to be corrected so that it might at last point beyond itself to a higher and better Law of the Kingdom, the Lord and Redeemer, who is Himself *ius divinum,* the only true law of God.[97]

Barth also reminds the Church that her exemplification of God's law remains *ius humanum* like other laws. Nonetheless, because it results from the Church's attempt to think of and acknowledge Jesus Christ, it is better and has advantages over all other human laws – even in her relative and broken formulation, or portrayal of this divine law. Therefore, the Church must keep on attesting and pointing to this *ius divinum,* which will come with the heavenly Jerusalem, "in the glory of eternal life," and will exercise its lordship "over every sphere of life."[98]

We now have come full circle in our exposition of Barth's conception of law. What has become clear is that he rejects any attempt to identify God's law directly with any human law (including the Church's law). The law of God, whose ground, basis, content and criterion is nothing other than God's grace in Jesus Christ, is beyong human reach, control, or formulation. The Church must proclaim and portray, represent and exemplify it to the world outside despite imperfections of its portrayals. Because the true law is the living Lord, who Himself is Lord over all laws in Church and state, any other law can, at best, attest only defectively to it. But any other law which does not come from, point to, or proclaim Jesus Christ directly or indirectly must be rejected because it is the law of another voice instead of the only one Word of God.

Barth's formulations are appealing. He not only has effectively grounded law and therefore the state, which administers law, in Christology, he has also provided criterion by which God's law can be distinguished from all corrupt "lawless" laws of secular governments. The break with the past, or traditional order of the law-gospel dialectic and the purification of the concept of law, with a definite content, has become total and successful in Barth's comprehensive reformulations of the Christian understanding of the law and state.

Barth himself expresses some satisfaction that his reorientation of theology has not only restored honour, integrity, and purity to the concept of divine law, but also that he has overcome the separation of law from the gospel, and of the temporal from the spiritual realm, by demonstrating that Christ is the Lord over the law and King over all men and all things (including the state). He sums up this triumph over Lutheran theology in this way:

> I have never been ready to call good that ominous Lutheran doctrine according to which there belongs to the state a "right of self-determination" (Eigengesetzlichkeit) independent of the proclamation of the gospel and not to be touched by it.[99]

Notes

1 *D. Martin Luthers Werke: Kritische Gesamtausgabe* (Weimar, 1883 ff), Vol. 36, 9: 24-31. Cited hereafter as WA.

2 This does not mean to imply that conceptions of the gospel have not changed; of course they have, but these changes have not been as radical as those of the conceptions of law because, with reference to the gospel, Jesus Christ still provides a common denominator and a point of reference.

3 For an illuminating discussion on this see: F. Edward Franz, *An Essay on the Development of Luther's Thought on Justice, Law, and Society* (Harvard Theological Review XIX, 1959), pp. 106-107.

4 Legal positivism is a complex technical term. Without going into details, we wish to define briefly what we mean by it in this discussion. By it, we understand the modern development of constitutional and legal arrangements in which the law is stripped from any metaphysical underpinnings and sometimes even separated from morality. Law is understood in a pragmatic sense of continuous attempts to transform rational demands

into legal enactments in order to meet human needs and to transform human conditions. Because God is no longer understood as a source of the law, the positivistic theory of law construes law as a purely rational product which derives from the "will of the people" in democratic states, or the will of the state in totalitarian states. At any rate, because legal positivism is mainly interested in the state, as a body which conceptualizes ethos and guarantees human freedom as society progresses, law is recognized formally as law when it has been produced by the will of the state, which may or may not derive its authority from the "will of the people." Law is that which people will and decree, and "the will of the people," or of the state, now assumes the role that was formerly played by God when law was understood to derive from Him (e.g., historically revealed law in the Bible which was viewed as heteronomous and unrelated to reason from the Enlightenment to the nineteenth century) who was the ultimate judge and administrator of justice. Under legal positivism, however, law and justice are not usually correlated. Nor is law correlated with morality. Rather, law is that which is formulated into a constitutional code, spelling out what the nation wants and what proper relation individuals must have to one another and to the state. Judges must interpret law professionally by unearthing nuances in what the written law says, and they may not differ from what the state has decreed. Unfortunately, it often happens that what the state may claim as the law is not a reflection of what wrong and right action is but merely of what the will of the majority is. Also, law may be a reflection only of the party that happens to be in power at the time, because through majority votes the party becomes a source of laws. Since the lawgiver is the ruling party or *junta,* positivistic laws may never be illegal because there is no higher court beyond what the existing legislation says, even though such legislations may be only an extension of the will of those who rule rather than a means of administering justice and righteousness.

5 For an elaborate statement on positivistic theory of law the reader is referred to: Carl. E. Braaten, "Reflexions on the Lutheran Doctrine of Law," in *The Lutheran Quarterly* (Vol. XVIII, February 1966), pp. 71–72f; Gerhard O. Forde, "Lex Semper Accusat?: Nineteenth Century Roots of Our Dilemma," in *Dialog* (Vol. 9, Autumn 1970), pp. 266–273; John R. Hanson, "Law and Theology: Who Cares?" in *Dialog* (Vol. 9, Autumn 1970), pp. 280f; Werner Elert, *The Christian Ethos* (Philadelphia: Muhlenberg Press, 1957), pp. 8f, 11, 50, 70, 86; Ernst Troeltsch, *The Social Teaching of the Christian Churches* (New York: Harper Torchbooks, 1960), p. 305.

6 Karl Barth, "Gospel and Law," in *Community, State and Church* (New York: Doubleday & Company, Inc., 1960), pp. 71-100. Cited hereafter as "Gospel and Law."

7 Hans Urs von Balthasar, *The Theology of Karl Barth* (Garden City, N.Y.: Doubleday Anchor Book, 1972), p. 83. He points to Barth's essay "Das Halten der Gebote" of 1927. Against this dating it must be pointed out that Christocentricism is already evident in Barth's commentary to the Romans.

8 Cf. Barth, *Church Dogmatics* I/I (Edinburgh: T. & T. Clark, 1936–), pp. 141–149. Cited hereafter as *Church Dogmatics.*

9 Barth, *Nein* (Theo. Exist. heute 14, 1934), pp. 19, 42.

10. Barth, *How I Changed My Mind* (Richmond, VA: John Knox Press, 1966), pp. 21–22. Barth expressed his horror at finding most of his teachers in this group.

11 Ibid., pp. 45–48; "Gospel and Law," p. 91.

12 Cf. A.C. Cochrane, *The Church Confession under Hitler* (Philadelphia: The Westminster Press, 1962), pp. 239–242.

13 Barth, *Church Dogmatics* IV/2, p. 31.

14 Barth, *Church Dogmatics* II/2, pp. 557-559, 563f, 566, 568, 606, 632.

15 Ibid., pp. 557, 559, 563; "Gospel and Law," pp. 77f.

16 "Gospel and Law," pp. 72–80.

17 *Church Dogmatics* II/2, p. 568.

18 "Gospel and Law," pp. 71, 77.

19 *Church Dogmatics* II/2, p. 566.

20 Ibid., pp. 563f, 587.

21 *Church Dogmatics* III/4, pp. 10, 37f.

22 "Gospel and Law," p. 91.

23 Ibid., p. 77.

24 Ibid., p. 77; *Church Dogmatics* II/2, p. 563.

25 "Gospel and Law," p. 77.

26 *Church Dogmatics* II/2, p. 563.

27 "Gospel and Law," pp. 72–73; *Church Dogmatics* II/2, pp. 591–593.

28 "Gospel and Law," p. 72.

29 Ibid., p. 73; *Church Dogmatics* II/2, pp. 568, 591–593.

30 "Gospel and Law," p. 73.

31 Ibid., p. 72.

32 Ibid., pp. 77f; *Church Dogmatics* II/2, p. 559.

33 *Church Dogmatics* II/2, p. 560.

34 Ibid., p. 560.

35 Ibid., p. 563.

36 Ibid., p. 563.

37 Ibid.

38 Ibid., p. 572.

39 "Gospel and Law," p. 80.

40 Ibid., pp. 71–72, 80.

41 Ibid., p. 80.

42 "Gospel and Law," p. 80.

43 Ibid., p. 73.

44 *Church Dogmatics* II/2, pp. 606, 632.

45 Ibid., pp. 594f.

46 *Church Dogmatics* IV/2, p. 100.

47 *Church Dogmatics* II/2, p. 564.

48 Ibid.

49 "Gospel and Law," p. 81.

50 *Church Dogmatics* II/2, p. 576.

51 Ibid., p. 586.
52 Ibid., p. 565.
53 Ibid., p. 595.
54 Ibid.
55 Ibid., p. 585
56 Ibid., p. 586
57 Ibid.
58 Ibid., p. 560.
59 Ibid., p. 583–584.
60 Ibid., p. 584.
61 Ibid., p. 588. (Italics added)
62 Ibid., p. 584. (Italics added)
63 Ibid., pp. 584–585.
64 Ibid., p. 593.
65 Ibid., p. 569.
66 Ibid., pp. 588–593. Here Barth takes up Pauline theology (especially Romans 7:1–25 and other texts from the Epistles) which supports the view that law "accuses, kills, and is death" until it is silenced by God's forgiving word of the gospel. Barth solves the apparent contradiction by introducing conceptions of misuse, misunderstanding, misinterpretations, and distortions of God's gift of law. His thesis is that the problem is not so much with the law as such – which in itself is good, holy, spiritual, and law of life – but with the fact that God's law is given to sinful human hands. When God accepted us in the "gift of the gospel and law," He entrusted his gift to our hands in spite of the questionable purity of our hands. Even in our possession, law remained God's gift. However, in our hands it can have both negative and positive consequences. It can be misused and distorted. Sin uses it as a springboard and becomes active while we become aware of it as sin in us (Rom. 7:7, 8, 11, 20, 23). By misusing and distorting this good gift, we can only turn the law against us. As sin takes over, deceives us, and causes covetousness to shoot up in us in the face of the law's 'Thou shalt not covet!', human beings try to overcome the burden of sins in their own lives. So they establish their own justification and, in doing so, sinners turn God's claims into human claims. Worse still, they claim that they can satisfy and will meet God's demands by themselves (cf. *Church Dogmatics* II/2, pp. 590–592). This is disobedience, Barth contends, because sinners arrogate to themselves God's role of judging between good and evil. In this distortion, misuse, and Pharisaic misunderstanding of law, what is best is concealed from us because now the law can only kill. For even in its misuse it is fatally effective and therefore deadly.

Barth calls our attention to the misuse of the gospel when it is in human hands. People try to manipulate, control, and direct it as a possession which they can readily use to comfort themselves. Christ is made a companion, the useful arm or stopgap for all our efforts towards our own self-justification and self-sanctification (cf. "Gospel and Law," pp. 90–91).

But since God cannot be mocked, his law can only kill the sinner by showing him the wrath of God. It prepares the sinner for death, it executes and excludes him from the house of the Father and from all goods, it tears him into two (cf. *Church Dogmatics* II/2, pp. 590f). Fortunately for us, some good still comes out of all this mess. While we are slaves to sin and the misused law which kills, the good news of God reaches us for the first time, and God's victory becomes really good tidings for sinners because He comes in to rescue us from the apparent condemnation under the misused law. Here Barth agrees with Paul that clearly law precedes the gospel; God kills us through the law in order to make us alive through the gospel when we become free from the law of sin and death. Just as resurrection is preceded by death, so the gospel is preceded by the misused law of sin and death. But while he concedes that law precedes the gospel, Barth retorts that this "is entirely unintelligible to us as an order. It can only be event and *fact* and we can of ourselves believe it only as the promise of what Jesus Christ does for us, and our belief will be a source of amazement to us" (Cf. "Gospel and Law," p. 97). By the use of categories of misuse and misinterpretation, Barth clearly has tried to answer accusations that his theology contradicts Pauline theology. For, if law accuses because it is distorted by us, it does not follow that God's law in itself is one of accusation. Moreover, this misused law precedes the gospel only to be superseded and excluded once we are liberated from it. Law of God remains essentially one which sets free, one under which we are placed by the gospel in our determination for existence in covenant partnership. And God's action in Christ frees us from old connections with misused laws under human control while God's true law is once again re-established in its purity as the law of life, whose form, content, ground, and basis is Jesus Christ.

67 Ibid., pp. 541, 569; *Church Dogmatics* IV/2, pp. 722–725.

68 *Church Dogmatics* II/2, pp. 563f.

69 "Gospel and Law," p. 79.

70 Ibid., p. 91.

71 Barth, *This Christian Cause* (New York: Macmillan Company, 1941), p. 3.

72 William H. Lazareth, "Luther's 'Two Kingdoms' Ethic Reconsidered," in *Christian Social Ethics in a Changing World,* (ed.) John C. Bennett (New York: Associated Press, 1966), p. 120.

73 Barth's letter to French Protestants (1939) in *This Christian Cause,* pp. 7–8. (Italics added)

74 A translation and citation of this letter is in Lazareth, "Luther's 'Two Kingdoms' Ethic Reconsidered," pp. 120–121.

75 Barth, "Church and State," in his *Community, State, and Church* (New York: Doubleday & Company, Inc., 1960), p. 103. This is an important essay for two reasons. It was written at the crucial time prior to the second World War during which Lutheran theology was defenseless before Hitler and his policies. Also, it crystallized Barth's attempt to ground both law and state in the gospel rather than in the doctrine of creation, and

provided a rather positive understanding of the state, the criterion by which it can be judged, and set limits to Christian obedience to the claims that a state can make.

76 While Barth addresses his harshest criticism to Luther, whom he sees as the forerunner of the *Deutsche Christen* movement which tried to sanction Nazism and distorted the law, his comments in his Christological grounding of law and state also are addressed to Calvin and others who follow Luther – when they made the law precede the gospel rather than proceed from Jesus Christ.

77 "Church and State," p. 108.

78 Ibid., p. 118. (Italics added)

79 Ibid., p. 113.

80 Ibid., pp. 113–114.

81 Ibid., p. 114.

82 Ibid., p. 120.

83 Ibid., p. 117.

84 Cf. Barth, "Christian Community and Civil Community," in *Community, State and Church,* pp. 147–171. Cited hereafter as "Christian Community and Civil Community."

85 Ibid., p. 132.

86 "Church and State," p. 126.

87 *Church Dogmatics* IV/2, pp. 680f, 720f.

88 Ibid., p. 689.

89 Ibid., p. 719.

90 For an elaborate list of these analogies, the reader is referred to Barth's "Christian Community and Civil Community," pp. 171–180ff.

91 "Church and State," p. 145.

92 Ibid., p. 145. He writes: "The assertion that all governments are equally compatible or incompatible with the Gospel is not only outworn but false ..... it is not true that a Christian can endorse, desire, or seek after a mobocracy or dictatorship as readily as a democracy" (p. 145).

93 *Church Dogmatics* IV/3, p. 893.

94 "Church and State," pp. 144f, 147f.

95 *Church Dogmatics* IV/2, p. 719.

96 Ibid., p. 721.

97 Ibid., pp. 720–722.

98 Ibid., p. 720.

99 Barth, *How I Changed My Mind* (Richmond, VA: John Knox Press 1966), p. 48.

Chapter two

Either the law or the gospel is God's last word to humanity but not both

Werner Elert is one of the twentieth century's most learned and towering figures in Lutheran scholarship. He was a loyal and confessional Lutheran theologian, a professor of both systematic theology and church history at Erlangen University. As a creative scholar with a broad historical knowledge, he was also an ecumenical churchman. He and Paul Althaus were central figures in the Lutheranism of the 1930s and 1940s in Germany, and this explains their joint participation in the drawing up of "The Ansbach Proposal as a Response to the Barmen Theological Declaration" (June 1934).[1] The Barmen declaration was written under the leadership of Karl Barth. The theology of "Ansbach Proposal" was a direct challenge to Barth's theology by Lutherans on the problem of law and gospel, and the relation between Church and state.

But it was in the essay entitled "Zwischen Gnade und Ungnade"[2] that Elert gave his most sharp and stinging attack on Barth's attempted reversal of the Lutheran and traditional order of law and gospel dialectic. First, by choosing a title opposed to the one Barth used, Elert wanted to make it unmistakably clear that he did not only disagree, but also wished to defend the traditional order. His contention was that Barth was farther from the truth when he claimed that it was *only* in the light of the gospel that humans could discover their sinfulness. Rather the opposite is true, namely, before we can come to understand what the gospel really is all about, it is necessary that we should know about God's law under which we stand condemned. That is, the human condition of sinfulness to which the gospel claims to provide an answer is a necessary presupposition or precondition for the understanding of the forgiving news of the gospel. Therefore, the law and with it sin must precede the gospel. Otherwise we would not appreciate the uniqueness of the gospel as an answer to the human dilemma which sin poses. Consequently, the gospel can only be the last word of God to humanity among whom the power of sin reigns supreme.

Secondly, in contrast to Barth's assertion that a theological response to modern "lawlessness" is the one which fully grounds our understanding of law Christologically, Elert contends that the adequate theological response to the modern "crisis of law" should be the one that grounds conceptions of the law in the doctrine of creation. Only when it is rooted in the doctrine of creative and ruling activity of God is it possible to purify the concept of law, something which, Elert claims, Barth has dismally failed to do.

2.1 LAW AND GOSPEL ARE MUTUALLY EXCLUSIVE

Elert's main thesis is that law and gospel are not only to be differentiated but also must be seen as mutually opposed ways of God's address to humanity. It is because we are not dealing here with mere words *(verba)* but with two realities with distinct contents or substances.[3]

He further adds that when they are distinguished but also dialectically related each will remain in its proper place and within its limits. The law will not claim to be the gospel, even as a form of the gospel (Barth!), and the gospel will not pretend to be the law. When theology fails to distinguish them, both the law and the gospel are rendered impotent and lose their reality, especially when Barth asserts that the "judgment of the law is also grace." And the result can be only to reduce their difference into a verbal one rather than a substantive (material) one. For the possibility that human beings can stand accused under the law, or stand forgiven by a gracious God through the gospel, is removed.

Elert charges that Barth is guilty of collapsing the gospel and law into one thing; he has smoothed out any substantive or material difference between them when it is asserted that the law is nothing but a form of the gospel. This assertion, Elert contends, fails to see that the two realities cannot exist in *friendly coexistence* nor could they talk in unison because the nature of the case is that law and gospel speak in contradictory lines.[4]

Elert is of the opinion that Barth was misled by his obsessional zeal to stamp out a theology which, since the time of Schleiermacher, had lost the distance between God and the creature. Barth's energies were directed away from a theological necessity to distinguish between the law and the gospel to another distinction which consisted of:

> ..... the ontic contrast between the Creator and creature and in the noetic contrast between divine revelation and human reception of the revelation.[5]

The result of this Barthian distinction can result only in blurring the issues, because now the essential thing becomes:

> not *what* God says, but *that* he speaks, not *what* man hears, but *that* he hears.[6]

As a consequence, the distinction between the material content of what the law says and what the gospel says in such a theology becomes insignificant, for in both cases divine speaking and human hearing make up for the necessary polarity.

The problem inherent in dialectical theology was compounded when the Confessing Church had to face the ''lawlessness'' of Hitler Germany. The Church was flooded with essays on *nomos, Volksnomos,* and *Volksgesetz;* and what surprised Elert was that, under Barth's leadership, theologians failed to counter the alleged false teaching by precise theological re-definition and purification of the conception of law. Such a move would have compelled Barth and his followers to discuss the distinction of the law and gospel.

However, under the leadership of Barth, theologians held tenuously to an unqualified concept of revelation, which was used as a criterion by which differing interpretations of the law being proposed by various factions were to be judged. Their only interest lay in stamping out anthropocentricism and traces of natural theology:

> The battle was not fought to maintain the purity of the concept of law. If it had been, this would have required some differentiation between the concept of law and ... gospel. Instead the battle was fought under the catchword "revelation" — true revelation vs false revelation, natural revelation vs. revelation through the Word.[7]

On this basis, the issue of the pure concept of law can never be raised nor settled. Also, these theologians worked under the illusion that by affirming absolute revelation through the Word they had finally built up an invincible bulwark against all heresies.[8] Yet, by affirming Jesus Christ as the exclusive medium of God's revelation, they were contradicting the Scriptures.[9] Elert was willing to sympathize with the intent of the Barmen Declaration, but he felt that these theologians, under Barth's leadership, went too far when they denied natural revelation.

The problem became serious when Barth, in his "Gospel and Law" of 1935, instead of correcting a deficiency inherent in the Barmen Declaration, talked about the law and gospel in unison, and designated them as one and the same Word of God — the content of which was the same. In this reductionism, Barth, then, claimed that in the law there was promise and therefore also the gospel. When God speaks in the gospel, the divine command is simultaneously expressed, and therefore it is the law. Hence Barth's famous definition that "the Law is nothing but merely a *form of the Gospel,* whose content is grace."[10]

Elert objected to Barth's assertion that the "very fact that God speaks to us, that, under all circumstances, is, in itself, grace."[11] Elert saw this as a confirmation of his own suspicion that, for Barth, what mattered was the fact *that* God spoke and *not what* the listener heard. This, Elert concluded, was a fundamental error in Barth's theology which assumed that God spoke grace *only!* Elert listed several instances from the Bible to show that Barth's theology was outright unbiblical: When God expelled Adam from paradise, this was never viewed as grace by the writer of Genesis, but as God's judgment. In the decalogue, God promised to visit iniquities of the father upon the children. This statement could not be understood as grace. Elert added:

> No exegesis can twist Isaiah's words about Assyria, Moab, and Egypt into declarations of *grace for the victims.* Or should the infants of Babylon destined to be dashed against the stones, and the women who were to be outraged, understand this somehow as the grace of God?[12]

Since Elert thought that Barth's assertion that God spoke grace *only* was unbiblical and destroyed the power of the reality of the law and gospel, we now proceed to analyze what it is that he (Elert) understood by the law. We will discuss this under his own sub-title in which he discussed the law in direct opposition to Barth and Calvin.

2.2 THE LAW ALWAYS ACCUSES

Elert, as a faithful Lutheran, discussed under this sub-title the theological use of law. But he also departs from the usual Lutheran way which discusses the first use of the law *(usus politicus)* before it goes on to discuss the theological or second use, *usus legis,* about which Luther writes: *"Secundus usus est, de quo dicit Paulus, quod lex sit paedagogus ad Christum"*[13] It is also called the proper use of law *(usus propius legis).*[14] By beginning with this reversed approach, Elert is posed for an attack on Barth who he thinks has misunderstood *what the law is.* He rejects any suggestion that law is a demand on us by God and that the life of faith is one of obedience.[15]

To define law as God's demand which humans may or may not fulfill, in Elert's opinion, is misleading. For it gives an impression that adherence to some law may make amendments for sin, and therefore that the "damage could be repaired, and the problem of destiny solved by human composure."[16] This falsely portrays God as though He were a human legislator who comes to give answers to human questions such as: *What shall we do?* Moreover, law is reduced to a rule of life, a *norma normans* of human behavior.[17] Elert sees both Calvin and Barth as those who define law wrongly as *"règle de bien vivre et justment."*[18] He sharply denounces this because then the law appears as:

> ..... a fence running alongside the straight path. We traverse this path on our journey through life – obviously on the right side of the fence, like a well-curbed horse. However, it frequently happens that the horse capers across the fence and thus lands in forbidden territory.[19]

Here sin becomes a deviation from a norm, implying a wanderer who strays from the right path, thereby exposed to danger. Also, sin is understood as a "trans-gression," a *transgrassio legis, aberratio* or *exorbito a lege divina.*[20] According to Elert, this definition of sin lacks the element of opposition to God's will which human disobedience implies and to which God responds in judgment through his death-dealing law.

Elert insists that law is the divine judgment on the quality of human life in its totality. This means that humans have to be seen and understood from God's point of view where they appear always as sinners. Thus, the theological use of law refers to God's manner of passing sentence of guilt.[21] As God's juridical activity, the law understood theologically cannot mean that we are on this side of the fence, but rather that we are already over the fence – "that our entire life from beginning to end is on the wrong side of the fence."[22] Elert believes that this is the way Luther and Paul understood the theological use of the law *(usus proprius, theologicus* or *spiritualis).* Also, he sees his view as in agreement with the Church's understanding of original sin, which, according to Paul says that beginning at birth we are already in the forbidden territory. The law was added because of transgressions.

Furthermore, Elert says that although Paul also mentions that the law was not given until four hundred and thirty years after Abraham (Gal. 13:17), this should not be understood to mean that the law was non-existent before its formal giving at Sinai. Rather, since death was already there, and it is the wages of sin (this Paul affirms),[23] it must be concluded that the law was already operative. This is the case because death ruled from Adam (long before Moses) until Christ came. Since the law (the Decalogue) was added because of transgressions, Elert concludes that human transgressions are presupposed by the formal legislation at Sinai.

The Decalogue made the law of retribution, which was operative, independent of and prior to Sinaitic legislation, more pointed because it now enlightens human conscience which is often blinded and darkened by evil works (Rom. 1:13–23). Therefore, Mosaic law did not in any sense produce a turn for the better by finally "giving men a rule of life, by which they could now organize their lives":

> Instead it revived sin, granting it new power by provoking it to opposition. At all events it was unable to do anything else than make sin apparent. It pursued its purpose of granting man insight into his opposition to God (Rom. 7:7ff; 3:20; I Cor. 15:16).[24]

Elert praises Melanchthon for his insightfulness when he coined and said of the law: *Lex semper accusat* (the law always accuses).[25] Elert thinks that this concise formula does not only underscore Luther's understanding of the law, but that it expresses Paul's view as well. For if the law is God's law – and God never assumes the role of human legisaltor waiting to see whether or how humans fulfill it – then it can never be a rule of life but is a manner of God's rendering a verdict. Through the law, God passes sentence on the sinner. The law always accuses, for if we truly listen to *what* it says to us, it never gives only information (as a rule of life) but constantly proclaims God's verdict about us which, measured against the law, is always condemnation.[26]

To clarify this even further, Elert argues that Barth's view of the law as the form of the gospel, the covenant law of the gracious God, is misleading. Barth, in Elert's opinion, overlooks the fact that the *promise* of the law, which, to be sure, the law contains, is not applicable unconditionally. Grace here is for those who love God and keep the law.

If we truly listen to *what* the law and gospel say, not merely *that* God speaks, and if the law is seen in the light of the gospel, this becomes clear: The law proclaims the *things that should have been done* and things that are left undone. It shows humans what they ought to be; that humans should do the good but not do what is evil. In contrast, the gospel proclaims that sins are forgiven and that everything is fulfilled and done. It is clear, Elert insists, that the law speaks contradictory things to the gospel. It is a threat. It is an accuser. It damns and kills, it is hell and confirms the fact that God is against us.[27]

What is more, the law has two sides (as if it were a coin). It is a conjunction of promise and threat. The gospel proclaims mercy to sinners but the law only to those who fulfill it. *The law is always the law of retribution* to both the good and the ill:

> The whole of Old Testament Torah, in the manifoldness of its contents, is from first to last the book of reward and punishment, not only in its actual legislation, but also in its paradigm of individual biography (Gen. 38:7) and of the history of nations (Num. 14:22f). The shedding of man's blood requires the shedding of man's blood (Gen. 9:6), "eye for eye, tooth for tooth, hand for hand, foot for foot .... wound for wound," etc. (Exod. 21:24f).[28]

On the basis of this evidence, Elert can only define the law thus: *"The law of retribution is God's law in the strictest sense of the word;* man as executor merely puts it into effect."[29]

Elert goes into a lengthy discussion to prove that the New Testament reiterated this Old Testament view of the law (Rom. 12:19; Heb. 10:30f;

Rev. 6:10).[30] New Testament writers know that life under the law is life under a curse (Gal. 3:10); God's law brings wrath because it is the law of retribution. Both the Old and the New Testament agree that the law is a system of rewards as well as punishments. Elert goes so far as to suggest that neither of the Testaments recognizes a law that is not a law of retribution.[31] Even Jesus' reinterpretation of the law in the Sermon on the Mount did not alter its accusatory element. His interpretation only heightened the demands of the law. Now it is no longer a matter of external demands – "Thou shalt not kill," "Thou shalt not commit adultery" – but even hidden hatred and evil desires are condemned (Matt. 5:22; 27–28).[32]

In Elert's mind, Jesus' interpretation, if anything, proves that the *law always accuses.* Jesus did not exempt anyone from this accusatory rule. That is shown by his call to repentance addressed to all people (Mark 1:15, Luke 13:3–5). Christ would not have made the confession of the publican a requirement for justification if an escape in the manner of the Pharisee were possible. The Lord's prayer, *"Forgive us our sins!"* in Elert's opinion, presupposes the guilt of all before the law:

> The Law always accuses. What adultery and homicide are I can learn from others. Hatred and evil desires ..... I must experience them myself to know what they are. The strict interpretation of the law reveals to the conscientious hearer what passions he harbors in his heart. It shows that opposition to God is not only possible but actual with him ..... The person who knows what Jesus speaks of when he refers to hatred and evil desires proves thereby his own guilt.[33]

In order to cut off any avenue for escape, Christ stated the subjective and objective criteria of love, of Godlike perfection. The demand for God like perfection vindicates, in Elert's mind, the statement that the *law always accuses.*[34] This is correctly understood by hearers of the gospel, for the gospel is not a demand but God's free gift of forgiveness and His message that He has become the friend of sinners and publicans. In the light of the gospel, we now fully recognize our pitiful position under the law and therefore the condemnatory or guilt judgment in the law. [35] Our position under the law before God *(coram deo)* is very negative in Elert's theology. We will now move on to consider his discussion of our position under the law *coram hominibus* (before our fellows).

2.3 THE LAW AS AN ORDER, SECURITY AND THREAT

Elert's most creative and constructive theological contribution on the problem of law comes to its clearest expression in what Lutherans traditionally call the political use of law *(usus politicus legis).* Here, his style is less polemical, and his theological reflection is at its best. Elert does not simply repeat what has been said by other Lutherans or by Luther himself but breaks new ground.

Trying to overcome what appears to him to be a non-biblical and deistic view of God's relation to the world[36] – which has resulted in "lawlessness" and the "crisis of law" because of its thrust toward immanentism and relativism, and in the absence of an attempt by Barth to purify the concept of law – Elert felt compelled to anchor the concept of law on something "eternal and unalterable,"[37] namely, the doctrine of God the Creator. He speaks of the law of creation *(lex creationis)* which brings into existence orders, conditions or categories of existence, and all of these derive from the hand of the Creator. In spite of his use of the language of the Erlangen theologians (theology of "orders of creation"), Elert's reflections on the purity and grounding of the law are very impressive.

The *usus politicus legis,* according to Elert, refers to the creative way in which God *brings order* out of chaos and *governs* the world, therefore making it possible for humans to live together in secure community and in relation to God. It is God who creates the conditions of life, and humans merely uphold and preserve the God-given order. In spite of the human tendency to disrupt God's created conditions of life, the law of God has proven itself effective by being able to preserve the natural order through the instrumentality of civil authorities' use of force and compulsion. This makes it also clear that God has not left the world (natural order) to the domain of the devil. Elert believes that the Bible includes humans in the total cosmos ordered by God's might. Humans are part of this order and must be dependent upon it, not because no other cause is possible, but because God respects the order already established.[38]

Elert distinguishes three types of orders. First, an existing situation *(Tatbestand* or *Seinsgefüge)* in which there is already a certain order of arrangement as, for instance, the arrangement of furniture pieces in a household where they relate and exist concurrently in their proper places. The opposite is disorder.[39] The clearest example of this is the parent–child relationship. A child cannot change place with the parent. These individual orders are embedded in general orders which apply to all individuals within a given category. Every child honours the parents; every child is subject to the same conditions. Disrespect of parents brings disorder into the parent–child order. We shall say more on this later.

The second type is called an order of rank *(Ranggefüge* or *Zeitfüge)* which involves an order of time. Here a person follows another. A parent comes before the child. Or someone goes into the physician's office because he has been in the line longer than the next person. Or one is born in his time, yet history has been going on before. The third type is called an issued order or directive, telling someone how things ought to be done. One behaves as ordered. For instance, a driver stops when the traffic light so indicates. The soldier marches when so commanded.[40]

Elert complains that many theologians have criticized the theology of orders because they identify an order with the third type, with compulsion and directive. Rather, what is of interest to him is the first type (and somewhat also the second) but not the third type of directive order because an order of creation does not stipulate how things ought to be but points to something that is already there and always exists.

For instance, without starting afresh, humans always find themselves in a family, as a woman or man, parent or child. An order is a place to which one is assigned by God in His capacity as Creator (one is born a girl or boy without having a choice), and this reminds us that we are responsible for others before God.[41] We are now going to discuss the law separately as an order, security, and threat in what follows with special reference to human relations.

2.3.1 The Law as an Order

As we have pointed out, the political use of law points us beyond the theological use of law, which consists only in our continuing conflict with God, to an element of order. This order is a clear sign that even though humans under the law stand condemned for sin, they still remain God's creatures. That is, God has not abandoned humans to loneliness, helplessness, and despair – which result in the face of condemning law apart from the gospel – but God has left them in communal relationships which are not arbitrary.[42] On the contrary, these relationships are orderly and purposeful providence.

The law of God, according to Elert, always relates us to our fellows who share our creatureliness.[43] We are placed in structured human interrelationships in which one is parent or child, ruler or ruled, teacher or taught, etc. That is, human society is an ordered existence. Consequently, all humans find themselves always as members of a community – and this existential category or order is true for both believers and non-believers, whether we honour them or despise them. They are already there before we appear on the scene as part of life and God-given forms of existence.[44] Elert writes:

> *Nomos,* law, is a category of orderliness which signifies a definite relationship of man to God but also to the total cosmos. Creation places man into the world, *nomos* binds him to the world ..... nomological existence under the law means only that we, like all other creatures, are subject to the orderly rule of God and that we do not live in the world of chaos and arbitrariness. Nomological existence is a controlled existence ..... As long as we are thus bound to God we cannot fall out of God's order. To be bound in the sense of being tied to God means security and safeguards against fear.[45]

Obviously, for Elert, this controlled existence is not an entirely negative thing but something that belongs to God's creative and gubernatorial activity and consequently to the realm of law rather than of grace.[46]

We have alluded to the way order, in the sense of things falling into their places, is understood by Elert. Elert also stresses that the nomological existence as a state, a condition or form of existence,[47] is something that transcends personal wishes. Divine law as compulsory order contains several kinds of bonds. Some, if not most, are involuntary; God places them there before individuals make a choice. God creates one a Jew or a Samaritan, one by birth belongs to a certain ancestry, family, nation, and citizenship. Even the people we relate to at times are placed before us without our choice. The "Good Samaritan" found a victim whom he did not place on the road but was there before he encountered him. Even this partial order (the victim and the Good Samaritan) is beyond human control.[48]

However, there are also voluntary orders. Elert points us to the marriage bond into which spouses enter voluntarily. One other such voluntary order is an economic order. Here, one chooses whom to enter into an economic transaction with.[49] Voluntary bonds or orders are as lasting as those which are involuntary, even though they (voluntary bonds) can, in principle, be terminated.

Discussing the relation between the Decalogue and the nomological orders of creation, Elert insists that we should not suppose that human interdependence in social relations is the result of legislation at Sinai. Rather, the Decalogue presupposes the existence of these relationships. The commandment: "Thou shalt honour thy father ....." did not create an entirely new and unique relationship, but it presupposes such human relations where one is a father and the other the son (or mother-daughter relations). Similarly, the law on adultery does not bring marriage into existence. If this were the case, it would read: "Thou shalt enter into matrimony!" Rather, it presupposes the human practice where an encounter between two sexes occurs or has already occurred. What it does is to prohibit the breaking of an order of marriage.[50]

In summary, the Decalogue presupposes the orders of creation, or categories of existence, wherein humans find themselves. Human autonomy consists only in disrupting this ordered cosmos, or rather these human interrelationships, into which God has placed us. Our opposition to God reveals itself within these orders because we fail to justify our responsible relationship to others before God.

The story of Cain is a sad commentary on how humans disturb or even destroy these orders. He commits "fratricide" and destroys the order of "brother-relationship" into which God had placed him. All the other commandments on the second table of the Decalogue refer to these interpersonal relationships and this agrees with Jesus' interpretation of them.[51] Adultery is not only a sin against an individual mate but also against the order of marriage and destroys it. Disobedience destroys the "father-son" order. Telling lies destroys the order of "truth"[52] etc., etc.

As we have seen, the Decalogue did not legislate that these orders be brought into existence because they have always existed universally wherever humans live. Rather they are God-given realities that belong to the creative and ruling activity of God. As the Creator, God creates and incorporates us into these orders *de facto,* and we are responsible for them *de jure.* The protective function of the law must be fulfilled by us.[53] This is what civil authorities do or must do since it is human duty to uphold the law (order) which God has created. The law shows that it can preserve and provide protection by its compulsion and retribution. This security which the law provides is discussed in the following subsection.

2.3.2 The Law as a Security

We have alluded to the fact that nomological existence is a controlled and complex but wonderfully ordered world by God's might. What is more, because the law always relates us to other fellows who share our creatureliness, we are ever in communal interrelationships which protect us from loneliness, isolation, and despair into which the condemning law can, when the gospel is not heard, throw us. These fellowships provide us with emotional and psychological security because it is in these orders or bonds that we express love and are loved in return.

The family is a typical example of this. It is here that physical security is given, as well as the nourishing of life itself. It is here that responsibility is also exercised by one spouse toward the other; by parents toward their children and vice versa. The state and nation also provide security on a larger scale. And here communal responsibility is exercised to protect life and property; it upholds the law and therefore God's order of creation. These interdependencies or categories of being *(Seinsordnungen)* of life, which Elert interchangeably calls orders, remind us that we are responsible for others before God because the law of God demands that we justify our relationships with our fellows.[54]

The law of God does not only signify a total reality (order) in which we find ourselves but also signifies an order of necessity, a necessity which addresses us as a request. "Everything is requested because everything is recompensed."[55] Further, Elert states:

> Through the law of God that creature which can hear and answer becomes responsible not for his deeds, not for a certain measure of goodness or badness, but for the totality of his humanity. As long as we live exclusively under the law, God is only a demanding God because he is the God of retribution.[56]

What God demands of us is responsibility for others because human life is such that we are always in some form of communal relationship. This responsibility is demanded because life presupposes that someone is my neighbour whose security and protection I must provide. It is within these relationships which give us security that our obedience or disobedience becomes manifest. This occurs when we oppose God by disturbing the orders or categories of life within which we are bound by God's law. Cain is an example of someone who is guilty against God's orders *(Seinsordnungen)* or categories of being, namely "brother-relationship order."

To interfere with these orders is to undermine life. Life is replete with destructive forces as exhibited by Cain's behaviour, but we must resist them even though these evil forces may transcend human control. God creates it but we are responsible for protecting life, and humans everywhere must have the will to guard and uphold God's law which provides security.[57]

Finally, the nomological existence provides security because the law also relates us to God. God knows and has given us names. This means that we cannot be swallowed up by masses, or attempt to run away from God to hide in a crowd, behind a tree, a nation, race, etc. God addresses and is related to us individually through the nomological order. Also, since our existence is a bound-existence through the law, it means that as long as we are thus bound, we cannot fall out of God's controlled and ordered cosmos. This means security and a safeguard against fear.[58] But, there is a question mark before this security. This we now take up in the following subsection.

2.3.3 The Law as a Threat

We have already pointed out that very often humans fail to be responsible for their fellows before God. They inject disorder and disrupt the relationships God has established.[59] This means that the security humans provide for one another is not absolute. It is constantly in danger of being destroyed by evil powers which transcend human control. Elert even suggests the existence of an order (lawlessness) bent on evil in the world.[60] This disorder has its own nomological structures with:

> ..... its own law (Rom. 7:12), its own psychological law (Rom. 7:7f; James 1:15), sociological law (II Kings 17:22), hereditary law (Rom. 5:29), law of tradition (II Kings 3:3; 10:29), law of accumulation (Isa. 30:1). *The most dreadful of these laws of evil is the law of demonization ... in which good is transformed into evil.*[61]

God has, to be sure, established the order of state to hold these evil forces in check, even by use of force; and as God's agent, the state administers the law of retribution (rewards and punishments). What is achieved by these human efforts, however, is but an external nomological order to the extent that the entire order is not completely wiped out by the evil forces. But as regards internal lawbreaking, which can be covered up by external behaviour (e.g., deception, hatred, and evil desires) the entire nomological order is defenseless. This poses a threat and reminds us of our vulnerability.

Finally, Elert goes back to the notion that God's law is the law of retribution in the strictest sense of the word. And this, above everything else, explains why the law is a threat to humans. God commands: "Thou shalt honor thy father and mother, love God and the neighbour, do good unto enemies, give food to the hungry, work, etc., etc."[62] Yet God lets us be born in the *state, order* of existence which is entirely in sin -- in the totality of our thinking and doing which makes the fulfillment of this "Thou shalt!" impossible for us.[63]

Elert concedes that God does provide some measure of security in the orders of existence (interdependences), and this enables us to carry our purposes for our existence – "but like the grass which flourishes today – here one hesitates -- is cut down in the evening and withereth."[64] At this point, our sense of security in the nomological order breaks down. The cause, here, is something that is beyond human control, namely death which, according to Elert, is the wages of sin. The law thus contains both the measure of security and threat. The *nomos* (law) both supports the rope on which we walk and also guarantees that some day it will break. Death is the direction in which life moves because it expresses God's anger with sin and therefore the wages of God's law of retribution.

Elert concludes by asking rhetorical questions: Why is it that in spite of human endeavour to do good, to be honest, to participate in useful community betterment, etc., there is still no single person who has fulfilled God's law? Why have idealists and reformers not achieved their goals long ago? Why is it that, even though Hegel long ago detected in history the increase of liberty from being the privilege of the few into becoming a property for the many,[65] we do still have so many people enslaved in our century? Why are there still barbarism, discrimination, and annihilation of humans by humans? Elert gives the following answer:

> Theological ethics cannot participate in the search for immanent criteria. It asks for God's judgment. God's law does not bind us only to his governing and creative activity, or to his legislative will. It places us under judgment. Only then will it fulfill the task which Christ and the apostles assigned to it: "The law always accuses" *(Lex semper accusat).*[66]

We have now come full circle in discussing the law in Elert's theology. Whether the law we talk about is the *usus theologicus* or *usus politicus,* it matters very little because the law always accuses. The law is always the *lex semper accusans.*[67] It must incessantly tell us that we are liars when we say we have no sin. The law incessantly exercises its "proper function" since it is always accusing (and it can never be anything but an accuser) to prove that all are guilty, and thus for all of us our mouths must be stopped first before we are driven to Christ who then moves into his "proper office" of speaking the word of forgiveness. Christ alone is the end of the law, for he has power to break the vicious circle in which humans find themselves under the law.

Forde has well summarized Elert's contention when he says:

> There is no escape from the law in that way. But there *is* an end to law far more real ..... the end that comes with the breaking in of the new in Christ, the end of the old Adam and the creation of the new. It is when man realizes that there is really and truly an end, a goal, a telos, that he can begin for the first time to listen to the law, to let it speak to him and hear what it says. When one sees the end, the goal of it all, has happened and is on its way through God's initiative one can begin to see the law in a positive light. For then one sees that law is not *for ever;* it is for this age, for this world.[68]

In what way is Christ the end of the law? Elert takes this up in his debate with Barth, and we wish to present his views below.

2.4 CHRIST IS THE END OF THE LAW BECAUSE HE IS GOD'S FINAL WORD

It is Elert's main thesis that the law always accuses and brings death because the law of God is the law of retribution in the strictest sense of the word.[69] He also knows that the law, too, is God's word and manifestation of God's will. We have already pointed out that for Elert the content of law and gospel are materially (substantively) different and, therefore, that the two ways of God's address to humanity are mutually exclusive. Thus, they cannot speak in unison.[70] Now Elert tries to unpack how the two are different and in what way the gospel is the final word of God.

Elert defines the gospel as "the message of Jesus Christ who was delivered for our sins and raised for our justification (Rom. 4:25)."[71] This definition is important because it underlines the difference Elert wants to make between the law and the gospel. The law is God's juridical action, a manner of passing judgment on sinful humanity, but the gospel has as its content a *person,* Jesus Christ. Further, it is not merely a story about a person that interests the believer, but it is what has happended to Christ; and this becomes "good news" insofar as it was done for "our sins" and for "our justification." The gospel has the concreteness of a person who is a bearer of grace, whereas the law was given through Moses and does not have a person as its content. Elert sees *no grace in the law* because it is judgment; even the judgment on the cross would not be grace had not God raised Jesus Christ for our justification.[72]

But because the gospel has to do with a person, the records about this person, namely the gospel, is of special interest to Elert. They alone transform us into "eye- and ear-witness of the earthly Christ, of his speaking and acting."[73] The life of Jesus is important for believers to know about because from it we learn how Jesus related himself to various peoples. Elert believes that, even though we have historical problems about the gospel writings, certain important events stand clearly and indisputably affirmed in the New Testament.

Two bear directly on the question of law and gospel: First, the New Testament agrees that Jesus did not come to abolish but to fulfill God's law (Matt. 5:17); for, by itself, it is holy law (Rom. 7). Rather, he heightened its accusatory interpretation in his Sermon on the Mount. He even died because he was accused of having violated this law. He preached good news to the poor (Luke 4:18f). And this news could not possibly refer to the law because the law does not distinguish between the poor and the rich, but recompenses the righteous, and punishes the evildoer. Without denying the law, Christ heals the blind and the lepers and preaches good news to the poor. These actions do not fulfill the law either, but they point to the person of Jesus and how he acted.

It is true that Jesus also begins his ministry by dividing the sinners and the righteous, but he identifies his person with one group, namely the sinners:[74]

> He became the friend of publicans and sinners. He likened himself to a physician who lives for the sick. He is interested as little in those who are healthy as they are in him. He is also the shepherd who leaves the sheep grazing in safety to seek the one that has strayed away.[75]

Jesus always found himself in bad company, in the fellowship of the sinners; he died on the cross between two malefactors. By his actions he annoyed the righteous. Also, he constantly attacked the Pharisees and scribes for their outward "righteousness" whereas within they were hypocrites (Matt. 23:28). Their acts, in Jesus' evaluation, were not righteousness in truth but merely in performance, "a theater" before men. Jesus attacked them because, by claiming to adhere to the law while in truth hiding their sins, they were refusing to confess that they, too, were sinners.

In other words, the Pharisees and scribes were afraid of truth. They lived "as-if" they were not sinners. They clung to the law, but they refused to listen to the pronouncement of the law, namely the divine juridical verdict that all humans are in sin. Paul, a Pharisee himself, after he had truly heard *what the law says,* concluded that the path of the law leads only to human self-evaluation of rightousness, not God's righteousness. He thus agreed with Jesus that the Pharisees and scribes were not truly listening to the law they clung to.[76]

In relation to the sinners, Jesus did not behave like an Old Testament Prophet or modern "hell preacher" with passionate threats of the law of retribution. Sinners were not exempted from repentance, even though Jesus showed remarkable mercy toward them. He often admonished them to sin no more. The result of Jesus' encounter with sinners became one in which sinners experience a distance between themselves and Christ. The distance is of a personal nature. The centurion of Capernaum says he is not worthy to have Jesus under his roof; John the Baptist says he is unworthy to untie the thongs of Jesus' sandals; Peter says he is too sinful to come close to Jesus.[77] These people were sinners in fact and truth, and Jesus acknowledged the presence of faith when they confessed this truth: that they were sinners. In response, Jesus, whenever necessary, forgave them.

In all these instances, Elert sees something qualitatively different from the way the law functions. Christ is not the enemy to be feared but a friend of sinners, a helper and healer. Christ is grace in person, for unlike the Law-giver, he does not condemn or threaten to punish but forgives. The wall between the saints (holy) and sinners with him is broken down. This reaches its climax when the "Holy One of God" sits with sinners at table in all his purity, innocence, and truth.[78]

Elert insists that the procedure Christ follows in dealing with sinners is not a nomological one for, according to the law, Jesus would be issuing threats. The publican, malefactor on the cross, and the adulteress would have been punished. But Christ went against the law by forgiving them all their iniquities. The gospel, Elert argues, differs:

> ..... from the law, not merely in the "clarity of its manifestation," but as day differs from night, as condemnation differs from pardon. They cannot simply be united. Nor is any compromise between them possible. Sinners are *either* forgiven *or* recompensed.[79]

Elert then inquires about Christ who, according to gospel accounts, died and how his death relates to the fact that he offers forgiveness in the face of the law of retribution. He notes with interest that even on the cross the earthly Jesus Christ did not change his attitude toward the sinners. And even during the last hours, he pardoned the malefactor, thus contradicting the law of retribution to the last breath. With reference to those who crucified him, he did not remind God that whoever sheds man's blood should have his own shed in return.[80] Instead he prayed to God to forgive his murderers.

His death also has another significance. Jesus died with the help of the law. Those who execute him act lawfully,[81] because he died according to Jewish law which he had violated by forgiving sin (making himself equal with God). Elert contends that, by dying voluntarily, Christ acknowledged that he was the friend of sinners (Mark 15:28). By taking human sin upon himself, Jesus became guilty of that sin. Since the sin of all sinners was upon him, and he died for it while he was also praying for forgiveness for all; and his death means that the circle is closed.

The law of retribution, which is the law of God in the strictest sense of the word, is now fulfilled, because Christ has in truth now taken the sin of the world.[82] The result of this death and God's judgment on Jesus on the cross means that:

> God pronounces judgment according to the law of retribution. Man's nomological existence is not only disclosed because the death of Christ brings the craftiness of all human legal systems to light. It is mortally wounded because atonement must be made. The atonement consists in the fact that he who restores the state of truth between God and man by making all of them sinners in truth must die for this deed. The judgment of God, to which Christ submits as the bearer of the guilt of all, proclaims that God has accepted the atonement. *The curse of legalism which rested upon mankind has been cancelled.*[83]

What is more, the reconciliation accompalished in Christ means that the new order of things is established. This is an order of forgiveness which *substitutes* for the law of retribution (nomological existence). It is an order of grace, and it stands in the place of the order of creation and thus of law.

In this order of grace, which is qualitatively new by virtue of the resurrection of Christ from the dead, an order anticipating eschatological existence, the *law has no longer any voice whatsoever.* Elert is persuaded that, with Paul, we can now say: "Christ is the end of the law, that everyone who has faith may be justified (Rom. 10:4)," because Christ is the end of a nomological existence and the originator of a new existence.[84] So, just as death is destroyed by his resurrection from the dead, the *gospel as God's last word reduces the law finally and conclusively to silence.* In the dialectical relation between the law and gospel in mutual conversation, this end of the law:

> ..... dare not be viewed as though yesterday God spoke one way, today speaks another way, and tomorrow will revert to the previous way again. Much less dare we imagine *that the one mode of speech says nothing different from another,* but only expresses it more clearly. What we must understand is that *in this conversation the gospel irrefutably and irrevocably has the last word.*[85]

Elert could not have stated his case more strongly against Barth than in the above citation. The law and gospel are such that their content is different and their messages are mutually exclusive; they can never be united nor speak in unison. This order of things is as true as death precedes life and the old precedes the new man. Indeed, Elert has so defined each that they cannot coexist, but can only remain exclusive orders of creation (synonymous with nomological existence) and orders of grace (synonymous with redemption or gospel). Each order has its own rules which do not apply to the other.

The immediate question that is posed to Elert is whether the law has any relevance for the Christian. What about the new obedience of the gospel to which Barth has called our attention, if indeed the gospel (or Christ used interchangeably) is the end of the law? In answer to this, Elert rejects any "third use of the law,"[86] He argues that true disciples of Christ need not be told *what they ought to do,* which *the law* in any case *is unable to do.* The believers in Christ need not be told that idolatry, adultery and bearing of false witness against the neighbour are sins. They know all these because they live in truth. Therefore, they do not have any need whatsoever for the law with its promises of reward and threats of punishment.

Further, Christ is active in the lives of the disciples through the sending of the Spirit. If this is true, Elert wonders,

> for what purpose do the children of God still need the law, since their distinctive trademark consists in their being "led by the Spirit" (Rom. 8:14)? What purpose can the law have for those who already walk by the Spirit and thus are protected from the desires of the flesh (Rom. 8:26, Gal. 4:6), for those who work miracles by the Spirit, for those whom the Spirit brings forth love which fulfills the entire law in joy, peace and faithfulness?[88]

Because they are under the Spirit's rule, they are no longer under the law (Gal. 5:18). Elert is trying to score many points against Barth, who, some theologians believe, needs a law which follows the gospel for a new obedience because he has no place for the work of the Holy Spirit.[89] Elert further adds:

> Just as law and grace stand in opposition to each other, so it is with law and Spirit. The law is bondage (Gal. 3:23), the Spirit, freedom (II Cor. 3:17).[90]

For Elert, the new life in Christ, in this new order of grace, is not some alleged new obedience, but freedom. This can mean only that once again the law and gospel are opposed to each other as death is to life. The law has served its purpose when it convicts all of sin, but once the gospel has spoken, there can never be any room left for the law. This is because the new creation described as regeneration or rebirth, which is solely God's creative activity through the Spirit, can never be the object of an imperative.[91] For Elert, therefore, the choice is clear-cut:

> Either the law or the gospel is the end of God's ways with men, but not both ..... It is the gospel in which we place our faith.[92]

Notes

1 The English version of this Declaration is found in *Two Kingdoms and One World* (ed.) Karl Hertz (Minneapolis, Minnesota: Augsburg Publishing House, 1976), pp. 189–192. This was a religious document that gave Hitler support at that time.

2 Translated as *Law and Gospel* by Edward H. Schroeder (Philadelphia: Fortress Press, 1967). Cited hereafter as *Law and Gospel*

3 *Law and Gospel,* p. 1

4 Ibid., pp. 1, 5.

5 Ibid., p. 2.

6 Ibid.

7 Ibid., p. 3.

8 Ibid.

9 Ibid., p. 4.

10 Barth, "Gospel and Law," p. 80.

11 Ibid., p. 72.
12 Elert, *Law and Gospel,* p. 6. (Italics added)
13 The citation is taken from Emil Brunner, *Man in Revolt* (Philadelphia: Westminster Press, 1947), p. 520, where he discusses Luther's understanding of law over against Barth.
14 *Luther's Works* (American ed., Concordia Publishing House and Fortress Press, 1955–), Vol. 26, pp. 308–309. Cited hereafter as LW.
15 Elert, *The Christian Ethos* (Philadelphia: Muhlenberg Press, 1957), pp. 15, 197f, 221. Cited hereafter as *The Christian Ethos.*
16 Elert, *The Structure of Lutheranism* (St. Louis: Concordia Publishing House, 1962), pp. 27, 34f. Cited hereafter as *The Structure of Lutheranism.*
17 *The Christian Ethos,* p. 15.
18 *Law and Gospel,* pp. 7–8.
19 Ibid., p. 10.
20 Elert, *Law and Gospel,* p. 10.
21 Elert, *The Christian Ethos,* pp. 18, 28.
22 Elert, *Law and Gospel,* p. 10.
23 Ibid. Elert cites Romans 5:16 for his view.
24 Elert, *Law and Gospel,* p. 11.
25 Ibid.
26 Ibid., p. 45.
27 Elert, *The Structure of Lutheranism,* pp. 21, 36–37, 56, 70.
28 Elert, *Law and Gospel,* p. 9.
29 Elert, *The Christian Ethos,* p. 53.
30 Elert, *Law and Gospel,* p. 9.
31 Elert, *The Christian Ethos,* p. 62.
32 Ibid., pp. 64–65.
33 Ibid., p. 65.
34 Ibid., pp. 65–66.
35 Ibid., pp. 16–17.
36 Ibid., pp. 7–11, 15, 32ff, 50, 70f.
37 *The Structure of Lutheranism,* p. 37; *The Christian Ethos,* pp. 18, 40f.
38 Ibid., pp. 18, 25–26, 50–51, 69.
39 Ibid., pp. 77ff.
40 Ibid., pp. 77–79.
41 Ibid., pp. 56, 67f, 82–83.
42 *The Structure of Lutheranism,* p. 37.
43 *The Christian Ethos,* p. 18.
44 Ibid., pp. 41, 56.
45 Ibid., p. 51; *Law and Gospel,* pp. 14–15.
46 *The Christian Ethos,* pp. 18, 67.
47 *The Christian Ethos,* pp. 18, 56, 67.
48 Ibid., pp. 40, 41.
49 Ibid., p. 79.
50 Ibid., p. 78.
51 Ibid., pp. 50, 67.

52 Ibid., p. 68.
53 Ibid., pp. 68–69.
54 Ibid., p. 67–69, 79, 82–123.
55 Ibid., p. 55.
56 Ibid., p. 55.
57 Ibid., pp. 40, 55, 68–69.
58 Ibid., pp. 25–26, 36f, 51, 55f.
59 Ibid., pp. 40, 67–68.
60 *Law and Gospel,* p. 15.
61 Ibid., p. 15. (Italics added)
62 *The Christian Ethos,* p. 140. Also cf. pp. 56–56ff.
63 *The Structure of Lutheranism,* p. 35; *The Christian Ethos,* pp. 145, 147f.
64. *The Christian Ethos,* p. 51f.
65 Ibid., p. 141.
66 Ibid.
67 *Law and Gospel,* pp. 7–15, 19, 36f, 48.
68 Forde, "Lex Semper Accusat?: Nineteenth Century Roots of Our Current Dilemma," in *Dialog* (Vol. 9, Autumn 1970), p. 274.
69 Elert, *Law and Gospel,* p. 9.
70 Ibid., pp. 1–3, 5, 26–27, 32, 48.
71 Ibid., p. 16.
72 Ibid., pp. 17–18, 30–32.
73 Ibid., p. 18.
74 Ibid., pp. 19–20; *The Christian Ethos,* p. 182.
75 Ibid., pp. 182–183.
76 *Law and Gospel,* pp. 20–21, *The Christian Ethos,* p. 186.
77 *Law and Gospel,* p. 20; *The Christian Ethos,* pp. 184ff.
78 *The Christian Ethos,* p. 187.
79 *Law and Gospel,* p. 25.
80 Ibid., p. 27.
81 Ibid., p. 28; *The Christian Ethos,* p. 192.
82 Ibid., p. 193; *Law and Gospel,* p. 28.
83 *The Christian Ethos,* p. 194. (Italics added.)
84 *Law and Gospel,* p. 30; *The Christian Ethos,* p. 194.
85 *Law and Gospel,* p. 30. (Italics added.)
86 Ibid., pp. 38–46. Elert goes so far as to suggest that regarding what we ought to do, the law, even the Decalogue, is helpless in political, societal, economic and practical life. Every decision will ever remain ours, no matter how hard we enquire after God's will in the law, and with *none* can we stand before God claiming to have done his will. See his discussion in *Law and Gospel,* pp. 35ff, 45ff.
87 *The Christian Ethos,* pp. 15, 197f, 221f.
88 Ibid., p. 33. Also see p. 24.
89 Cf. Brunner, *Man in Revolt,* pp. 517f.
90 Elert, *Law and Gospel,* p. 33.
91 Elert, *The Christian Ethis,* pp. 221f.
92 Elert, *Law and Gospel,* p. 48.

PART TWO

A critique and appraisal

Chapter three

A need for an adequate definition of law

It has been pointed out already that Elert is not at all persuaded by Barth's theological program which, in his opinion, has dismally failed to appreciate the fact that two distinct realities – with two different substances or contents – are involved when a theologian talks about law and gospel. In order to preserve this difference, especially of their formal as well as their material contents, Elert argues that a dialectical dialogue must be maintained between law and gospel.

However, since Barth has failed to do just that, the consequence has been both a *blurring* of material or substantive content of law and gospel, and also a failure to *purify* the concept of law. This purification, according to Elert, is possible only when a theologian takes the trouble to think through and distinguish what the concepts of law or gospel mean. In order for this to happen, of course, a clear definition of these concepts must be made because only then do we know what the law is, and what its content is (formally and materially), in contrast to the gospel.

However, as it will soon become clear, the issues are not as simple as Elert's charge would seem to suggest. Indeed, they are far more complex; they involve more than just a question of definition. As it turns out, it is Barth above all who has shown greater interest toward a redefinition of law, offering thereby a novel and very original conception of law, when he holds that the law is nothing else than a necessary form of the gospel whose content is grace. Indeed, contrary to what Elert's charge would make us believe, Barth has gone further than any of his contemporaries towards purifying the concept of law – despite the problems that his definitions create.

The fact still remains, however, that Elert has laid his finger on the crucial and sore point, namely, the need to define what the law is, and to spell out what its formal or material content is. The implications of such definitions of law are crucial for theology, and so are the contents that the law is understood to have. As Barth and Elert try to define the law and its content, both the deep-rooted differences in their positions and strengths as well as weaknesses in each theologian become manifest – as the following discussion shall demonstrate.

Elert defines law, as we have already seen, *formally* as God's manner of passing judgment. The context in which this formal definition is given is one in which God's judgment is understood to be two-fold: God's judgment is either condemnatory, as guilt-judgment is meted out through the law, or judgment of forgiveness, as the divine or Christ's righteousness is imputed upon the sinner through the preaching of the gospel. In other words, the concept of law – correctly understood in this formal sense – does not refer to a *thing* (known as law), but rather to an existential situation in which human beings, as sinners, stand under the scrutinizing "eye" of God.

The implication of Elert's definition of law in its formal sense means that the divine law is rightly understood only when its meaning is restricted to the so-called "theological use of law," where it mainly functions to reveal sin and to accuse the sinner before God. Consequently, law is God's juridical activity, or a passing of senctence of guilt. Put differently, law is nothing else but a portrayal of man as God sees him in the totality of his being, not just a judgment of series of events in life. This can mean only that a theological talk about the divine law has as its view the description of human life as judged "exclusively by God's standards."[1]

The upshot of Elert's conceptualization of law, understood in its "correct" and formal sense, is that law has been lifted out of the immanental sphere to the transcendental realm, that is, to the level where only categories of the sinner's justification before God, not humans, apply.[2] This explains why Elert stresses the fact that the criteria by which the quality of man's life is judged, when the divine law is rightly talked about, refer unequivocally to "God's exclusive standard." Within such a framework, the meaning of the divine law is discontinuous with the secular or immanental laws by which external behaviour is judged either as good or bad in society. For, according to Elert, the primary question is: Seeing that "we are by nature children of wrath, born into life under law," how do sinners – as we are – stand *coram Deo?* When the law is understood in this formal sense, Elert believes, *the inevitable answer* to such a question is that "God's law condemns man." The intensity of the condemnatory judgment of the law is driven home, especially, when the extent of our sinfulness "enters our awareness" through the event of Jesus Christ, who, as the Holy One, "communicates with us."[3]

From these observations, Elert draws the conclusion that portrays the divine law with a startling formal content, when he holds that "the *law of retribution is the law of God in the strictest sense of the word.*"[4] The upshot of this assertion is that God is wrathful through the use of law because God is the God of law which is, in principle, inherently retributive. Consequently, the divine law makes sure that sinful human life should end in death, because death is the reward of sin. When the law is defined formally, as Elert has done, it comes as no big surprise that God's law has no love, no creativity, no mercy, nor grace in its use.[5] Not only is love ruled out as the content of law, but also Elert polemicizes against Calvin who, in his opinion, disarms or depotentiates the law when he injects grace into his discussion of law. By doing this the notion of retribution, which is the content of law, is removed or smoothed over. For if the law is also grace then it is deprived of its divinely uttered retaliatory threat.[6]

Elert, to be sure, concedes that Jesus summarized the double-command of law by love of God and love of the neighbour. Also, he says he is aware that "in I John 3:23, faith, to be sure, appears together with love as the content of the divine commandment."[7] But he adds that this does not mean that faith and love are identical. Nor should they be collapsed into each other. This need not be the case because it does not make any sense to say faith is love and vice versa. Neither does anyone get any clarity by insisting that faith, as love, is obedience because such an assertion leads to legalistic misinterpretations. Furthermore, Elert argues that the law of love is foreign to the Decalogue with its retaliatory threats. Therefore, it is wrong to assume that the double-command of love by which Jesus summarized the law warrants us to say that the Decalogue has love as its content. According to Elert, as we have shown already, the law of love is so new and unprecedented that it is both unknown in that double-meaning in the Old Testament and goes beyond the Decalogue by demanding one-sided love of the enemy — thereby excluding rewards and punishments which constitute the Decalogue.[8]

The heavy-handed manner in which Elert removes love as the content of the divine law raises serious problems. It is true that his position clearly distinguishes the law from the gospel because the latter has grace as its exclusive content; but it is not clear at all that Elert has succeeded in purifying the concept of law — as he claims. He starts out by accusing Barth of a lack of clarity and of precise definition of law, but he ends up giving us a generalized, imprecise, and misleading definition of law, a definition that is totally negative and lacking of any positive element. Indeed, nothing can be more negative and general than to say that *the law of retribution is the law of God in the strictest sense of the word.* To complicate matters even further, Elert adds that, while vengeance is God's, humans are the ones who execute the retributive function of the law as executors.[9] The problem does not lie in his saying that humans carry out these punishments, but in the general meaning which this formal definition has. Law as that which condemns is so general that it can virtually be identical with each and everything that condemns or accuses human conscience. Elert tacitly acknowledges this generality by affirming both that God's law is identical in content with natural laws because they all accuse the sinner in his/her opposition to God, and by conceding that "natural law is not a coherent system in which all parts fit together."[10]

What is frightening is Elert's denial that love is the content of the divine law. His refusal to spell out what the positive content of law is, apart from its retaliatory function, means that we have no criterion by which God's law might be differentiated from the laws of Baal because the important thing is that a true law must always accuse. In one of his most disturbing sentences, Elert has this to say:

> *Our problem* at the moment *is not the citizens who will have to obey the law* but "those responsible" who determine its content. *Whether these laws owe their origin to a king or parliament, a dictator or a plebiscite makes no difference.*[11]

This citation sounds ominous despite Elert's assurances that the Decalogue should be reflected upon responsibly when laws are made. The problem is that — since the Decalogue is itself God's most retributary law in the strictest sense of the word and refuses to be changed into the law of love, mercy and grace – we have no positive criterion whatsoever. Consequently, no amount of reflection upon the Decalogue – no matter how serious the effort – can save us from the dilemma in which we find ourselves, were we to accept the formal definition of law that Elert gives. This is because, in the final analysis, it makes "no difference" what the content of the law is (love, wrath, death, etc.) and where they owe their origin (dictators, kings, etc.), as long as we keep in mind that:

> The law of retribution is a fundamental principle of every form of nomological existence especially of the social use of the law as wielded by the state. It is not only basic to criminal law but also serves civil law as *justitia commutativa.*[12]

It is our contention that Elert's lack of interest in the content, origins and, finally, *the citizens who have to obey the law,* is very dangerous; for it lends itself well to all kinds of distortions from which he had intended to purify the law. To be sure, Elert suggests that preservation of human existence is also served by the law, but his indifference to the contents of various laws, or where laws owe their origin, or the quality of preservation that laws intend to serve, or the implications of a demonic law to the citizens who reel under its oppression, ignores the experience of how tyranny and fascism can do all kinds of things in the name of the preservation of human existence, or "Christian" civilization, or a "pure" race, and/or law and order.[13]

Moreover, Elert's assertions that God's law is fundamentally retributive for it both preserves life and also to ensure that we must finally die;[14] that "even the destructive, disrupting, depleting reign of death" proceeds according to God's law in judging human life; that the "tragedy which is inherent in the political existence of the nations" as well as imperfections and breakdowns of treaties point to *lex quae semper accusat;*[15] that wars and afflictions are God's instruments in carrying out punishments; that the preservative function of law must also be qualified by its inherent retributive principle;[16] that a retrogression of civilization to barbarism through annihilations of humans in the twentieth century somehow has to be understood as judgment by God's law which accuses;[17] all of them make it abundantly clear that God's law is either demonic or that the divine law is *not at all different* in content from all other oppressive and destructive laws that are inherently deadly and demonic at the hands of tyranny and fascism. For history shows that oppressive and dictatorial laws can, in fact, destroy or suppress humans in the name of saving them from real or imagined leftist ideas.

One wonders whether Elert's assertion, that God's law is fundamentally retaliatory, something for which we must be grateful even though it turns us over to death, expresses a true understanding of what the divine law is all about, or simply mirrors his personal pessimism about human history which, in his view, is a "history of man's revolt" against God.[18] Or is this perhaps an indication that by defining law as he has, Elert has gone beyond a point where no room is left for a positive function of the law of God, one which can, in fact, be different from other demonic laws? An inevitable conclusion to which his position leads us is that either Elert's definition of law is a gross misunderstanding or it is so inadequately defined and formulated that no other dimensions of God's law, with positive aspects or uses, can find accommodation and expression.

Indeed, Elert leads us into a situation where, if his views are accepted, we are unable to say *what it is* that basically distinguishes God's law from other laws and obligations, such as laws of Baal, Nazism, or worshippers of racism. For it seems clear that, according to Elert, our faith has no illumination in this matter either. Consequently, humanity appears totally defenseless before claims and counter-claims, incapable of questioning, challenging, or rejecting these contradictory voices, because there is no basis or criterion of any positive content of God's law by which these other claims might be relativized.

Put differently, Elert gives the impression that even believers in God through Jesus Christ have no norm by which judgment can be made between distortions and laws that truly attempt to express the divine will, because all laws must in principle express a retributive activity of God.[19] It may be that Elert is right in his contention that none of us can stand before God, claiming to have known and done God's will fully. Nonetheless, Christians have always maintained that some norm, though limited, can be found in God's revelation in Jesus Christ. Absolute knowledge they do not claim to possess, but this need not lead to cynical conclusions that no criterion whatsoever is available to distinguish between demonic and good laws – as if humanity were in darkness, or "night in which," as Hegel observes, "all cows are black."[20]

Reflecting the opinion of most Christians that God has not left humanity in total darkness as implied by Elert's position, Nürnberger, in one of his insightful observations, echoes the justifiable criticism that Barth has often levelled against Lutheranism in general for courting a danger exemplified by Lutherans, such as Elert, and writes:

> The danger ..... is that there *seems to be no distinction between the will of God in himself and all sorts of other worldly obligations,* and the Gospel doesn't give any guidance either. The result is that the Gospel itself seems to have no impact in the world, while all sorts of secular and religious obligations may assume the status of divinely instituted laws. Law and Gospel break apart and the Law becomes the decisive thing, without any criterion of what its legitimate contents is![21]

It may very well be that the guidance Nürnberger believes exists from the gospel, and the hope that problems might be solved when biblical faith is distinguished from other religions, are oversimplifications of what these aids can actually achieve.[22]

Nonetheless, he puts his finger on the decisive question, namely, one of *the legitimate contents* that just laws might be expected to have, in contrast to demonic laws with all their "illegitimate" contents and obligations. For it is when questions of legitimate contents of laws and criteria are ignored, as Elert does, that Christians have often found themselves supporting highly questionable courses (if not outright injustice and oppression) in the name of law and order. Indeed, where law and order are the only major concerns without asking what the contents of these laws are, and the quality of the order that is being defended is, and when the stress is placed merely on the need to curb chaos and sin – as Elert does – then almost anything that effectively checks chaos, in the name of law and order, can easily become a possible candidate that must now be identified with the law (will) of God (including totalitarianism and fascism which, incidentally, appear effective in containing alleged disorders in a given society).[23] These errors are traceable to Elert's attempt to give a formal definition of law whose content is totally negative, when it is expressed in concepts such as retribution, retaliation, judgment, and death. Above all, in his zeal to maintain the difference between law and gospel, Elert overexaggerates his claims when he holds that the law of God as the law of retribution cannot be changed into the law of love. Moreover, when he eliminates love (and perhaps rightly the heavily loaded word "grace") as the content of the divine will which is expressed through the law, and makes retribution the only content, Elert's program becomes highly vulnerable to distortions of every kind because retribution can be claimed for many oppressive courses which, in fact may be gross violations of the very law of God.

To be sure, the Old Testament laws seem to contain some elements of retribution, such as Gen. 9:6, Exod. 21:24f, etc. But it is not clear that we should rule out love as the content of God's law. Even more, it becomes problematic when retribution is substituted for love as the content of divine law because this defeats the very purpose that any purification of the concept of law is supposed to achieve. There is yet another weakness which shall be pointed out later after we have discussed Barth's position because they share it, namely, the attempt to define and restrict the meaning of law within the framework of justification of humans before God, a move that hardly does adequate justice to the social uses of the law.

The question of the content and purity of the concept of law, as we have already indicated, was of particular interest to Barth. In his attack on Lutheranism, Barth spared no effort to think through it again and again. In a way, his theology offers a much needed corrective to Elert's weakness, when it comes to the question of content and criterion by which judgment could be made concerning various laws. As we have seen, Barth's most basic and formal definition of the law, simply stated, is: "Law is nothing else than the necessary *form of the Gospel,* whose content is grace."[24]

In other places, Barth adds that law as grace is identical with Jesus Christ. That is, Jesus Christ is both the gospel and the law because He is the One eternal Word of God. Or, put differently, the person of Jesus Christ is both the grace of God and also its form and therefore, He is both the gospel and the law.[25] By defining the law formally as the grace of God in Jesus Christ, and by arguing that Jesus is both the form and content of law and, therefore, that *He must be the criterion of all laws,*[26] Barth shifts the dialogue in a decisive manner. He refuses thereby to separate the discussion of law from its ground, content, and criterion, namely Jesus Christ. Whether Barth is correct, by holding that grace is the content of God's law, and therefore that Jesus Christ is the only form of the divine law by which God confronts us, is another matter we need not take up at this point.

Rather what interests us is the bravery with which Barth faces the question of the criterion, indeed, of the legitimacy of the content that God's law must have head-on. For, by defining the law formally in such a way that makes it identical with Jesus Christ (God's grace), Barth establishes a decisive criterion by which various laws might be judged, questioned, and even rejected, or disobeyed. Unlike Elert, who cares little about the origins of laws and their contents as well as about the citizens who must obey them, Barth believes the origins of laws, their uses or contents in the society matter. His special concern in all these is clearly manifest when Barth cautions us against certain laws and writes:

> Submission to all other demands, even if made in the name of God, can only be provisional and not binding, and it always involves a risk of error. *The criterion by which all other demands are to be measured is whether they, too, proclaim indirectly the life and rule and victory of Jesus. If they fail to do this, if they do the very opposite, they are definitely wrong,* and when we know this, *it is only with a violated conscience that we can submit to them.*[27]

Barth rightly rejects any suggestion that we have no knowledge of God's will, or law and, consequently, anything can qualify as a candidate for God's law. He is persuaded that *God wills nothing really different from Jesus* in whom He directs and claims us "for Himself."[28] Indeed, he knows that many other laws do not simply express God's will as this is revealed in Jesus Christ. Consequently, it is important for those who must obey various claims and counter-claims that they should distinguish law from laws, demonic claims that oppress and violate our integrity from God's law whose content is grace (the gospel or Jesus).

The criterion Barth gives is a decisive guidance which can, if applied, make the difference between one's obedience to the laws of Baal, nationalism, racism, and the law of Yahweh. Another landmark Barth gives believers, as a useful criterion by which various laws can be distinguished, is one of freedom. According to him, God's law never binds, but sets free. It never appeals to human fears, but to human courage, while other laws function differently, appealing to human fears, weakness, and prejudices so as to achieve their oppressive and destructive ends. Indeed, these other laws use "these fears to appeal to him, instilling them into him and holding him in grip. In essence, their bidding is a forbidding; the refusal of all possible permissions,"[29] Because these oppressive laws, which are by nature demonic and unjust, never open up dimensions of freedom and liberation for humanity, they differ very sharply from the real command of God, which is characterized by the giving of permissions — the granting of a very definite freedom. For the God who claims us through the law is not a dominating tyrant or fascist, but rather a gracious Lord whose aim is to quicken and liberate.[30]

There is no doubt that Barth's landmarks or definitions of God's law, with explicit content and criteria, have strengths that might correct weaknesses inherent in Elert's theology. For, by stressing the qualitative difference in form, content and function between the law of Yahweh and other demonic laws, Barth has injected a discontinuity between biblical faith and other religions, or laws, or obligations.

This is made possible by the fundamentally different contents that are constitutive of various laws. Furthermore, Barth stresses the corrective function of faith which must distinguish between true laws, that express God's will, and distortions to which laws might be subject under oppressive, fascist, racist, and totalitarian regimes.

However, while Barth's overall formal definition of law has obvious advantages and strengths over Elert's, it does raise serious problems when questions of the material content of law are posed. Because Barth wanted to make good his word, that God's law – in virtue of its form, content and function – must *be distinguished not just relatively but absolutely, with the distinction of heaven over earth,* he had to lift God's command from the immanental realm to a transcendental sphere where it is not only identical with God's active commanding, but also becomes incapable of propositional formulation.[31]

What makes it even more serious is the fact that now it becomes unclear how in real life God's command is related to the empirical, historical laws, that have resulted from human deliberative reason and constructions. In order to restate the nature of the problem, the best place to begin would be to focus on how God, in calling or commanding us in the event of grace, simultaneously establishes or gives the law to us.[32] In doing so, Barth joins both the gospel and the law. What is more, just as the gospel is grace, so is the law. This graciousness of the law now means that, like the gospel, it becomes something that is beyond human control both in form and content. The reason is that Jesus is the law's form as God's grace, or content. Consequently, the control of when, how, and where we may receive God's law is all in God's hand, who, from time to time, chooses to give it to us in the event of grace. And we may not anticipate what the law shall be in advance of the actual revelation, neither can we *thingify* it into codes of laws (written or unwritten); for it is pure grace, a pure event.

Barth does not tire of emphasizing again and again that God's law is pure grace, a pure event that is not at human disposal to be manipulated by moralists.[33] By emphasizing the fact that God's command is grace, or pure event, Barth wants to exclude – as far as it is humanly possible – any trust in "inner and outer laws" which may now be thought of as *the* correct formulations of the divine will (law). Rather, Barth goes on to assert, God's true law defies any human formulations of it; indeed, to try to formulate it leads only to legalism or error.[34] This, to repeat, is because God's law, as an *event,* can never be separated from God who speaks it in the event of revelation. For God deals with us as the living, active, and commanding personal God, who continuously issues commands.[35] To be more precise, it is not to abstractions of laws, conceived and formulated by humans but to the divine, active overlordship that the theological notion of the law points us.

Consequently, Barth argues that the "One who really commands is the living, *eternal God who repeats his claims anew for every man."*[36] And Because God and his divine commanding are inseparable, apart from the concrete commanding and living God, there is no law, new or revolutionary, to which believers are subject. Indeed, any law that can be separable from the personal God who gives concrete commands in every situation is a false absolute or "spurious Infinite" which need not be obeyed.[37] For Jesus Christ, as the law of the Kingdom, is the only law which believers and unbelievers are called upon to obey.[38] Of course, this law is distinguishable from all other laws, both by its form and content, namely, the commanding grace of God in Jesus Christ who is its ground, origin, and criterion. By contrast, all other laws are capable of being called into question because they are never free from distortions, perversions, and absolutizations that laws, founded in ognorance of Jesus Christ, are subject to.[39]

Once Barth has identified the law with God's active commanding rule in Jesus Christ who, as the law of the Kingdom, is not *ius humanum* but *ius divinum,* it now means that an absolute discontinuity has been created between God's law – in the person of Jesus Christ – and any empirical, historical laws which are all *ius humanum.* And, just how God's law is related to these human laws that are always historical, relative, and linguistic constructions and innovations, becomes one of the thorniest problems in Barth's theology. The question is whether such a transcendent law in the person of God can at all be expressed in a broken human language.[40] The way Barth tries to answer this question of continuity between law and laws, one *ius divinum,* and the other *ius humanum,* and the extent to which he succeeds or fails, is one which shall be taken up in the following chapters.

Notes

1 Elert, *The Christian Ethos,* pp. 6–7, 141. Also see pp. 16–17, 26, 298f.

2 Ibid., pp. 2–7, 16–17, 141. Elert, in order not to leave any doubt that categories of justification operate, separates moral behaviour from this qualitative judgment by God of the totality of human life. There moral standards do not apply, and a move from human judgment to the divine judgment has to be made.

3 Ibid., pp. 16–17, 185–187, 298–302.

4 Ibid., p. 53 (Italics added)

5 Ibid., pp. 28, 51ff, 62, 294, 301f. As if Elert takes pleasure in the fact that law formally defined is always accusing, delivering us to death, he retorts: "As the law of retribution, the Decalogue resists all attempts to change it into the law of love" (Ibid., p. 62).

6 Ibid., p. 302.

7 Elert, *Law and Gospel,* p. 47.

8 Elert, *The Christian Ethos,* pp. 59–60, 61–64.

9 Ibid., pp. 52–53, 68–70, 73f, 101–103, 160–168.

10 Ibid., p. 76. For an elaborate identification of all laws (Decalogue and natural laws) see Ibid., pp. 70–76.

11 Ibid., p. 112. (Italics added)

12 Ibid., p. 113.

13 The "master race" idea of Nazism during the insanity of Hitler's reign, through which Elert has lived, should have served as a warning. Other examples abound, such as dictatorships in East and West, or racist regimes that use law for separatist ideology because God's will requires such a separation of races.

14 Elert, *The Christian Ethos,* pp. 51–52, 294.

15 Ibid., pp. 52, 70.

16 Ibid., pp. 108, 113.

17 Ibid., p. 141.

18 Ibid., p. 28. Also cf. pp. 29–35, 53–67.

19 Elert's position, by claiming that God's law is intrinsically retributive and by implying that there is no positive criterion to differentiate between laws (for love is not a content of any law), drew a sharp and almost angry retort from Dr. Kaufman, who, in one of his tutorial responses to a draft, among other things asked: How can such a law whose essence is retribution be an order of creation which supports us, and gives us security as Elert claims elsewhere? Can such a demonic retribution as described by Elert be attributable to God? Can this portrait be reconciled with the Christian view of a loving God? The answer to all these questions is simply no! Indeed, it shall be the burden of this study to prove our contention that there is no basis for Elert's view in the biblical testimony; nor is the God who is portrayed by him identical with God our Redeemer in Jesus Christ.

20 G.W.F. Hegel, *The Phenomenology of Mind,* translated by J.B. Baillie (New York: Harper Torchbooks, 1967), p. 79.

21 Klaus Nürnberger, *Dogmatics I,* Appendix to Chaps. 7–9 (unpublished lectures, South Africa, Mapumulo: Lutheran Theological College, 1971–72), p. 99. Cited henceforth as *Dogmatics I.*

22 Ibid., p. 100. He assumes that faith and religion are unrelated, and ignores the influences of culture, mores, values, and prevailing beliefs in which faith is formed — as if faith transcends its cultural milieu.

23 Elert's tendency to stress law and order, at the expense of legitimacy, justice that law expresses and the quality that is supposed to result when order is maintained, explains in part his involvement in the drawing up of the "Ansbach Proposal as a Response to the Barmen Theological Declaration" (June, 1934), which, in fact, gave Hitler's regime a tacit support. Also, his preference for a stable, ordered world, whose best forms he found in German institutions of the past, underscores his dislike for social change and his commitment to the politics of the Weimar Republic. His theology of "orders of creation" is nothing but a rehash of this lost "golden age" which had to be defended theologically at any cost.

24 Barth, "Gospel and Law," p. 80.

25 Barth, *Church Dogmatics,* II/2, pp. 557–59, 553, 566, 568, 606, 632.

26 Ibid., pp. 568, 606, 632.

27 Ibid., p. 568. (Italics added) It is clear that, for Barth, there is a sharp distinction between demonic laws that might be obeyed with a violated conscience and God's true and just law, which can be obeyed with free and willing conscience.

28 Ibid.

29 Ibid., pp. 585, 587.

30 Barth stresses freedom and even makes obedience lighter by comparing it to an invitation to a feast, a wedding. It is a law of liberty that "orders us to be free." It instills courage in a disarming manner, so as not to leave us with excuses for not becoming free for God (Ibid., pp. 586–88).

31 Ibid., pp. 588, 602–603.

32 He writes: "Ruling grace is the commanding grace. The gospel itself has the form and fashion of the Law. The One Word of God is both Gospel *and* Law ..... the Law has the form of grace. As the grace of God is actualised and revealed, He claims men. His love commands" (Ibid., pp. 511, 566).

33 Barth's position here has an obvious affinity to Elert's already critized above and concerning which more will be said. Both believe that the transcendental law of God is beyond the immanental laws that have to do with penultimate and limited good advocated by moralists in society.

34 Barth, *Church Dogmatics* II/2, pp. 602–603, 672ff, 700.

35 Ibid., pp. 672–700; *Church Dogmatics* III/4, pp. 5–6.

36 *Church Dogmatics* III/4, p. 16. (Italics added)

37 *Church Dogmatics* IV/2, p. 547.

38 Ibid., pp. 547ff, 683, 710f, 715, 721–722.

39 Ibid., pp. 721–723.

40 It has been observed already that Elert, too, operates with a law which has been lifted out of the immanental sphere to the transcendental realm. It is for this reason that he conceives of law as an *infinite, absolute,* or *divine standard* by which human life is judged. This law operates within the categories of justification before God where any fulfillment of it, by humans through external behaviour, is impossible. In both cases we have conceptions of law which have nothing in common with historical laws which regulate human behaviour in society.

Chapter four

Law and God's will: a problem of material content of the divine law

How, and the manner in which, the will of God is disclosed to humanity and, consequently, the medium by which this will is communicated and thereby known, have been and still are among the most controversial issues in theological discourse. Taken together, they pose the question of material content which the divine law is believed to consist of. In other words, very often theologians do not merely limit their definition of law to its formal meaning but also try to spell out how *materially* God's law appears to humans to whom the divine will is revealed.

As theologians try to flesh out concretely what this material content consists of, a considerable disagreement becomes evident regarding the nature of the medium by which God's will is made known. That is, theologians are not agreed on what this medium materially is. Therefore, some theologians take the Ten Commandments as the primary form in which God's will is materially known, and the fulfilment of the Decalogue is thereby understood to be an obedience of the divine will. Other theologians, however, supplement the Decalogue by talking about a general revelation through which natural laws are generated, and it is believed that some knowledge of the will of God can be culled from such a revelation as well. Those who take the latter route find their support in St. Paul who seems to suggest that even heathens (non-Jewish peoples) could do the works of law and, therefore, that the will of God is not completely hidden from them (Rom. 2:13–15).

It is against this controversial background of divergence of opinion among theologians, namely: whether the will of God should be identified exclusively with the special law given to believers in the Old Testament or it should be identified also with natural laws, believed to have been written on human hearts, in addition to the special revelation, that the discussion of the relation between the law and the will of God and, therewith, the question of the material content of law by Barth and Elert should be understood. That the will of God is somehow known, therefore, is not debatable. But whether the Decalogue, or written codes, may be a material content of the divine law remains largely unresolved.

Elert, like Barth, holds the view, as we have observed already, that the will of God is revealed to humanity through the divine law.[1] But when he is pressed to spell out *in what,* materially, this law consists of, that is, the form that the *lex quae semper accusat* has, Elert becomes noncommital. Defensively, he argues that such a demand for spelling out what the material content of the law is is misguided, for it asks the wrong question. Indeed, this demand assumes that God's law and theologians must give answers to human questions, such as: What ought we to do? What is it that God wants when the divine will is revealed through the law?

Elert is convinced that God's law does not answer such questions. If it did, it would imply that the divine law is a demand placed upon individuals from outside like any other heteronomous moral imperative. Further, it would imply that God's law demands an external good or behaviour from humans, a behaviour conforming to an existing legal structure according to which a judgment can be rendered by a "third party, a judge or a jury."[2] Yet, the truth of the matter is that God's law, truly understood, is never a body of "norms by which the Christian believer can be guided in his daily activities." That is, God's law is not a rule of life which theologians can formulate to "enable" the believer to "practice his Christian convictions in actual life situations."[3]

One could conclude from these negative answers that Elert denies the validity of any suggestion that the divine law is known to humans. However, he assures the reader that this is simply not the case. Rather, what he questions is the assumption that human life is a response, or obedience, to some law whether human or divine.[4] This is false because, as we have observed already, Elert does not believe that God is a legislator who gives the divine will in laws, codes, or prescriptive precepts. Indeed, were God a legislator for human conduct, it would imply that there is a place where we may read of such divine will, a divine will found in codes for the purpose of giving ultimate answers to penultimate human questions.[5]

However, the truth of the matter is that such a divine will that can be codified is not available. And to think that it is available merely courts the danger of legalistic understanding which complicates rather than solves the problem. For the result can be only endless theorizing about laws "written on hearts" which need to be supplemented either through written codes in Scriptures or a synergistic combination of individual effort to fulfill the law and the help that is given by grace in Jesus Christ, because of the persistent reality of sin. In reality, however, Elert believes that no one lives according to such ideals, *norma normans* of all human behavior.[6]

Once he rejects the view that human behaviour is lived according to some revealed law in which God's will is encapsulated, Elert launches an attack on Barth and Calvin, who, as he claims, thought that God's law answers human questions, such as: *What ought we to do do?*[7] Indeed, unlike them, Elert is very pessimistic about just how much material content of the divine law can be culled and systematized and known with certainty from biblical laws. According to him, the "notion that the Holy Scriptures are a collection of moral precepts is misleading" because "under no circumstance can we define this ethos as the unqualified acceptance of imperatives."[8]

Elert justifies his pessimistic conclusion by returning to his basic contention that *God's law, after all, is never meant to supply us with information about what we should do.* Rather its function, as the *lex quae semper accusat,* is one of constant exposure of sin and to hold sinners in check. For it presupposes the reality of human sinfulness in all aspects of life and, as a consequence, it is a means by which God renders judgment of guilt to "every single individual, for the godless as well as for the so-called righteous, and also for the regenerate."[9] The Church, therefore, preaches the law not to guide the "new man" in Christ but to destroy the "old man" who participates in the sinfulness of Adam. For, the law must incessantly tell us that we lie when we say we have no sin, because God's law is never anything but an accuser who must always convict the sinner.[10]

Elert is somewhat gratified that his conclusions are supported by a Reformed theologian, Emil Brunner in his book on law and social order.[11] He refers specifically to Brunner's awareness that humans need a divine law that could supply them with information in their struggle against social ills. But after thoughtful reflection, Brunner was led to an inevitable conclusion – similar to that of Elert – that, *regarding what we ought to do, the law can by no means help.* Instead of giving prescriptions and guidelines precisely at those places where the law touches upon human relationships, it offers only prohibitions.[12] To be sure, Elert concedes, Luther was a bit hopeful in this matter because he tried to elicit positive sides of the law. But he draws our attention to the fact that even Luther was forced to issue the rejoinder that the Decalogue was retributary in his explanation of the first Commandment.

Moreover, even if such positive elicitations, such as Luther made, were possible, the conclusions we would draw from these laws would forever remain human decisions.[13] And, consequently, these conclusions would be burdened with the same dubious character as all human conclusions as far as practical questions of life are concerned. To underline the relativity of all human conclusions and problems that one encounters in decision-making, Elert takes as his example one of the difficult texts in the New Testament and writes:

> According to Romans 13, the authorities exercise their official power to restrain evil. But whether God demands a government constituted in a particular manner, and which one that might be – this we are not told. *No matter how eager we are to be obedient in our inquiry after the will of God at this point, the risk of decision is, ultimately, always our own responsibility.*[14]

It is obvious from these considerations that Elert not only refuses to spell out *what material content* the divine law might possibly be said to have, but also tries his best to eliminate any desire on the part of believers to seek after such divinely commanded law. The reason he gives is that every decision is ultimately human and, therefore, no law qualifies unequivocally as *the candidate* for the material content of divine law. More importantly, it is clear that Elert is unable to discuss law without tilting toward categories of justification before God *(coram Deo),* where none of our decisions can claim to have conformed to the divine law. Elert's view may be correct if by arguing

— as he does — we try to avoid *direct identification* of any empirical laws with God's law. But if it means that no law or norm whatsoever exists to differentiate demonic laws from God's law in society, this can be dangerous as we have already pointed out.

Indeed, Christians in Hitler's Germany, or in other totalitarian states — were Elert's dictum to be accepted as the whole biblical truth — would have no basis whatsoever to oppose repressive laws, or governments in the name of God's revealed law or will, however imperfect their perception of God's Absolute truth or law may be.[15] Nor would the powers that be need justify their actions because it would not matter, in the final analysis; for with none of their actions can they stand *coram Deo* claiming to have fulfilled any known will or law of God. Moreover, his position rules out the very idea that there is a will or law of God which must be obeyed, because it would hardly make any sense to demand obedience to a law which is not known.

Against Elert, it must be contended that the witness of the Churches, or believers in the Old Testament, such as the prophets who fought against social ills, contradict the assertion that we are totally ignorant about the will or law of God; for, were it unknown, it would be unintelligible to demand obedience to it by prophets. Even Luther, on whose authority Elert makes these claims, had to oppose the Roman Catholic Church on the grounds that somehow he knew God's will and, therefore, that it was possible to distinguish aberrations from genuine obedience to God's law. One cannot escape the impression that Elert's assessment of the law was made deliberately negative because in this way it could be harmonized with his formal definition of law, a definition claiming that God's law is always retributive.

Consequently, instead of allowing other meanings of the law, such as those which have to do with the positive actions for social justice and righteousness, to challenge and correct his conceptions, Elert defines the law exclusively in negative terms in advance of any consideration of these other meanings. The result is that he forces every other meaning of law into this "strait-jacket" conception of law, while he anxiously tries to persuade us that no other positive content of the divine law is either formally or materially known. For this reason his talk about divine law which is also protective of life rings hollow and unconvincing, because in the final analysis it, too, must, in principle and of necessity, be retributive as the law that serves *justitia commutativa.*[16] And it strikes us as rather strange that he would talk about God's nomological structures which are in conflict with nomological structures of evil, each with its laws. For, if no positive content of the divine law exists, how does one distinguish one nomological structure from the other seeing that the content of law is the same, namely retribution? Also, if humans are the ones who execute these laws, is the danger not more multiplied by the fact that – by virtue of their limited insight – they might be administrating nomological structures of evil rather than those of God, especially if no norm is there to evaluate which of these laws express God's will that is known?

Finally, Elert reassures us time and again – in his discussion of the orders of creation – that God's law points us to the total cosmos ordered by the mighty hand of God, a cosmos in which each of us is placed at birth so that none might fall away from God's hand. This cosmos is dependable and offers us security.[17] But if, in fact, God's law includes the totality of the cosmos which is ordered by divine might for our security, are we not entitled to question Elert as to whether his negative definition of law, the *lex quae semper accusat* the human conscience of sin, is not perhaps too narrowly based? That is, must we then extend this human experience of pangs of conscience to the totality of this ordered cosmos through the mighty hand of God, the law – presupposing existence of moral qualms of conscience and agonies of judgment outside the social sphere?

Indeed, if sin and the experience of the condemnatory function of *lex quae semper accusat* are purely human psychological or spiritual phenomena, is it not a mistake to project them on to other creatures that are included in the totality of the cosmos? If these experiences are unknown among the animal kingdom, for instance, is it not unintelligible to still insist that the law of retribution is the law of God in the true sense of the word? That is, if nomological existence means to live in a cosmos ordered by God's might for the protection of life (among humans and other creatures), is it not a distortion of language to claim that such security, as the divine law might provide, means the same as retribution – merely to satisfy Elert's theological bias that God uses law *always* to accuse? Elert, for all practical purposes, has given us a one-sided and defective understanding of law both in its formal and material sense. The mistake seems to lie in his discussion of law always within the framework of human justification before God. Hence his declaration that with none of our decisions and actions can we stand before God claiming to have fulfilled the divine will (law).

This may be true, but do we need to stand *always coram Deo* rather than *coram hominibus* having not only discharged the duties of our vocations responsibly and faithfully but also, by doing so, become instruments of God's creative love? Is this not what Elert himself affirms when he says: "When we love someone God loves through us," and that "our brethren do not compete with God for our love because we cannot love God without loving our brethren"?[18] It is clear that, if love for the brethren is the content of human obedience that the law requires, so that possible, penultimate, or relative justice might be procured, then these positive functions of law cannot be given adequate expression in Elert's theology which limits and confines its conception of law to the framework of justification. Indeed, his theology anchors the understanding of law so narrowly on so small a place that other uses of law in other areas, in which God's ordering of the cosmos continually takes place, are rendered impossible to understand. We shall return to this later, after considering what in Barth's view constitutes the material content of God's law.

We have shown already that Barth, unlike Elert, affirms as true the fact that God gives commands to humanity and, therefore, that they are not left to their own devices. According to Barth, the command of God gives answer to the human question: "What ought we to do"?[19] On their own, humans cannot discover what goodness or rightness are. Rather these are told them by the living God who reveals this knowledge in the event of commanding grace. Also, Barth rejects as unfounded a complaint, such as Elert makes, that we are ignorant of God's will or law, that the will of God has not been given us unequivocally and that, therefore, we cannot stand before God claiming to have conformed to the divine law with any of our decisions.[20] This is, Barth adds, a futile evasion of the fact that God, in his Word as King of kings, is so present to the world and each individual that He confronts him or her in the smallest step and thought through his commands.[21]

Normally, one could conclude from this flat rejection of Elert's claim that Barth will be more forthright and willing to spell without equivocation what the material content of this law that God gives us is, so that each of us can be guided in our obedience. However, Barth does the contrary; he is the first to caution us against such a conclusion. The reason is simple: In his formal definition of law, Barth contends that it is a mistake to separate, isolate, and *thingify* God's commanding grace. Grace is grace, and can never be "something" that exists independent of the living, acting God. This grace of God, which is both the form and content of law, is the person of Jesus Christ. As such, this commanding grace of God is given neither once-and-for-all nor in such a way that it is subject to human control, so that it might be reduced into propositional or general rules of conduct.[22]

At this point, therefore, Barth is in agreement with Elert that *material content* of God's command, which can be known and constructed prior to a concrete situation of decision-making in which the command is given in the event of revelation, is not simply available. For Barth, however, it is not because the divine will (law) is unknown, as Elert alleges, but rather because God controls both the formal and material content of his command. Hence Barth declares:

> His commanding is not the *empty positivity of commanding that this or that should be done. And that is why it cannot be left to our whim how we are to fill it out,* in what special way we are to obey God. There is no divine claim as such in itself. There are only concrete divine claims. For it is the grace of God which expresses itself in these claims. *It is always God in Jesus Christ* who, as He puts these claims, wills to have us for Himself.[23]

In this and many other paragraphs, Barth closes all doors to any demand that he should spell out what the material content of the law consists of. For God's law *in itself* is never found in general laws, or moral maxims which, as such, could qualify as the material content of God's command, because the real command is never separable from the God who speaks it in the concrete situation in which his ruling grace is issued. Therefore, neither the Decalogue nor Jesus' Sermon on the Mount is such a material content.[24] Much less, then, can we believe that such a material content exists outside God's revelation in Jesus Christ – as moralists are inclined to make us believe. Further, Barth contends that, even if such material content were found in codes, these laws would remain abstractions that no one lives according to and, therefore, would have still nothing to do with the real command of God. For the real God who is the Lord over both the formal and material content of His command of grace:

> ..... does not confront us in the guise of rules, principles, axioms and general moral truths, but purely in the form of concrete, historical, unique and singular orders, prohibitions, and directions. Their common import consists in the fact that it is always the same divine Overlord who in this confronts various men ..... to conform in their actions at a definite time, a definite place and in a definite way to the history of the covenant and salvation controlled by Him.[25]

In general, Barth does not deny that either the Decalogue or the Sermon on the Mount, to which moralists appeal, do in their own way reveal God's will. Rather he rejects any direct identification of God's will with them in such a way that they now can assume independent existence – as material content of law that functions apart from the context in which they were given or from God who gives them to particular individuals. Were this to occur, the commanding grace of God would be destroyed as grace or pure event, because it would not only mean that God's will is encapsulated in a propositional rule or axiom, but also that these laws replace, or stand between the believer and the living God who commands. The consequence of all this can be only that the believer or moralist would be tempted to set himself on the throne of God, trying to distinguish between good and evil, and "always to judge things as one or the other, not only in relation to others but also to himself."[26]

Once Barth has warned us against the temptation of tinkering with the law – as if humans are the ones to judge between good and evil in human behaviour or action – he offers a new way of appropriating biblical injunctions. He suggests, for instance, that the Decalogue and the Sermon on the Mount are *typical forms* which God's command takes when it is addressed to his people. But these commands are never given generally to be valid forever. Rather, He issues them to specific people in concrete situations or contexts, such as God would issue commands to Aaron and Moses but continues to demand specific decisions that are not and may not be related to the Decalogue. Also, God gave specific orders to Noah that are different from those He gave to Abraham or Lot; and, again, He gave commands to Peter and John that were not repetitions of past orders. Consequently, God's commands must be understood as always individual and specific orders that demand purely *ad hoc* "actions and attitudes which could be thought of as historically contingent and as such the acts ..... which must be performed on the spot.[27]

However, Barth does not say that we should discard the codified commands in the Bible. Rather, we should understand them in the context in which they were given, the context of covenant. That is, these pictures of God's dealings with his people mean to point us beyond themselves, to a frame of reference, or a contextual standing place where we, too, can expect to hear and receive God's commands. And who pointing beyong themselves, they mean to bring us face to face with the living Lord of the covenant who stands beyond the multiplicity of laws, ideas, or moral principles.[28]

However, because God is not a tyrant that is totally unpredictable but faithful in his dealing with his people, these pictures are useful and may apply to us. Not that in themselves they are normative for all times, but because the God who acted there and then is the God who may confront us here and now; and the content of what He commands may not be entirely different from *what* these pictures consist of. After all, a God of any other description than the one given in these summaries does not exist.[29] And, once these pictures are understood as what they are, namely, as pointers, sign-posts for standing places, they can rightly and legitimately be adopted and used by us – provided that:

> ..... we do not expect to find here something more or other than a framework and programme of the divine action and corresponding human conduct ..... God will command ..... within these limits and not elsewhere. But His commands and prohibitions will not consist simply in repetitions and applications of the Decalogue.[30]

Here Barth's position summarises the extent to which he accepts and limits the uses of biblical ordinances. While he does not directly identify the material content of God's command with the Decalogue, there is no question that Barth ascribes to them uniqueness. For, in the final analysis, *whatever God may command may and will not significantly differ either materially or formally from* the Decalogue or the Sermon on the Mount.[31]

Barth's strength lies in his strong desire to resist a fusion of God's law directly with any empirical, positive law. This allows him to affirm the transcendence of the law of God, which is inseparable from God's grace in Jesus Christ through whom the Creator claims us. Also, it makes possible the questioning of any historical law regarding its adequacy as the medium by which God's law may come to us. The problem arises when Barth goes to extremes by erecting unbridgeable gulf between God's command and other commands, in his demand that distinctions between them be as heaven is over the earth. For once this discontinuity is made it becomes very difficult to see how such a transcendent law might intersect with historical laws.[32] Even where Barth tries to bridge the discontinuity between God's law and the human laws through which the former comes to us, his efforts are frustrated by his excessive zeal that tries to protect the divine command from human distortions and manipulations. His vehement attack on all of general ethics is based upon this anxiety to protect God's law from some alleged human control.[33]

As he tries to protect the "purity" of God's law from human misunderstanding and distortion, Barth simultaneously attempts to offer us an alternative but a disembodied portrait of the law that is not related to civic uses of law, as these operate in society to produce penultimate good and justice.[34] Moreover, Barth fails to relate his conception of law to the divine law as it generally functions to order the totality of the cosmos, where its ordering can hardly be said to be in danger of being manipulated by lower creatures in their attempt to justify themselves. Barth's reluctance, as in the case of Elert, to spell out what the law of God consists of materially is symptomatic of how defective his understanding of law is; for his formal definition of it is so narrowly anchored that he cannot make necessary connections between it and other empirical laws. For if the *real* command is identical with the grace (gospel) of God in the person of Jesus then it is not without justification to conclude that the historical, positive, or empirical laws are not laws in the *real sense* of the word – unless this transcendental, idealistic *ius divinum* were to be connected miraculously with the *ius humanum.*

The second problem, related to the one of formal definition, is Barth's attempt to cast his conceptions of the law within the framework of justification or election of man. As we have seen, this is the same problem that Elert has when he claims that law always accuses; it renders qualitative judgment on the totality of human life rather than on a series of external conduct, or behaviour that is open to human evaluation by a third party, it is an exclusive God's standard by which guilt is rendered on the sinner, and that with none of our actions can we stand *coram Deo* claiming to have conformed to God's will. All these statements point to a framework of human justification before God rather than before our fellow humans. That is, the content of human obedience is specified always with reference to religious justification rather than to social righteousness *coram hominibus.* And before such an *Absolute* standard and demand humans will always fall short and the law will be for them *lex quae semper accusat* because they cannot be justified religiously by the works of the law – as Elert does not tire to remind us.

To be sure, Barth's position appears on the surface to be different from that of Elert's. But the content of human obedience is also specified with reference to religious justification before God, as it shall soon become evident. For, it is Barth's basic thesis that the law of God has as its goal, that is, it is concerned with, the sanctification of man. It is a judgment of grace by which God elects humans when, within the framework of the covenant, God enters in to save, help, emancipate and redeem and, thereby "conferring salvation on man."[35] It is clear that, for Barth, the command of God functions within the framework of human justification or salvation by God. For the command not only frees, delivers and snatches the sinner from the "old man" who tries to work out his own self-purification, self-justification, and self-sanctification, but also grants the "new man" permissions, or releases; it quickens, refreshes, and invites him for fellowhsip with God, when the Creator declares that He is for us.[36]

Because Barth casts his theological conception of the law within the categories or, rather, a framework of justification, he is extremely sensitive to any possible misuse, or distortion that might result when humans use the law to justify themselves. His polemics against general ethics is intelligible only when it is remembered that Barth understands the law strictly as an instrument that has to do with our righteousness before God – pretty much in the same sense as Elert.[37] This explains his declaration that:

> It is Adam, the sinner himself who perverts the Law to a rule of human self-purification, self-justification and self-sanctification, that is condemned ..... *When the Law of God frees itself from misused, corrupt and pernicious form of the Law of sin and death, the man who is liberated in and with this event,* who belongs to Jesus Christ, *is cut loose from the distress which this Law necessarily causes him .....*[38]

However, if both Barth and Elert had broadened their conceptions of law so as to take into account the social uses of law in the ordering of the social and natural world, and if they had separated questions of religious justification before God from social righteousness *(iustitia civilis)*, their anxiety that human beings necessarily misuse the law for their self-justification – which is impossible in any case – would have evaporated. For, as we have already observed, to assume that the social uses of law lead to a "despicable security" of Pharisaic moralism that refuses to acknowledge one's sinfulness before God,[39] and to assume that the use of law leads to distresses, perversions as humans try to work out their own self-purification, self-justification and self-sanctification,[40] is to distort the intention of those who are trying to solve social problems, especially because their concerns are never directed at a religious justification. Therefore, the problem with these two theologians is that they operate with only a *partial and one-sided view* of the law, a view that ignores the other creative functions of the divine law in the totality of the created cosmos. Indeed, they seem incapable of conceiving of the divine law that humans cannot misuse as they try to save themselves. For instance, Barth pretends as if other uses of God's command do not exist and lists as the first command the ordering of Adam to multiply and fill the earth. The second command is the one that God gave to Noah to build the ark, and the third to Abraham.

Noticeably absent are the other commands, such as God uttered when the cosmos was created, or when the earth was ordered to give forth fruits and living creatures – all of them uttered before the appearance of Adam.[41] Also, absent is the command God gave to Adam to till the earth and care for it, a command clearly underscoring the creative and positive functions of the law – functions which can hardly be done justice to when the law is forced into the framework of religious justification, as if this is the only function of law, and as if the law is given exclusively for the human world. Indeed, both Barth and Elert seem to think in dualistic terms: For them, God is active only among the humans, and only there does the Creator give commands. Consequently, the natural order is separated from the sphere of the sanctifying command (Barth) and the sphere of the accusing law, which is given to sinful humanity to render guilt-judgments (Elert).

Against both Barth and Elert, it should be contended that their conceptions of law – construing it as given only to humans – are defective and one-sidedly dualistic. For their claim that law either sanctifies, liberates, elects, and invites for fellowhsip with God, or that it *always accuses* the sinful conscience, do not seem to include the creative works of God in the ordered process of nature. Indeed, to hold that God's law is one of permission and obligation makes sense only for the human world, where these concepts have meanings. This holds true for Elert's view that law accuses, because it is unintelligible to claim that the pangs of conscience are experiences that are known among lower creatures.

Also, to suggest, as Barth does, that the divine law is apprehended *only* through faith is to make an exclusive statement that is totally misleading outside the human world, where the concept of faith may be meaningless. This is also true about the claim that God's law is a good gift that is now perverted through human attempts at their self-purification and self-justification, because such a claim excludes *automatically* the entire cosmos where God's creative works are not lacking and, certainly, where it would hardly make any sense to suggest that the lower creatures misuse the law to judge between good and evil. Claims as these can be made only by dualistic theologians, such as Barth and Elert who still hold to the view that humans are the centre of the universe – a position surely dubious in the modern world; it does no longer seem tenable to limit God's activity through the law to the human world, when divine works extend far beyond the human world to the entire universe.[42]

Finally, one might have expected that, because Barth and Elert have restricted their understanding of law exclusively to the human world, their discussion of law would give greater illumination to the creative and positive dynamics of the divine law as it operates among humans and in their social interrelationships. But, in fact, the opposite is true. Indeed, their excessive pre-occupation with a "theological use of the law" *(theologicus usus legis),* the use that deals primarily with human standing before God rather than other humans, dominates their discussion to such an extent that, when they try to move from the formal definitions of law to its horizontal dimensions, they are almost incapable of discussing these social uses without tilting toward the framework of religious justification.

The best example of this is found in Barth, who argues that the "true man and his good action can be viewed only from the standpoint of the true and active God and his goodness."[43] He rules out the possibility that there is an immanent goodness in human deeds and, therefore, that human action can carry any substantive significance, no matter how hard humans try to do good.[44] That is, man even in the horizontal relationships has no good action except as he is an obedient hearer of God's command. To underscore his point, Barth not only dismisses all casuistry and general ethics (just as Elert does) as useless attempt to act like God, but also imposes an interpretation that makes sense only within the framework of justification on the entire meaning of the Decalogue, by specifying the content of obedience with reference to human self-offering to God and sanctification. He does all this by making the third/fourth commandment the prologue to the entire horizontal ethics.

In justification of his interpretation, Barth argues that just as the gospel must precede the law so the *Sabbath takes precedent over and explains all the other commandments.*[45] All this may be fine and good, but in his haste to exclude social activities as the content of human obedience to God's law, Barth wrongly finds it necessary to attack both Calvin and Luther, who argued that the Sabbath was necessary also for the purely physical and human need to rest "which nature teaches and demands." Against the Reformers, Barth retorts angrily that Jesus' saying (Mark 2:27), that man is not made for Sabbath, does not mean humanitarian needs exhaust the meaning of the Sabbath – the result of which can only be boredom.[46] Barth may be right that humanitarian needs do not exhaust the meaning of Sabbath, something the Reformers would agree with anyway. But his tendency to dismiss the significance of human needs against an explicit statement of Jesus Christ betrays his bias toward an exclusion of social activities as the possible and necessary component part of the content of human obedience to the divine law.

This bias is even more explicitly expressed when Barth tries so hard to twist the meaning of the so-called second table of the Decalogue, so that it might fit into his narrow definition of God's command, one that confines law within the framework of religious justification. For instance, he tries to fuse the meaning of the commandments into one, even where this clearly does violence to the text, when he contends that the second table of the Decalogue requires that man should be a covenant-partner of God, that is, by allowing himself to be loved as a covenant-partner; it reveals man's failure to love his neighbour because he does not belong to Jesus; it demands total obedience in the sense of the first table of the Decalogue, that is, to live as the one who is chosen and loved by God, and to confront the neighbour as the one who is utterly bound to this gracious God; it requires one to follow Jesus and live according to Jesus' directing.

All this harmonization of the two parts of the Decalogue is justified by Barth in his contention that God's command cannot be atomized into different commands for various epochs, social groups, economies, customs, rules, and political dictates.[47] Barth even tries to simplify the Decalogue by reducing its parts to a minimum single meaning, when he declares:

> Follow me. This is again, and decisively, the interpretation of the commandments of the second table as they are supposed to be known ..... and fulfilled ..... The freedom for God which they demand from man is freedom for Jesus. And the freedom for one's neighbor which they demand is again freedom for Jesus. They aim at the true God and true man when they aim at God and man.[48]

It is our contention that, if Barth had clearly separated religious righteousness of faith from social righteousness, it would be hardly necessary to twist the meaning of the second table of the Decalogue into a "strait-jacket" of the first table of the commandments, because each of these two righteousnesses has its own role and, individually, is a content of obedience to God's law, and thus need not compete with each other. However, Barth does not allow the social uses of the law to have their full place and, consequently, fulminates against Calvin who often included the social righteousness as a component element of the content of one's obedience to the divine law. Against Calvin, Barth retorts:

> At this point, we cannot agree with Calvin ..... who softens the important to mean that Jesus loved him as God loved Aristides and Fabricius on account of their civil virtues and therefore on

> account of the *commune bonum* of this world: *quia illa grata est humani generis conservatio, quae iustitia, aequitate, moderatione, prodentia, fide, temperantia, constat.*[49]

It would seem, therefore, that Barth has become a victim of his own theological definitions, definitions that have thrown the conception of law into the framework of justification. As a result, any suggestion that social righteousness *(iustitia civilis)* be considered a component part of human obedience to the divine law has become unintelligible from his point of view. For the law, according to him, is identical with God's grace in Jesus and is exclusively the means by which God elects the sinner. Such a view of law has lost any connection with laws as they operate on the horizontal sphere, producing an attainable temporal good in society by humans for their fellows. Had Barth drawn a line between the social and religious righteousness, it would be hardly necessary to accuse Calvin and other moralists for playing God through casuistry because their interest in the cultivation of virtue and good behaviour is not intended to challenge or compete with salvific acts of God -- unless one confuses morality with religious self-justification. And such a confusion between temporal good (morality or virtue) and human justification before God can very easily occur, if one were to agree and contend with Barth that "when you ask about the good, you step before the seat of the Judge from whose verdict there is no appeal to a higher court," and that "you are asking what is good in the sight of God – in the One who is the good."[50]

However, any collapsing of the two issues into one (issue) ignores the importance of temporal good which is continually being done not before God but before humans. It is true that ultimately it is God who judges, but when the focus is on the horizontal sphere, such statements become partial truth, because statements that are true in the framework of justification need not be transferable to social righteousness without further qualification. It is not without purpose that prophets, too, called for obedience but, unlike Barth (for whom the law sets free, liberates or sanctifies) and Elert (for whom the law accuses), they specified the content of obedience not within the context of religious justification – in which God is equally active – but primarily with reference to social justice and righteousness. In uttering commands, God does not always demand religious obedience, as Barth alleges, nor does He seek to condemn, as Elert contends. Rather, God seeks to involve our mature humanhood in the creative dynamics of divine creative love.

The law does not become an exclusive tool God uses to expose sin or declare external righteousness, but also God, through the use of the law, involves humans creatively to promote social structures that nourish and preserve life. In this sense, the demands of God's command are characterized by the divine goodness that points us to God's creative activity -- using the creative genius of finite human agents – which results in structures (legal institutions, etc.) that serve the well-being of finite creatures. This aspect of the law is not done justice to by either Barth or Elert who restrict its meaning to theological uses, that is, they confine the law to the framework of justification, as a result of which the law can be used by God either to condemn the sinner (Elert) or to save, help, emancipate, and redeem him by conferring salvation on man (Barth).

In spite of their apparent differences regarding how much is known of God's law materially, both positions suffer from the one-sided and defective definition given to the law, which does not adequately include its social uses as well, uses which were in effect as long as creation itself, and long before the Fall and God's need to punish or save sinners. Elert's position is negative because, for him, the content of the law is retribution and lacks a criterion by which one law can be distinguished formally or materially from another. But because he does not claim that God has given humanity laws, his position does not get entangled in the problem of how God's law is materially related to empirical or historical laws. Barth's position, on the other hand, is positive because it stresses the salvific function of the law, and the fact that God himself is the law, the living law of the Kingdom, who continually gives commands. He provides a criterion, but his conceptions raise the problem of how such a transcendent law is related to historical laws.

This problem defies solution because Barth tries his best to exclude every human creative activity from the use of the law; for the law is an exclusive tool of God for the redemption of the sinner. Yet, law is effective only in the historical form, a form which is the very production of human linguistic innovation. Because Barth seems to overlook the fact that all laws are linguistic innovations and, therefore, human constructions, it will become clear in the following chapters why we cannot follow Barth even though his formal definition is more appealing than that of Elert. Any discussion of the law that tries to exclude God's employment of finite human agency, as Barth does, is bound to be inadequate. This is as true for Barth as it is for Elert for whom the law is God's manner of passing sentence and never anything else that is creative. In real life, law does not always function as they have so narrowly defined it (accuses, or redeems, or sanctifies). Is their inability to correlate their definitions with any positive laws effectively an indirect admission that materially there is no corresponding reality of the law as defined by them? The answer will be given in the following two chapters of our evaluation.

Notes

1 Elert, *The Christian Ethos,* pp. 5f, 14ff, 54–62, 73, 112, 141–145.

2 Ibid., p. 3.

3 Ibid., pp. 4–5, 295, 300–302.

4 Ibid., p. 5.

5 Ibid., pp. 53–54. Also see *Law and Gospel,* pp. 35, 45f.

6 Elert, *The Christian Ethos,* pp. 15–16.

7 Ibid., pp. 63–64, 301–302.

8 *Elert, Law and Gospel,* pp. 9–10. In one of his explicit statements, regarding any law that can be thought of as a material content of the divine will, Elert expresses his cynicism in this way: "Neither the little questions of our earthly life – whether and whom we should marry, which vocation we should select – nor the practical questions of social policy in the realm of labor, taxation, in inheritance, nor the great political questions of communism, socialism, or liberal democracy can be answered from the Decalogue" (Ibid., p. 35).

9 Ibid., p. 11

10 Ibid., pp. 36–37.

11 Brunner, *Justice and the Social Order,* translated by Mary Hottinger (New York: Harper and Row, 1945).

12 Elert seems oblivious to the fact that the fourth/fifth commandment does indeed give positive commands to the children to "honour father and mother," and therefore that this command is not necessarily retributive. Also, even if it were true that all other commands are retributive, it is not clear at all that we should draw the conclusion that they tell us nothing about what we should do. Commands such as, "do no steal, lie, kill, etc.," do say something, though perhaps less directly than we may want.

13 Elert, *Law and Gospel,* p. 46.

14 Ibid., (Italics added) Elert's pessimism leads him to add: "With none of our decisions can we stand before God with the claim that any of them conforms to the law" (Ibid., p. 46).

15 Elert's own detailed "orders of creation," which he believes are derivative from the creative and rule of God through the law, are inconsistent with his claims that nothing positive is known about God's will or the law formally or materially. If so, where does he get his material for the detailed portrayal of these "orders of creation," which are nothing but a form of the material content of the divine law – as he conceives it?

16 Elert, *The Christian Ethos,* p. 113. Also see pp. 105–108 above. One is left with the impression that Elert talks about the political use of law merely because Luther also spoke about it. But, in reality, the political use of law whose aim is to produce social righteousness has little room in his theology, because demonic and retributive laws cannot protect life.

17 Ibid., pp. 50–51, 80–86

18 Ibid., p. 281.

19 Barth, *Church Dogmatics* II/2, pp. 646–59, 662, 669.

20 In his most explicit statement on this matter, Barth has this to say: *"The objection is obviously futile that God has not really given, and does not and will not give, His command with such wholeness, clarity and definiteness that it only remains for us to be obedient or disobedient, and not to try to discover what the divine command really is ....."* (Ibid., p. 669). (Italics added).

21 Ibid., p. 669.

22 Ibid., pp. 602f, 646, 664, 674–75.

23 Ibid., p. 556 (Italics added).

24 Barth is persuaded that it is a distortion of facts to claim that the material content of God's law consists of "a prescribed text, which, partly written and partly unwritten, is made up of biblical texts in which there are believed to be seen universally binding divine ordinances and directions ..." *(Church Dogmatics* III/4, p. 6).

25 Barth, *Church Dogmatics* III/4, p. 12.

26 Ibid., p. 10. Barth says the moralist claims that "in a *summa* of ethical statements compiled by him and his like from the Bible, natural law and tradition, he can know the command of God, see through and past it, and thus master and handle it ..... so armed with this instrument he may speak as law" (Ibid.).

27 Barth, *Church Dogmatics* II/2, pp. 673f.

28 Ibid., pp. 686–88, 697–705; III/4, pp. 15–6.

29 *Church Dogmatics* II/2, pp. 702–703, 706.

30 Ibid., p. 702. Barth summarises the content of these pictures and says that the first four commandments deal with all the how and in what God always will to be honoured, while the last six deal with the how and in what God wills humans protected against fratricidal strife and self-destruction. Only within these limits does the God of the Bible command and nowhere else.

31 Ibid., pp. 574, 706.

32 Ibid., pp. 584f, 684–706; III/4, p. 12.

33 It is ironic that Barth, who attacks the nineteenth century theology for trying to defend the cause of God and, thereby, for not letting the Word take its course since it is self-authenticating and needs no defense, should now try to protect the purity of the Word through a systematic device. The gimmick he uses is one of erecting dualisms between general ethics and special ethics, the command of God and other commands, where conceptions of misuse or distortions dominate his reflections. Cf. *Church Dogmatics* II/2, pp. 513–542, 583–606 and III/4, pp. 6–16.

34 We have suggested that Barth's conception of law gives us a disembodied portrait of law because, unlike other laws that are always conceptually embodied in statutes, or codes, Barth claims that God's law cannot be reduced to a propositional rule of conduct without it being violated as grace. Hence God's law has nothing in common with *positivity,* or empirical laws. Cf. *Church Dogmatics* II/2, pp. 602f, 655; III/4, p. 12. How such a disembodied law of non-positivity is related to social and other civic laws remains one of the sore problems in Barth's theology.

35 *Church Dogmatics* II/2, p. 562. Barth also has this to say about the function of law: "... man is at once condemned and acquitted and thus becomes free for eternal life ..... and *this freeing by God's judging grace is the final goal, the real work and therefore the original purpose of the command of God. It is man's sanctification" (Church Dogmatics* III/4, pp. 4–5. (Italics added).

36 *Church Dogmatics* II/2, pp. 585–87, 590–92. That Barth conceives of the law primarily as the medium of election (which is the same thing as justification or liberation) is underscored by his assertion that it: "..... circumvents the person who would save and purify and justify and sanctify himself ..... it circumvents his retreat into himself, the further exercise of his office as the judge of good and evil ..... and therefore to be like God" (Ibid., pp. 596–97).

37 Cf. our critical evaluation of Elert above.

38 *Church Dogmatics* II/2, p. 574. (Italics added.)

39 Elert, *The Christian Ethos,* pp. 64–66, 72, 208, 284, 299ff.

40 Barth, *Church Dogmatics* II/2, pp. 574, 585–87, 590–92, 596f.

41 Ibid., p. 673.

42 Harold P. Santmire, *Creation and Nature: A Study of the Doctrine of Nature with Special Attention to Karl Barth's Doctrine of Creation* (unpublished dissertation, deposited in the Adover-Harvard Library, Harvard University, 1966), pp. 57, 136–40, charges that Barth's theology is non-inclusive and anthropocentric because, as a theology of election, it involves only man. He concludes that Barth's theology is closer to that of Ritschl in its disregard of nature. His critical observation, in our opinion, rightly applies to the theology of Elert as well.

43 *Church Dogmatics* III/4, p. 3.

44 *Church Dogmatics* II/2, pp. 578–579. There is a closer affinity between this and Elert's view that: "..... qualities with which we and others credit ourselves ..... the notion of every moral person that he can observe improvement within himself has no standing before God" *(The Christian Ethos,* p. 208).

45 Barth writes: "It is to be placed at their head. By demanding man's abstention and resting from all his works, it explains that the commanding God who has created man ..... is the God who is gracious to man in Jesus Christ. Thus it points him away from everything that he himself can will and achieve and back to what God is for him and will do for him" *(Church Dogmatics* III/4, p. 53).

46 *Church Dogmatics* III/4, p. 61.

47 *Church Dogmatics* II/2, p. 721.

48 Ibid., pp. 621–622. Also, Barth equates obedience to the law with faith that looks up to, follows, and endorses Jesus' own and our righteousness and glorification. Hence, there is nothing higher that humans can do than to love Jesus. Indeed, Barth adds, God's law has nothing to do with plans for world-betterment or programs, because "follow me, is issued and is there and valid quite independent of what is done or not done ....." (Ibid., p. 570. Also see pp. 558–559.)

49 Ibid., p. 617

50 Ibid., p. 614.

Chapter five

The law in ethical decision-making: God as the source of morality

In theological discourse, the problem of the relationship between salvation and ethical decision-making often arises because – even though it is generally accepted that God's activity in the Christian life does have some impact on the moral transformation of the believer – most theologians agree that two distinct issues are involved here. In other words the questions of salvation and morality – though closely related and, perhaps, even inseparable in the actual life of the believer – are by no means the same. For, salvation has to do primarily with God's redemptive activity in Christ while morality (ethics) interests itself primarily with the active shaping and directing of the believer's moral existence, which in itself may or may not have been brought about by religious justification.[1]

The upshot of all this is that while the goal of justification is sanctification, it does not mean that salvation *per se* is a solution to, nor does it imply a possession of knowledge concerning, complex moral issues that are involved in life situations. Because the two are seen as different, the discussions of salvation and morality often constitute two distinct levels of deliberation. Ethics is thus discussed in close relation to the divine law (understood as God's demand for a certain kind of moral posture), while salvation is discussed in relation to the gospel (understood as God's gift, forgiveness or imparting of external righteousness to the sinner without merit or works).

If our observations about Barth and Elert are correct, namely, that they have defined and confined the meaning of the law within the framework of justification or election — where law functions only to set free, to elect "man" or to accuse the sinner — then a question arises as to how God's law is understood to be actively involved in ethical deliberations which, for all practical purposes, are not solved by the justification that is declared upon the sinner. That is, in what sense do Barth and Elert understand God's law as the source of morality in human life? If we agree with Barth, on one hand, that the "Law that really binds has been fulfilled once and for all in Jesus Christ"[2] — by virtue of Christ's divinely elected representation of mankind, whose fulfillment of the law is universally vicarious — in what sense could human behaviour be regarded as a fulfillment of the demands of the law embodied in norms, rules and moral principles existing concretely and historically in society, which are thus understood to be expressions of the divine will?

If, on the other, we agree with Elert that those who are in Christ need no law, need no longer be told not to practice idolatry, to bear false witness, or to commit murder and adultery because they are led by the Spirit,[3] in what sense could believers understand demands of political or social righteousness as expressions of God's law or will that must be fulfilled in their lives?

The answers to these questions by Barth and Elert reveal startling similarities in their understanding of the law despite differences of detail. This similarity has already been shown above, where we pointed out that they have narrowly achored the meaning of law within the framework of justification in which law becomes an exclusive tool that is used by the Deity either to condemn (Elert) or to liberate (Barth) the sinner. The consequence of that understanding is that the religious justification is accented at the expense of the social righteousness of one human being before others. Also, the positions of Barth and Elert revealed a weakness that incapacitates their theological reflections to make smooth transition from the vertical dimensions of the functions of the law to the horizontal plane. This, in turn, poses serious questions as to how God's law, embodied in historical and concrete propositional rules of conduct, could seriously be understood as the source of human morality. We now turn to consider these problems in greater detail.

5.1 CASUISTRY AS A MASTERY OVER GOD'S COMMAND

It is one of our contentions that both Barth and Elert fail to separate questions of human justification before God from those of morality (i.e., social righteousness *coram hominibus).* As a result of this failure, they find themselves forced to wage a war on general ethics or casuistry for its alleged competition with the gospel.

As we have seen, Elert constantly sets law in mortal opposition to the gospel to such an extent that nothing positive or creative remains to be said about the law: it is totally devoid of mercy and grace. Indeed, he seems to be working under a false assumption that the law has no other meaning except as a means of retribution, or a "ladder" (so to speak) which is the way to salvation. Unfortunately, because humans are sinners or fail to climb the "ladder" to achieve salvation, they stand guiltily condemned before the divine law.[4] What complicates his reflection on the law even further is Elert's tendency to think in *either/or* alternatives. For him, the law *either* is true and, therefore, must always accuse, *or* else the law is fictitious, if it does not accuse. In our opinion, such an approach to law prevents Elert from finding anything positive about the law as the instrument of God's love – even in its social uses.[5]

What he affirms in the *either* is automatically excluded in his *or* alternative. Had Elert been working with a *both/and* approach, it would have been possible to let the positive aspects of the law stand on their own right, even though these positive elements (in matters of justice and social righteousness) fall away when a move is made from the horizontal to the vertical – where a human standing before God becomes the decisive thing, and human work does not contribute toward justification. However, Elert's insistence that either law must be true and retributive or else, if it does not accuse, it is fictitious,[6] would not let him recognize the fact that the law is related to questions of faith righteousness in a different manner than it is to questions of morality or social righteousness between human beings. Instead, Elert prefers to sacrifice the positive meanings of the law in order to protect his either/or alternatives.

Not only does Elert fail to separate questions of spiritual righteousness from those of morality but also rejects any suggestion that Christian behaviour is a response to, obedience to, some law, whether human or divine.[7] This follows from his thesis that God cannot be said to be the author of human morality because the Creator is not a legislator who, like humans, issues rules of life to guide human action in the Kantian sense of categorical imperatives.[8]

Elert's moves lead him into a direct conflict with casuistry, which he accuses of legalistic ethics or deontological moral thinking.[9] First, Elert launches his attack within Christian quarters against those who hold the view that there is Christ's law which serves to guide Christians on their way to sanctification. His attack here is based on two counts. On one hand, he rejects deontological thinking because it portrays God as a law-giver who answers questions like: What shall we do? According to Elert to think that God gives us *norma normans* for human conduct can mean only that God is reduced to a level of a spectator who waits to see if this or that behaviour fulfills this law. On the other, deontological ethics wrongly advocates for third use of law creating the impression that the law is now a friend of the regenerate, performing only the informatory task of telling the believer what to do. As merely an instructor but not an accuser, law is a companion that does not threaten the Christians with its threats of punishments or retributions. Moreover, Christian life is understood legalistically as a life of obedience to the law of Christ.

Indeed, this law of Christ is seen as intended for the "new man" or the "spiritual man," and as an arbiter of the relationships between God and humans.[10] But, because Christian life is one of obedience to this law which regulates God-human relationships, the law becomes the only decisive thing to which the gospel is subordinate as a servant, adding "substance to the shadow," namely, the promise. For this reason, law is seen as manifesting God's grace, a "form of the gospel whose content is grace."[11] Expressed differently, deontological ethics collapses law and gospel into a legalistic understanding of Christ who is made to function as a law-giver. According to Elert, norms are constructed but the gospel is destroyed as the differences between law and gospel are smoothed over. The end result of this process can only be a "despicable security of the Pharisees" among Christians as well as an imperialistic moralization of the world because the salvific plan is thought of in terms of divine command and human obedience.[12]

Against Christian deontological ethics, Elert contends that casuistry overlooks the Christian insight about original sin. According to this, insights, when the law is truly listened to *what* it says, is never purely informational but accusatory to the guilty conscience.[13] And this accusation is not just a passing or momentary one but a constant threat. Moreover, to define a law as though it were a demand humans *may or may not* fulfill is misleading because a false impression is given that adherence to the law or rules of conduct may make amends for sin and, therewith, the damage of human sinfulness "could be repaired, and the problem of destiny solved by human composure."[14]

Against this, Elert concludes that we look in vain in the Scriptures if we hope to find a collection of imperatives or precepts which could be reduced to a rule of life – as casuistry deludes itself. After all, Elert contends, "not all things that must be fulfilled were written in the law" of the Old or New Testament.[15]

Secondly, Elert's rejection of Christian special ethics leads him to attack all of philosophical ethics as well. Many reasons are given for this. Firstly, deontological ethics (philosophical ethics is one of these) focuses attention on "certain forms of behavior" that are either lawful or unlawful. Human conduct, accordingly, is believed to conform to a norm: social or political, a norm in relation to which an individual can, if he/she wishes, misbehave or disregard this standard rule of behaviour. What is implied in all this is that while moral demands or social sanctions require a certain behaviour, they do not determine it. So deviation is always possible. The divine law thus is a *relative* rather than an *Absolute* claim upon human life, according to deontological ethics.

Secondly, according to Elert, a study of existing moral conduct and the relativity of all laws and mores belongs to history and sociology rather than to theology. And this follows from the fact that theological ethics is interested in a qualitative rather than a quantitative judgment of human life.[16] Thirdly, philosophical ethics, in his opinion, has lost interest in qualitative judgments that apply to concepts of good and evil. Instead, this ethic judges according to externals: style of living, cultural taste, books one reads, power or weakness, beauty, etc. These externals, Elert goes on to assert, do not interest God's law in the very least; for God's judgment of the totality of human life cannot be impressed by these immanental criteria.[17] In one of his important statements, Elert underlines the separation between God's law and morality or external behaviour, when he asserts:

> *The law* of God *does not recognize* "man as such." *It knows nothing* of the "duty which man owes to himself," a concept which is of importance in some systems of ethics.[18]

By separating external human conduct, as this conduct is expressed in actions that are observable by others in society, from the law of God, it becomes obvious that Elert cannot say anything meaningful about social righteousness as a component element of human obedience to the divine law. As a consequence, Elert can only urge us to be disinterested in social righteousness, consisting of externals of human conduct, because theological ethics – in his opinion – cannot participate in the search for immanental, relative, and penultimate standards. Rather it seeks for God's absolute standards before whose judgment:

> ..... qualities with which we and others credit ourselves ... the notion of every moral person that he can observe improvement within himself has no standing before God.[19]

While, in the final analysis, this may be true, one must ask Elert whether his dogmatic assertion is justified, namely, that because "theological ethics cannot participate in immanental criteria" its real task *"is not to describe man as he is or counsel people to live respectably but to make clear how God judges man."*[20] His answer is, as always, God's law always accuses and is never the author of human morality.

By denouncing all prescriptive ethics, and by failing to say what is and what is not an acceptable behaviour before God that is a necessary component part of the content of human obedience to the divine law, does it mean that Elert's position is antinomian? The answer he himself gives is "No!" In sharp contrast to casuistry, Elert advances the ethics of responsibility before God and our fellows, and bases this on his belief that humans were responsible before the Fall but became irresponsible only afterwards. Salvation in Christ restores this responsibility, or *imago Dei.*[21] This new "man" is *beyond* all old relationships, and his ethics are totally new; they are ethos under grace — which can only be received from God who must be continually depended upon. All works that are done under grace must be attributable to God's work, even though humans do them. Because the Spirit is the originator of this new birth, the transformed existence of the "new man" is so new that it cannot be equated with human self-consciousness. Nor can it be open to psychological study because it is God's unconditional *creatio ex nihilo* as the first birth.[22]

The works of the justified sinner are good not only because God remains the subject and originator of the new birth, but also because the will of this "new man" is attuned to the will of God. Consequently, antinomianism never poses a threat to him because the Spirit abides in him, guiding and leading him, so that this new creature might not go wrong in his freedom from the law.[23] The acts of the believer remain, however, acts of faith, not sight, for life in Christ does not mean receiving direct commands from God.[24] As works of faith, they bear the marks of adventures, adventures that must continually be taken and be justified ever anew *coram Deo.* The last judgment is to be left to God because every human action (conduct) is a risk, and our hope lies in God's forgiveness.[25]

Elert has denied that God is the author of morality through the law because, under the law, humans are *totally sinful* before God and can never do anything that is good. But it turns out, after all, that God is the author of morality in the life of the justified sinner, through the Spirit which restores us to our "original" responsibility, our *imago Dei.* Before we question Elert as to whether such an absolute discontinuity between the ethics of the "new man" under grace and the "old man" under the law is plausible or tenable – expecially because all humans are shaped by, and are products of, culture – let us outline briefly what Barth has to say on law and morality

Barth's position, even in its attack on casuistry, contradicts that of Elert. For instance, he brings God directly into the decision-making process by arguing that there is not good apart from that which is commanded by God. That is, humans are not left to their own devices, to seek after and to find the good by themselves. Only God in Christ, who is the light that enables humans to view the self and the world in their proper perspective, can tell them what the good is through his commands.

However, Barth's discussion of the relations between the command of God and ethical reflection is more subtle and complex. It is full of contradictions and ambiguities traceable to the fact that he couches his ethics in theological rhetoric that – in its similarity to Elert's position – lifts morality from immanental judgment to the transcendental realm of justification of humans before God. As we have already seen, Barth's basic thesis is that *the law that really bind has been fulfilled once and for all* by Jesus Christ. The upshot of this is that the law comes to us as the law that has already been fulfilled. This can mean only that ethics is not a description of human external behaviour. Nor is it a description of human attempt to figure out how they ought to fulfill the good as defined by them. Rather ethics concerns itself with the good and right conduct as these are determined solely by God in what He has done in Jesus Christ.[26]

Hence Barth contends:

> There is no realization of the good which is not identical with the grace of Jesus Christ and its voluntary or involuntary confirmation. For there is no good which is not obedience to God's command.[27]

But if what we ought to do has been done in Jesus Christ, what is it that the command still requires as the good which is identical with the right action of God in Christ? The answer to this moral question is given in theological concepts that are appropriate to the language of religious justification. Barth contends that what is left for us to do is not to re-enact what Jesus has done, or to try to be little Christs to others as Luther thought, or to try to be little gracious creators to our fellow humans in the hope of distributing grace.[28] Rather, we must confirm, obey, follow and accept as right God's judgment when He made Christ our justification and our righteousness in whom all obligations to the law are fulfilled, and who is the enabler to do the good, as the living Commander.[29]

Once Barth, like Elert, has removed the questions of good and morality from the locus of the temporal sphere, where moralists try to evaluate what is good and what is not, he launches a stinging attack on general ethics and casuistry. Barth not only warns us against casuistry, but also goes on to reject any use of general ethics, or casuistry. He justifies his rejection by saying that such ethics leads to temptations in which humans try to play God, when moralists think that they are the ones to judge between good and evil. According to him, moralists are wrong because they manipulate God's law, rushing to tell the doubter and themselves what they ought to choose as good. In doing so, they are pre-occupied with something from which Christ has redeemed them.

Indeed, to try to work out what is good and right apart from God's grace is sinful denial of this grace; for it is to behave as if humans were not the object of God's grace, as if Christ has not fulfilled the law, as if they must ask and decide for themselves what is good and how to achieve it, and as if they were free to pick and choose what they think is right.[30] Such a possiblity must be rejected, in Barth's opinion, because it has been taken out of human hands by what has happened to Jesus Christ. Barth is so fearful of casuistry and of human attempts to formulate the material content of what God requires into propositional rules of conduct, hoping thereby to apply them in concrete situations of decision-making, that he is led to make a rather startling assertion, when he says:

> When God confronts man with his commands, what he wills is purely *ad hoc* actions and attitutdes which can only be thought of as historically contingent even in their necessity, acts of obedience to be performed on the spot ..... pure decisions the meaning of which is not open to discussion.[31]

If the moral conduct required can never be anticipated – because

God wills *ad hoc* actions that must be performed on the spot, actions that are not open to ethical reflection or discussion – it seems that Barth has effectively rendered useless casuistry, ethical norms, and other cultural mores that have shaped the individual's personality. The reason is simply that the content of what the command will require from us in day to day life-situations can never be predictable; it cannot be learned from the society in the hope of applying such knowledge to the actual moment of ethical decision.

The warning both by Barth and Elert against excessive reliance on ready-made moral rules is laudable because, when these are worked out to minute details to cover every aspect of life, casuistry can, in fact, blunt our moral sensitivity. But one wonders whether the emphasis on discontinuities between the "old man" and "new man" (Elert), and between what a person knows or has learned from society and the command of God that is given in the event of decision (Barth), does not lead to excessive individualism. Indeed, individualism is courted when Elert, for instance, rejects all casuistry (including special ethics for Christians) but carves out a *special area* where the believer as God's unconditional *creatio ex nihilo* led by the Spirit, is said to be beyond "all biographical contexts, all human environmental influences and circumstances"[32] in his/her practice of virtues that are no longer under the ethos of law (i.e., casuistry of both the general and special ethics). That is, the believer acts out of the dictates of the Spirit rather than under the guidance of society whose rules of conduct he/she may have learned.

This tendency towards individualism becomes even more explicit in Barth's emphasis on the uniqueness of every situation, and on the contingent character of God's command. For, as Barth himself notes, God's command is not given to mankind universally as a general good to be applied by them. Rather, God's law:

> ..... is always an individual command for the conduct of this man at this moment and in this situation; a prescription of this case of his; a prescription for the choice of a definite possibility of human intention, a decision and action.[33]

Also, this individualistic ethics is accented by Barth, when he contends not only that God's command is given for specific action – which by the nature of the case is unrepeatably singular for willing purely *ad hoc* actions to be performed on the spot – but also that God commands in such a way that "man" is told *how* "to think and act here and now," and *what* specifically "is to take place inwardly in his mind and thoughts and outwardly in what he does or refrains from doing."[34]

Surely, any individual who is controlled by God both mentally and physically as to how one should act or refrain from acting in this or that way (Barth), and anyone who is directly led by the Spirit in such a way that he/she cannot go astray under the ethos of grace which is free from compulsions of the law with its "thou shall nots" (Elert) — such a person needs no social aids in his/her ethical decision-making. Indeed, by rejecting rules of conduct which could enable us to make informed ethical decisions, Barth and Elert seem to suggest that we approach each and every situation *de novo.* That is, their rejection of all cultural aids implies that situations in social life are so dissimilar that the "past accumulation of moral wisdom"[35] of humanity, a wisdom holding the view that there is a universal character in human relations with a fairly predictable ethical relationships (e.g., parent-child, husband-wife, brother-sister, ruler-ruled relationships, etc.), is so useless that the only option open for the "new creature" in Christ is individualistic ethics based on one's risk of faith.

We, for our part, cannot agree with them at this point. We know very well that believers, as H.R. Niebuhr has persuasively argued, are also products of their culture and time and, as such, are completely penetrated by the culture whose air they breathe. Indeed, as persons whose personalities, attitudes, perspective and value preferences — all of which influence ethical decisions — are shaped and molded in culture, they cannot speak or think without the aid of a particular language or culture.[36] Consequently, the discontinuities which both Barth and Elert want to make between the "old and the"new" creature in Christ are neither possible nor tenable.

The impossibility of their task is underscored by the fact that their portrayal of *a*social and abstracted individual who, in his/her ethical deliberation, is completly free from the society's rules of conduct and acts spontaneously at the instigation of the Spirit (Elert) or the commanding grace of God (Barth) is as unconvincing as it is unrealistic. For, in real life, no such individual exists who *always* acts intuitively without any guidance whatsoever from a particular cultural ethos or parts of it. Therefore, it is very difficult for those who take social sciences seriously to accept as intelligible Barth's contention that in a moment of ethical decision the believers must

> ..... approach God as those who are ignorant in and with what they already know, and stand in dire need of divine instruction and conversion ..... ready, with a view to our next decision, to bracket and hold in reserve all that we think we know concerning the rightness of our past and present decisions, all rules and axioms, however good, all the inner and outer laws.[37]

What Barth here advocates is something more than humility before God, for the individual he has in mind is clearly an abstraction for whom the moral laws of the society have lost all their value. Indeed, he believes that the very personality of the believer – which is constituted by a cluster of values, habits and attitudes developed in the psychological, political, and socio-economic history of the individual who is about to make decisions – can be wiped clean. This would be possible if one were to be completely free from the society that has molded him/her. That is, if one were, to borrow Elert's rather startling metaphor, to be led by the Spirit in such a way that one could be said to be *beyond* and outside all the biographical contexts as well as human environmental influences. But, as we have repeatedly pointed out, in reality no one exists who can effectively "bracket and hold in reserve" what he/she knows about the good and right (i.e., what the law or social rules says he/she ought to do), thereby meeting and interpreting new situations *morally* without any aids of the language, thought patterns, and categories of meanings that a particular society provides.

Niebuhr is more right when, in one of his illuminating statements, he sharply rebukes excessive individualistic abstractions by theologians who portray the believer as though he/she approaches every situation *de novo,* unarmed by culture, and succintly observes:

> The picture of the radical doubter who sits down before natural events like a little child to be freshly taught ..... could be painted only by a generation which had made no study of little children, had paid little attention to the way in which language transmits interpretations, and knew nothing of the social, historical character of our knowledge.[38]

Niebuhr's words were not directed against Barth and Elert as such, but they raise important questions as to how much they take seriously the formative functions of the society and culture in shaping or molding of the very stuff of the human conscious self. Indeed, were social values to be bracketed and held in reserve, as Barth wants, and were one to exist in abstractions of the nature Elert talks about (beyond and above all social influences) so that individuals might be taught by God directly, there would be no differences in preferences, tastes, perspectives, and choices between a Swiss believer and Chinese or African Christian. However, experiences of differences between people of varying cultural values, or even within the same culture but with different spirituality (e.g., Roman Catholic or Protestant), argue against the contentions of both Barth and Elert, because we cannot wipe clean our historical and cultural contexts that have shaped us without violating the integrity of our very selfhood, or self-consciousness.

There is a further problem which complicates, especially, Barth's reflections on law and ethics, namely, his inability to conceive of God's command as something that can be both historically ascertainable and not mastered, or controlled, by humans.[39] He wants to say that God is the source of morality directly because God commands the good that has to be done by us. But Barth is unwilling to go all the way and to assert that this command of God is known in society and, therefore, can be conceptualized into propositional rules of conduct in order to guide the young in the cultivation of virtue.[40] Barth refuses to go that far because this would destroy the discontinuities between God's command and human laws that he wants to maintain.

This leads him to see casuistry, or any other social guide in moral reflection as an immediate danger to the supremacy of God's law which must not be conceptualized or codified into rules.[41] He wants to protect this supremacy by attacking the very past and present knowledge which constitutes our conscious selves, rooted in history and culture. In the process of excluding all psychological and social influences on ethical decisions, Barth's position almost reduces humans to a level of dummies.[42] The upshot of this claim can be only the preclusion of any usefulness of social values and norms in ethical deliberation or preferences regarding what the best action would be in a particular situation. For, to think that deliberation is possible leads to distortions in which humans usurp God's prerogative of judging what is good and what is evil. In order not to leave any room for such manipulations of God's law in ethical decision-making, Barth suggests not only that God controls what we are to think and do, but also that the divine law is specific and clear in a manner that requires no further application or discretion.

For instance, he writes:

> God's command leaves no room for application or interpretation ..... If God's commandment *is not clear, definite and concrete to the last detail,* then it is not God's commandment. Either God does not speak at all or else He speaks to us definitely as He spoke to Abraham ..... and Moses.[43]

If God's law is clear to the last detail, as Barth claims, then it might be protected from human abuse that can result from reading meanings into it that God never intended. But is it true that the divine law is heard clearly to *the last detail* by all those who are objects of God's address? The evidence from most people's experience points to the fact that Barth's affirmations are not conclusive; for these people (believers included) find life in its empirical givenness rather more complex than Barth is willing to admit.

As Meynell correctly points out:

> It is questionable whether Barth is correct in maintaining that God's command is always perfectly clear and unambiguous – for so *many people agree that they do not know what God's will for them is. The conclusion would be either that such people are insincere or that God has no command to give them,* something which Barth may not readily endorse.[44]

Indeed, it turns out that Barth disagrees with any suggestion that there are people to whom God does not give His command; for He is the Lord of both the Church and the people outside. And since Christ does not idle outside the walls of the Church but does His work, and since no humanity exists outside the lordship and humanity of Christ,[45] it seems reasonable to conclude that God's command is clear to the last detail in its prescription of what human conduct should be in every moment, by telling them what to think and act, and that this is equally true of all addressees of the divine law.

In fact, Barth seems to agree with such a conclusion, when he admits that the ambiguities and obscurities, which people claim there are, do not occur because God's law *per se* is not clear and definitive, but because humans try to run away from the real confrontation with the command of God by substituting human laws for it.[46] However, Barth's reply to critics like Meynell does not seem to satisfy even his most sympathetic interpreters,[47] because it overlooks complexities involved in human moral decision-making process.

Lehmann, without directly entering into a dialogue with Barth, underscores Meynell's point regarding difficulties that are encountered in ethical deliberation, and summarizes his observations thus:

> ..... however self-evident and valid it may be to urge upon men the doing of the will of God, this is only half the truth. The other half is that the "will of God" is not a simple answer to a simple question but a complex answer to a complex question. To assume that the question, What am I to do? is a simple one ..... is not only naive but irresponsible. *The fact is that men ask concerning the will of God, not merely evasively, pretending that they do not know, that they are to do the will of God when they really know, but because they are genuinely perplexed by the diversity and complexity of behavioral options which make up the stuff of the ethical situation.*[48]

The complexity of the actualities of the ethical situation, to which both Lehmann and Meynell point, is one Barth seems to overlook rather too often, when he claims that God's law is so clear, and unambiguous that the only thing that remains is "instant obedience," or disobedience.[49]

Barth's problem seems to lie in his definition of the law about which much has been already said. There it was pointed out that the command of God reduced to its most basic and simple material form is: "Follow me!" This, Barth says, is the most decisive interpretaion one can give to the law of God. This "follow me!" is identical with our acceptance of Jesus as our own justification and righteousness. When the law is reduced to that form, it makes sense when Barth complains, against his detractors, that it is "futile" and dishonest to say that this law is not given with clarity, wholeness and definitude. Barth may be correct in so far as no Christian can claim that Jesus has not died for us in order to be our righteousness and justification, and that following Him is the way to salvation. The problem, however, arises when Barth, having defined the law in this narrow sense and confined it to a framework of justification, wants to assume that analogies of following Jesus in faith can be transferable without further qualification to the horizontal sphere where ethical matters are complex and not as clear-cut as in matters of religious justification.[50]

As we have already observed, while the goal of justification is sanctification, it does not follow that salvation or justification *per se* is a solution to the complexities of moral issues, as Barth seems to suggest. That is, while salvation may be received in faith (viz., obeying in faith Jesus' call to follow Him), moral decisions still require our active use of sheer human and finite insights. Therefore, to talk about "instant obedience" to God's law in ethical decisions, implying thereby that "God's command leaves no room for application or interpretation," is as misleading as it is unhelpful to believers who often find themselves in moral predicaments. Therefore, Barth's attempt to preserve the purity of God's law in the manner he does raises more problems than it solves.

To conclude, a total rejection of casuistry or general ethics in moral reflection by either Barth or Elert — as if the Holy Spirit would supply us with intuitive insights — is unconvincing. Moreover, such a rejection only limits freedom of action in determining what the best action might be in a particular situation. Also, their arguments are misplaced because salvation is not the major focus of general ethics or casuistry. In addition, they ignore the fact that God may be involved in human attempts to find, through cultural creativity, the best possible means to structure and order human life for the well-being of all. And if casuistry is the product of human activity behind which God stands as humans try their best, by means of general ethics, to construct structures that protect and nourish life, and if God's command is not *directly* received in every situation requiring a moral decision, then casuistry is perhaps a better evil as an alternative to antinomianism — provided caution is exercised in its use.

Moreover, as Burtness rightly points out, many articulate and informed believers do not think that ethical decision-making must always be spontaneous and miraculously given directly by God either through the Spirit (Elert) or through specific and definite commands (Barth) for it to be gracious.[51] It is gracious enough of God to have seen fit to work great things through human hands and creativity. Culture, and through it casuistry or general ethics, is one of God's tools by which the Creator works with and among humans as their social world continues to be structured.

5.2 THE ROLE OF LANGUAGE IN MORAL DECISION-MAKING

In our criticism of Barth and Elert above, we drew attention to Niebuhr's rejection of abstractions of the believers's self-understanding which is not dependent on either the Church or the human fellowhsip in society and culture, a culture which supplies him/her with language, words and logic of piety or categories of meanings or some such aids that help one's interpretation of reality. In criticizing them for rejecting general ethics, we were drawing attention to the importance of language in transmitting meanings, whose importance cannot be emphasized enough. This importance of language is overlooked by Elert when he insists that there must be a total break between the "old man" under cultural influences and the "new being"who soars above cultural, biographical contexts, and all human environmental influences — as if the Spirit will supply such a person with new language and concepts to interpret reality. Yet, Elert goes on to talk about ethics of responsibility. What he assumes is that everybody knows what responsibility is in human relations; he assumes that each person invents the content of what it means to be responsible, and assumes that the word "responsible" is clear, self-interpreting, and without ambiguities. He ignores the formative function of language as well as social norms, values, and mores in defining what right conduct is, what responsibility is, etc.

Indeed, Elert seems to be oblivious to the fact that responsibility or moral action does not happen by chance. Rather, these virtues are brought about by habituation and practising of discipline in the process of socialization and internalization of social norms and values. To tell someone to be responsible in relation to others without defining the content of what it means — namely, responsibility as it is understood by a particular society — is useless if not irresponsible. For as Niebuhr points out, we enter into relationships from childhood which have meanings and have been interpreted by others before us. Through language, we are introduced into these meanings, and as we try to understand ourselves and engage in ethical deliberations, we do so not as abstract individuals but as beings fully armed with categories, the grammar and logic of the language of the society in which we were raised. Consequently, we look to our fellows not only for categories to interpret reality but also for verification as to whether what we do is indeed correct, good, right or, to use Elert's metaphor, whether or not what we do is responsible.[52]

The same criticism can also rightly be levelled against Barth who, more often than not, overlooks the significance of language in transmitting meanings. As we have seen, Barth claims that God's law is so specific, clear and unambiguous that it needs no interpretation because "even to the smallest detail it is self-interpreting."[53] A claim such as this can be made only by a theologian who has little regard for the way meanings are transmitted by a language of the society. For, if God's commands are to have meaning at all to the hearer, it is absolutely necessary that somehow God would have to employ concepts, words, categories of interpretations and classification that are already understood or have meaning to the addressee. And because of the role language plays in transmitting meanings in society, it makes no sense to suggest that God's command is self-interpreting when it confronts the believer. For, it makes sense only to talk about God's law, liberation, salvation, forgiveness, election, permission, etc., etc., to the people in whose vocabulary these concepts have meaning.[54]

Yet Barth seems to imply a discontinuity, when he holds that we must bracket what we know about good and right so that God's command can tell us what to think and do here and now, and that we must hold in reserve all of our knowledge, namely, the social values and norms whose meaning are transmitted by language, so that we might approach God like those who are ignorant and are in dire need of divine instruction. Do claims, such as Barth makes, mean that somehow God supplies us with new concepts and categories of good and evil that have no connection *even in the least* to what our language has taught us about good and evil?[55] We fail to see what Barth hopes to gain by giving an impression — though perhaps unintended — that somehow discontinuities occur when God addresses us after we have held in reserve all that we think we know about good and evil. For, if such discontinuities were to occur, a complete breakdown of communication would result between God and humanity.

We cannot follow Barth and Elert at this point; for we believe with Kaufman that:

> Man is a thoroughly historical being: all that we experience and understand is shaped by ideas and language that structure our consciousness.[56]

Indeed, if what Kaufman says about experience, understanding and structuring of our consciousness is true (as we believe it is), then precisely what Barth says should be held in reserve and bracketed, namely, cultural ideas, concepts, axioms and categories that have shaped our notions of good and right, become exactly what we necessarily must have -- if God is to communicate with us meaningfully. Also, Elert's claim that "new" beings in Christ are above and beyond all the social or human environmental influences is similarly unintelligible. Our language which gives meanings to concepts, such as good and right, cannot be shelved, or left behind with the "old man" in our encounter with God, for the result would be a total absence of self-consciousness (i.e., structure of our consciousness shaped by language itself), understanding and meaningful dialogue.

Sociology has given us a deeper understanding of the extent to which we are products of the cultural process in which language fundamentally shapes us in transmitting meanings and interpretations of events by previous generations. Our very conscious selves are shaped in social interaction and communication in a social and cultural context. Selfhood emerges through our active involvement in a society where – through language – we learn and know what roles to play, how to relate to others, and what is expected of us as children or as parents in a community, or as citizens in a nation.

Thus, it is through language that one can know what right or deviant behaviour is, as well as what it means to be responsible. Only when this role and linguistic system of meanings is internalized does it become possible for individuals to be guided by values, norms, and moral rules of culture – imparted to them by a particular society. Kaufman has aptly summarized the role of language in mediating selfhood, when he says:

> Both language and the role-system are created and shaped in the developing history of a society; and they may be regarded as ..... providing the context or matrix within which selves emerge. Maturing into selfhood ..... is achieved through learning the language and internalizing the roles of that community. The linguistic- and role-system of the culture – the very reservoirs, as it were, for values, ideals, ideas, attitudes, and ways of doing things which men have developed over many millennia – thus give structure to the self. Moreover, language provides categories by which the self perceives the world ..... it supplies a ready-made system of possible kinds of relationship between these realities .....[57]

The close relationship between meanings language transmits and the shaping of our very conscious selves, which Kaufman has so ably articulated, makes it all too clear why we believe that Barth and Elert have not taken the role of language seriously, when it is recommended that we bracket what we know in ethical reflection, and when it is claimed that the believer should rise above human environmental influences in the event of decision-making. For, were this to happen, our language – as well as the ways of doing things that constitute moral wisdom gleaned from the painful experience of the human race, the wisdom giving structure to our very selves, and thereby guiding us in our approach to moral situations – would also be shelved or discontinued within the life of the Christian. Indeed, there seems to be no way of shelving or leaving behind with the "old man" what we know without also shelving or leaving behind the language which mediates knowledge as well; for language is constitutive of what we know. And, a new language would become very necessary if dialogue were to become possible between God and humanity.

However, as some theologians have been quick to point out, even Barth himself has had to use common language because he has not succeeded in founding a thoroughly Christocentric language,[58] a language unpolluted by all that humans think they know about the rightness and goodness of their ethical decisions. Strangely, Barth confirms their observations by conceding that continuities are perhaps inevitable, for we cannot do without the language of the common culture. Of course, he does not admit his failure explicitly. Rather he talks about the conquering of general ethics and uses strong metaphors, such as "annexation of the kind that took place on the entry of children of Israel into Palestine," "invasion" of the territory of Cannan (meaning general ethics) *"not as a foreign country which did not belong to them, but as the land of their forefathers."*[59]

These metaphors underline the radical transformation that general ethics must undergo in Christian faith, but these are transformations of the *language which already belonged to them as language of the forefathers, of common culture.* These concessions mean that the bracketing of what we know may not, after all, be that easy or even possible. One is almost tempted to ask whether Barth's tendency, in his ethical reflection, to try to derive a democratic form of state – consisting of the legislative, executive, and judicial branches of government, based on Christianity's one baptism, one Lord, and one Spirit – instead of the Nazist slogan of *Ein Volk, ein Reich, ein Führer,* is not itself an indication that he himself has not really succeeded in wiping clean all that he knew and had shaped him as a citizen of the democratic state of Switzerland.[60]

Indeed, is Barth's protest so vehement against Nazism, which he saw as a temptation to Christianity while he counselled everybody to keep cool against reactionary responses to communist domination of Eastern Europe, really one of an ethical decision made after he had bracketed everything he knew about good and right? Is it not more correct to suggest that, for a German Swiss, Nazism (which was not the gospel to other nations that were excluded by this German superiority) would be more tempting to his Christianity while for everybody else communism or nationalism for that matter may really be the temptation to their Christianity?[61] The evidence seems to refute Barth's assertion that our heritage in historical and cultural context could, in fact, be held in reserve; for it is on the basis of values and preferences learned there through language that the German Christian could choose Nazism over communism as good news or vice versa. Similarly, one wonders whether Elert's conservative theology of "orders of creation," which equates the existing European (one can even say German) social structures with a directly willed or divine creations, is not, in reality, influenced by the European culture which has shaped him rather by the guidance of the Spirit — as he claims? Once more, it is clear that real poeple cannot hover above and beyond all "human environmental influences" no matter how they try. This leads us to our last point: Personality.

5.3 THE INDIVIDUAL PERSONALITY IN ETHICAL DELIBERATION

Already in our criticism of both Elert's and Barth's disregard for the formative function of cultural values embodied in the linguistic- and role-system or ethical rules of conduct, we made references to the way selfhood emerges through the process of internalization. An in-depth discussion of personality is beyond the scope of this chapter, and the reader is referred to better works on this subject.[62] Rather, we wish to underscore the importance of personality, or character, which so heavily influences our choices, preferences and value-judgments in every decision-making situation.

We have seen how Elert portrays the personality of the "new being" in Christ, who is said to be totally new and unconditionally God's *creatio ex nihilo* to such an extent that he/she is exclusively guided by the Spirit and, consequently, that being under its sway he/she is above and beyond all "biographical contexts and all human environmental influences" in the moment of ethical decision. That is, because he/she is no longer under the law with its compulsions where the "old man" lives in common culture, there is discontinuity between the ethos under the law and ethos under the grace. Similarly, Barth claims that God's command not only gives specific and definite orders regarding what we should do, but also tells us what to think and how to do the good here and now.

This is achieved, Barth goes on to say, when in commanding, the divine commandment

> ...... creates the situation and all the conditions of the situation in which we have to obey, so that there is no place for any further waiting for a developing situation or suitable moment, nor for any further consideration, appraisal or selection of different possibilities, but only instant obedience.[63]

This statement is loaded and claims quite a lot for God's command; and if its claims were true, human actions would be no different from those of puppets or robots because, without "consideration, appraisal or selection of different possibilities" in ethical decisions, all cultural, psychological and subjective moral values and habits would be without any influence on what they decide and do. For God would be pulling them with their noses through the commands and they would have no choice whatsoever of their own to make. Of course, Barth would protest against a conclusion such as this since it contradicts his own view of human freedom for God.[64] But, if it is true that God's law is self-interpreting, it tells us what to think and do; it creates circumstances of its own fulfillment and, therefore, leaves nothing to human choice or preference, then one wonders what other conclusion is possible.

Barth's claims show how far theologians can go in their abstractions of the individual. As a result, both Barth and Elert very frequently ignore the analysis of the essential nature of human behaviour with its complexity of its motivations. As it often happens their thoughts are removed from the realities of the actual and empirical human life,[65] where decisions are largely dictated by dispositions, moods, habits, preferences and values that have been transmitted by culture and now constitute the very stuff that is called personality, conscious self, or character. The best statement on personality that I know of comes from Cross, who writes:

> Human personality is a cluster of values. We cannot think of human persons apart from what we call "character." Character is a complex of traits and attitudes, habits, and reactions, developed in the psychological and social history of the person. Moral attitudes determining decisions

> are bundles of entwining opinions, habits, tastes, and attitudes. *Moral values are always the product of biological inheritance. They accumulate in us from infancy forward by impressions made by ..... hundred other sources of influence ..... We digest the inherited, heteronomous derivation of values, and interiorize and personalize them, making them intimately our own. This is the meaning of conscience: a personalization of derived and institutional moral guidance.*[66]

We have cited Cross at length because his statement gets at the heart of what personality, or character, or moral conscious self, or decisions dictated by one's conscience, is all about. This understanding of the essential nature of human behaviour is missing in Barth, who seems to believe that we can approach new situations that demand ethical decisions as those who are ignorant, waiting to be taught freshly by God after we have bracketed all of our knowledge. This is no less true of Elert, who believes that the "new being" in Christ is above all biographical contexts and outside all human environmental influences in his/her ethical deliberations. Indeed, Elert prefers to wage a war against the insights of all social sciences rather than enter into a meaningful dialogue with their analysis of the essential nature of human behaviour, in order to preserve his faulty, *asocial* and unhistorical understanding of human personality and conscience.[67]

However, what Barth and Elert seem to overlook is the simple fact that in moral decision-making *humans are not always guided by their overruling loyalty to God or to Jesus Christ or to the Spirit.* Rather, the fact of the matter is that, more often than not, they rely on the interior structure of values which make up the stuff of human personality, character, or conscience.[68] This does not mean to suggest that the role of judgment or assessment of the particular situation is excluded. Neither does this exclude the fact that God's grace or Spirit might be actively present. Nor is it a correct assessment of the situation to suggest that the help of God's grace or Spirit merely operate in a *vacuum, an empty head.* Rather, it must be asserted against Barth and Elert that they (the grace or Spirit of God) become aids to the self here and now making decisions, as the self that is already shaped by a cluster of values, as the self with definite dispositions, habits, intentions and preferences.[69]

Precisely because of these tendencies to act in certain ways, these dispositions and habits which play a larger role in our ethical deliberations than we realize, we cannot follow Barth and Elert, who advocate for instantaneous obedience based on direct instigation of the Spirit, or the commanding grace. On the contrary, we believe that Gardner's observation comes closest to the realities of life, when he writes:

> Moral choices are not matters of chance; they are not fortuitous and completely unpredictable. A person whose actions were free in this sense would not be good, for his actions would be unstable, and there would be no basis for confidence that his future actions would be of a certain kind, either good or bad.[70]

Gardner here has laid his finger on crucial issues, when he suggests that actions must be stable and predictable. This does not mean to imply that determinism is advocated; for people would be no different from robots, or puppets, if they were merely to be shaped by society without their, in turn, shaping and influencing cultural values. The existence of deviant behaviour and continuing breakthroughs in cultural innovations argue against cultural determinism.[71] But what is here being argued is that society does mould individuals in such a way that – despite obvious personality differences that would emerge, for no two persons are exactly the same even if they come from the same parents, or society, or community – they end up acquiring, through interiorization of values, some kind of stable, if not lasting, behaviour patterns that are considered by the society to be moral and acceptable.

It is on the basis of such patterns that predictability of human conduct in relation to others is based (e.g., husband-wife, parent-child, friend-friend relationships, etc.). Moreover, it is on the basis of the possibility of moulding human behaviour into a stable, and therefore predictable character, that discipline of the young – through education and learning of virtues or habits and also through effort and practice in civilized society by adults – is predicated.

To argue, as Barth and Elert do, that we are to shelve what we know and dissociate the "old self" in culture from the "new creature" in Christ in moral decision-making process is very misleading, because it is to ignore the major role that is played by individual character or conscience (which itself is a constellation of civic and moral rules of conduct). In fact, it should be argued that were conscience not present in moral action, God would have no contact with which divine laws might re-direct and correct our conduct. For it is precisely because conscience (personality or moral conscious self) is not bracketed or left behind that God, or society can effectively appeal to, or employ, its moral authority to guide or chasten us, because it is common knowledge that it is when this internalized reservoir of the linguistic- and role-system of values (now personalized as conscience) is contravened – "because of appetite, passion, or compulsion," or weakness of the flesh or shortcomings – that "we experience the psychic dissonance of pangs conscience and moral qualms."[72] Without personality or conscience, the Word of God would have no impact whatsoever on our moral conduct, as Luther observed long ago.[73]

The warning given us by Barth and Elert that we should not trust general ethics or casuistry too excessively is valid in so far as it is a mistake to identify directly either the *sensus communis moralis,* or cultural ethos, values and norms, and indeed human conscience with the divine law itself. But it is a mistake to go on and suggest that they could not be employed by God in dealing with humans, or that they could not point to the divine will. To be sure, God's will cannot be identified directly with historical rules of conduct or structure of values that exist in any particular epoch and culture. But without a double dialectical sense – in which God's command could be said to be present in these cultural activities and constructions that give rise to mores, rules of conduct, social values or norms and social structures in human community, such as the linguistic- and role-system of values, all of which give structure to the self, personality or conscience while at the same time the divine command transcends them – it would be impossible for humanity to hear the *real* command of God which hovers above the empirical, historical and concretely human laws and social structures that continually shape human selves and influence their moral conduct.[74]

To sum up: the problem with both Barth and Elert, as we have pointed out often enough, lies in their conceptions of the law, which are so defective and narrowly lodged within the framework of human justification before God at the expense of human righteousness before other humans that they dismally fail to separate the function of law in matters of salvation (election) from its function in ethical conduct or deliberation. As a consequence, they pay little attention to the complexities that are involved in the dynamics of ethical decision-making process, because their conceptions of law take no account of the penultimate, relative, and temporal good that humans, under the guidance of general ethics, or social structure of values, can actually achieve in their relation to their fellows.

Yet, as we have already remarked in our opening remarks, a clear recognition should have been made that there two issues which are neither identical nor in competition with each other are involved: one deals with human standing *coram Deo,* and the other with human standing *coram hominibus.* When each is given its due place and dignity there is no reason to wage a perennial war against casuistry as Barth and Elert do, especially because social righteousness is also a necessary element of the content of our obedience to the law of God.[75]

Notes

1 The concept "salvation" will be used almost interchangeably with "justification" in this chapter. The same applies to the concepts: "morality" and "ethics" or "ethical deliberation."

2 Barth, *Church Dogmatics* II/2, p. 563.

3 Elert, *Law and Gospel,* pp. 32–33.

4 Elert's contention that *lex semper accusat* because a God-like perfection is not achievable makes sense only when the law is understood within the framework of justification. It is not clear, however, whether social righteousness – which, to be sure, is not identical with God-like or Christ's righteousness – is equally unachievable. If this were true, why did prophets require it?

5 We are aware that Elert also talks about the political use of the law elsewhere. But, instead of reflecting positively on that use, he sees it only as a convenient way by which law ultimately will deliver us to death; for by providing security, it also insures that finally we must die. In doing so, Elert blurs the distinction between *theological* and *political uses of law.* The positive use serves the negative use in the final analysis. Cf. *The Christian Ethos,* pp. 51–53, 62, 69, 113, 282–295, 298–300.

6 Elert, *The Christian Ethos,* pp. 298, 303.

7 Ibid., p. 5.

8 Ibid., p. 15.

9 For a lucid statement on "deontological" ethics, cf. H.R. Niebuhr, *The Responsible Self* (New York: Harper and Row, 1963), pp. 66–67. Cited hereafter as *The Responsible Self.*

10 Elert, *The Christian Ethos,* pp. 296–302.

11 Ibid., p. 302. He cites Calvin and Barth and notes their agreement here that grace is the content of law.

12 Ibid., pp. 299–302.

13 Ibid., pp. 298–299. The law, according to him, says that we are already in sin in our totality at birth even before we break this or that rule.

14 Elert, *The Structure of Lutheranism,* pp. 27f, 34. By bringing the problem of destiny in ethical discussion, Elert confirms our contention that law for him operates within the categories of justification.

15 *The Christian Ethos,* pp. 49, 54.

16 Ibid., pp. 2–3, 6–7, 9–11, 16–17, 141.

17 Ibid., pp. 7, 141, 208. It is important to note that Elert is able to reject prescriptive ethics because he has separated external behaviour from the demands of God's law. General ethics, or casuistry is rejected because

it does not use "God's exclusive standards" in which humanity is seen as sinful and subject to the retributive law of the Creator from beginning to last. Special ethics (Christian obedience to the new law of Christ), like philosophical ethics, is denounced because it concentrates on the external behaviour rather than the guilty conscience and leads to Pharisaic moralism and a denial of one's sin before God.

18 Ibid., p. 18. (Italics added) If Elert's position were correct, God's law would be disinterested in the way we behave towards others as well as in our personal integrity; for it would be blind to questions of social justice and injustice both personal and communal. Fortunately, his conclusion does not have any support from the Old Testament prophets.

19 Ibid., p. 208.

20 Ibid., pp. 141 and 63 respectively. (Italics added) This and the preceding citation make it abundantly clear that Elert has become a victim of his own theological system, a system that has defined and confined law to the categories of religious justification. For the idea that an ethical posture *has no standing* before God means that ethics is lifted out of its normal usage with reference to human conduct in society to a level where law determines one's standing *only before God.* Further, if ethics does not describe "man" as he is in his social, historic, and concrete setting, hoping thereby to clarify how an acceptable conduct differs from non-acceptable behaviour, what else does? Must ethics really concern itself with abstractions rather than with "man" as he really is and how he lives? Where else would *lex quae semper accusat* meet and accuse "man" concretely except as he is found *as he is* in society where he tries to live respectably in his individual and communal relationships? Because Elert does not focus on law as it produces some good in society, his eyes are always on human justification before God.

21 Ibid., pp. 26–35, 44–46, 11f, 141. Responsibility and the image of God are used almost interchangeably by Elert.

22 Ibid., pp. 206, 209, 211, 213, 216–217, 226.

23 Ibid., pp. 216f, 254, 292, 297–299.

24 Ibid., p. 252. Elert does not tire to remind us that the believer's life is full of struggles and temptations that must be resisted, because, even though we live under the Spirit who leads us into correct ways, the fact remains that there are no easy decisions because we live by faith and not by sure knowledge or sight.

25 Ibid., p. 255.

26 Barth, *Church Digmatics* II/2, p. 538. There is an interesting similarity between the views of Barth and Elert. They both agree that ethics has no interest in external human conduct but rather in that which God does on the sinner, which is the same thing as justification before God. See footnote 21 above in this chapter.

27 Ibid., p. 538. As we have seen already, this good, or obedience is portrayed as one's response to Jesus' bid that we should follow him.

28 Ibid., pp. 577–579.

29 Ibid., pp. 536f, 540, 543, 565, 665, 670.

30 Ibid., pp. 517–518, 636f, 673–75, and III/4, pp. 6–11.

31 *Church Dogmatics* II/2, p. 674.

32 Elert, *The Christian Ethos,* p. 206.

33 *Church Dogmatics* III/4, p. 11.

34 Ibid., p. 12. Barth, of course, would protest against any suggestion that his ethics is individualistic. But if his own words are to be taken seriously, one wonders how individualism can, in fact, be avoided. For the person he talks about is, like Elert's "new man," beyond and outside cultural and social contexts which have shaped him/her. Cornelius Van Til's cautious charge that Barth courts individualism is not without justification. Cf. *The New Modernism: An Appraisal of the Theology of Barth and Brunner* (Philadelphia: The Presbyterian and Reformed Publishing Company, 1946), pp. 315, 319ff.

35 Henlee H. Barnette, "The New Ethics: 'Love Alone,'" in *The Situation Ethics Debate,* ed. Harvey Cox (Philadelphia: The Westminster Press, 1968), p. 139. Hereafter cited as *The Situation Ethics Debate.*

36 Against Barth and Elert, we agree with Niebuhr's insightful observation that Christ *never claims us outside but always within* cultural contexts. For, as he rightly contends the Christian "..... cannot dismiss the philosophy and science of his society as though they are external to him; they are in him ..... He cannot rid himself of political beliefs and economic customs by rejecting the more or less external institutions; these customs and beliefs have taken residence in his mind"; cf. *Christ and Culture* (New York: Harper and Row, 1956), p. 69. It can be argued that the believer undergoes some religious transformation, or conversion, when Christ is accepted. But this should not be understood to mean that cultural influences are wiped out in such a way that no differences would remain regarding one's past as a German, American, or Chinese, Christian who has been shaped by a particular culture. And because cultural roots go much deeper than some Christians are willing to concede, it cannot be claimed that one's decisions and action are "purely" Christian and are without any traces of the social milieu of which the believer is a product.

37 *Church Dogmatics* II/2, p. 646.

38 H.R. Niebuhr, *The Responsible Self,* p. 81.

39 Cf. Cornelius Van Til, *Christianity and Barthianism* Philadelphia: The Presbyterian and Reformed Publishing Co., 1962), p. 427.

40 Barth's ambiguity at this point approximates that of Elert about which we have repeatedly complained, especially his refusal to affirm that God's will is known in society so that we can rightly claim that some of our decisions have conformed to it.

41 *Church Dogmatics* II/2, pp. 585, 588, 602f, 646f, 663–80, 700ff.

42 In one of his startling statements Barth says that the divine law "..... commands not only how man is to think and act here and now, but also quite specifically what is to take place inwardly in his mind and thoughts and outwardly in what he does ..... It leaves nothing to human choice or preference. It thus requires no interpretation to come into force. To

the last and smallest detail it is self-interpreted" *(Church Dogmatics* III/4, p. 12).

43 *Church Dogmatics* III/4, p. 14. (Italics added) Elert's position here, despite its weaknesses in some areas, offers a needed correction to that of Barth, when he says that Christians do not receive commands from God *directly* in order to "spare us personal planning and decisions in changing circumstances of our lives" *(The Christian Ethos,* p. 252).

44 Hugo A. Meynell, *Grace Versus Nature; Studies in Karl Barth* (London: Sheed and Ward, 1965), p. 185. (Italics added)

45 *Church Dogmatics* IV/2, pp. 722–725 and II/2, pp. 541, 569. This is the basis of Barth's criticism of Luther who, as he claims, has failed to ground the law Christologically, when the Reformer left free reign to the magistrates by separating the gospel (Christ's spiritual rule) from the realm of law.

46 *Church Dogmatics* II/2, pp. 646–654f, 663–705 and III/4, pp. 11–14.

47 Cf. Robert E. Willis, *The Ethics of Karl Barth* (Leiden: E.J. Brill, 1971), p. 430. Cited hereafter as *The Ethics of Karl Barth.* John H. Yoder, in his *Karl Barth and the Problem of War* (New York: Abingdon Press, 1970), is skeptical about Barth's claims and asks: "Does this church exist? Is the Swiss Reformed Church ..... capable of speaking with this degree of clarity, of examining and understanding situations with this degree of certainty, of making her voice heard at the right time to say now 'peace' and now 'war' in such a way that both church members and politicians can count on it?" (p. 108).

48 Paul Lehmann, *Ethics in a Christian Context* (New York: Harper and Row, 1963), p. 76. (Italics added)

49 *Church Dogmatics* II/2, p. 669; IV/2, p. 542.

50 *Church Dogmatics* II/2, pp. 618–620, 622f, 717, and III/4, pp. 12–14. In all these places Barth twists the meaning of the texts to fit his understanding of the law within the context of justification. He goes so far as to oversimplify law and obedience within social relationships as well.

51 Cf. James H. Burtness, "Life-Style and Law: Reflections on Matt. 5:17," in *Dialog* (Vol. 14, Winter 1975), p. 14.

52 Cf. H.R. Niebuhr, *The Responsible Self,* pp. 79–80.

53 *Church Dogmatics* II/2, p. 66, and III/4, pp. 12, 14.

54 Heinz Zahrnt is more right in arguing for some preliminary idea and knowledge of basic meanings of concepts, words with which God's revelation in Jesus and in religious language could make contact. Cf. *The Question of God: Protestant Theology in the 20th Century* (New York: Harcourt, Brace & World, Inc., 1969), pp. 59–62. Cited hereafter as *the Question of God.*

55 I do not want to imply that our encounter with God does not result in a transformation of language, but merely to point out that it transforms words that already have meanings in the common culture as a whole.

56 Gordon D. Kaufman, *Systematic Theology: A Historicist Perspective* (New York: Charles Scribner's Sons, 1968), pp. 14. Cited hereafter as *Systematic Theology.*

57 Ibid., p. 24.

58 Cf. James M. Gustafson, *Christ and the Moral Life* (New York: Harper & Row, 1968), p. 28; Edward L. Long, Jr., *A Survey of Christian Ethics* (London: Oxford University Press, 1975), p. 30. These theologians complain that Barth sweeps clean general ethics, casuistry and legalism only to bring them back under other auspices and new names. Casuistry is rejected in the name of freedom in Christ only to become "permissions" or "practical casuistry," etc. The impossibility of Barth's venture is best summarized by Niebuhr, when he writes: "In our time the effort to achieve a completely Christocentric and solely Christomorphic form of thinking and acting has been confined to theology, most notably to Karl Barth's theology ..... Barth ..... attempts to dismiss all analogies, all metaphors, all symbols from Christian speech and conduct except Jesus Christ. But, of course, he cannot interpret the meaning of Jesus Christ without the aid of other metaphors and symbols such as Word of God, Son of God, Servant, Lord ..... *Particularly in speech about Christian ethics he must employ non-Christian though not non-Biblical symbols, such as commandments, law, obedience, and permission" (The Responsible Self,* p. 158). (Italics added)

59 *Church Dogmatics* II/2, pp. 518–522. (Italics added)

60 Zahrnt, in *The Question of God,* has illuminating suggestions about Barth's theology, especially pp. 181–182.

61 George W. Forrell argues persuasively that Barth's ethical decisions were not free from parochial vision, bias and personal preferences of a non-pluralistic cultural setting. Cf. "Can we endorse the Barthian Ethics?" in *Dialog* (Vol. 3, Winter 1964), pp. 55–56. In a similar vein, more illuminating questions are posed by Will Herberg in his introduction to Barth's three essays: *Community, State, and Church,* pp. 43–67. John Yoder's reply in *Karl Barth and the Problem of War,* pp. 119–131, does little to improve Barth's weakness and his idiosyncratic approach to ethics.

62 Cf. Niebuhr, *The Responsible Self;* Kaufman, *Systematic Theology;* and Gustafson, *Christ and the Moral Life,* etc.

63 *Church Dogmatics* III/4, p. 12 Also cf. II/2, p. 665.

64 Barth rejects the view that God relates to humans in a tyrannical manner. Rather God acts to free us all from tyranny, and he believes that human life has to be defended even for the most villainous brother; for he is Christ's brother too. Cf. *Church Dogmatics* II/2, pp. 553f, 620–663, 716f; *The Humanity of God,* p. 53.

65 Willis, in his *The Ethics of Karl Barth,* pp. 195–201, 430, 432, 439–441, persuasively demonstrates how Barth often ignores the empirical data provided by social sciences in preference of insights that are given directly by God.

66 Wilford O. Cross, "The Moral Revolution: An Analysis, Critique and Appreciation," in *The Situation Ethics Debate,* p. 163. (Italics added)

67 Cf. *The Christian Ethos,* pp. 30–35, 206, 211–213, 216–17. Elert's main objection to scientific definitions of conscience is that social sciences tend to relativize the law, the "ought" by giving the impression that it varies from culture to culture. Also, he objects to the view that conscience is something that belongs to human natural quality, an endowment that is found in all "men," or that it is something that guides us regarding what we should do. Rather, conscience refers to the knowledge of God, or an awareness of past deeds which accuse the sinner. Hence there is no such thing as a clear or "good" conscience because of the experience of guilt which accompanies the sinner. Because the conscience brings home the reality of sin and its ultimate meaning for human life, it constantly reminds humans that before God all men are without excuse when they lack the fear of their Creator; for no amount of exercises of Kantian "good will" nor pursuits of virtues in response to "duty" remove its accusation.

68 It is for this reason that, were they to shelve and bracket all that they know about good and evil or part company with their "old" self rooted in culture, humans would not be any more moral than animals, and their actions could hardly be called ethical.

69 This explains in part why people who come from the same culture, not to mention those from other cultures, differ so much when a Christian response is called for in a given situation. One in America, or South Africa, becomes a racist, the other anti-racist. One becomes a pacifist, the other, from the same church, believes that war – even nuclear annihilation – does not violate Christian beliefs. James Cone, in his *God of the Oppressed* (New York: Seabury Press, 1975), pp. 39–88, underlining Niebuhr's observation on the relativity of all persons, rightly contends that theology tells us more about the dreams of the believers than it does about God, the Creator of heaven and earth.

70 E. Clinton Garner, *Biblical Faith and Social Ethics* (New York: Harper & Brothers, Publishers, 1970), p. 3. Cited henceforth as *Biblical Faith and Social Ethics.*

71 A clear example of indeterminism is the Reformation period with a different set of ideas and values. So, also, are dissidents or civil rights activists in repressive and totalitarian states.

72 Cross, "The Moral Revolution: An Analysis, Critique and Appreciation," in *The Situation Ethics Debate,* pp. 163–164.

73 *Luther's Works,* Vol. 40, p. 97.

74 Cf. Brunner's insightful remarks about the necessity to understand God's law dialectically in *The Divine Imperative,* pp. 147, 208.

75 The relation between the positive claims that have been made here about the social structure of selfhood in society – where an individual is expected to act morally and thereby attain justice and civic righteousness in relation to others – and the problem of law and gospel may not be obvious, as others have remarked. However, if one follows the unfolding of the argument carefully, the relation is there. The connecting link between this chapter and the preceding chapters is not so much the gospel as it is

the creative activity in which God involves humans through the instrumentality of the law. Our contention is that God's goodness and willingness to give life and all that sustains it, which reached its climax when the Creator gave Jesus Christ for the world, is the motivating factor behind God's creative use of the law in social relations. For God involves humans through the law in the creation of structures whose purpose it is to nourish and sustain life Therefore, God's use of the law is characterized by the divine love that is actualized only as fellow creatures are served. When Barth and Elert define their conceptions of law within the categories of justification, excluding thereby God's interest in social justice and righteousness, we felt it necessary to criticize them because our thesis is that the content of human obedience to the divine law has to be specified with reference to achievements of temporal good and right in society. What this chapter demonstrates is that conceptions of law as held by Barth and Elert are so inadequate, deficient, and one-sided that they fail to do justice to the positive and creative aspects of law in society; they fail to make sense of questions of ethical decision-making, the role of selfhood in ethical situations, and how language mediates between human selves and the external world. Indeed, Barth and Elert have no theology of culture, one which could understand God to be standing behind human creativity in culture, and which conceives of cultural creations, such as the linguistic- and role-system of values, laws and norms as well as the social structures, as tools *God creates together with humanity by involving them through the command in the divine creative dynamics, and that God freely utilizes these cultural media to reach and communicate with human creatures.* The manner in which God is involved in human culture and the extent to which human agency is employed by the Creator, as the command is used to involve finite beings in the dynamics of divine creativity, will be made more explicit towards the end of the next chapter and through the constructive chapters of Part Three.

Chapter six

Beyond the positions of Elert and Barth: where have they gone wrong?

It seems appropriate at this point, before we move on to the constructive part of this study, to examine the context within which the command of God is understood in the theologies of Barth and Elert. It is, in our opinion, as we fully understand the reasons that have led these two theologians astray – in their formulations of such inadequate and imbalanced conceptions of law that lodge the notions of the law within the framework of justification of humans before God at the expense of human righteousness before others – that we may avoid similar mistakes and be in a position to correct and move beyond their untenable views.

The nature of the discussion here is much more one of further examination of the data, a theological excursus rather than one of a further critical evaluation as such. It is a necessary exposition because it will try to locate some of the basic root-causes of the problems that haunt the theologies of Barth and Elert, thereby serving as a warning that theological understanding of the law cannot be expressed adequately unless that understanding is grounded in the dynamics of the divine will itself which is essentially creative and characterized by the divine love.

To be sure, there is always more than one root-cause to any problem. But we want to suggest here that the basic root-cause of the one-sided and inadequate conceptions of the law in the theologies of Elert and Barth are attributable, for the most part, to their failure to ground their notions of law in the dynamic and creative will of God, or in the doctrine of creation which is highly charged with dynamism and activity.[1] This failure can be traceable, we believe, to the specific but mistaken conception of creation against which the divine law was understood. It is mistaken because it is static and fails to take into account the fact that creation is a continuing process here and now through cultural activities in which humans are involved.

As a result of this static notion of creation, for Barth and Elert, what is created seems to be a finished product; things are as they were created and unalterable for the better, so to speak; and what remains for the Creator to do is to save them from the blemish of fall and sin. That is, only in salvation does God appear to be actively at work in the present. Consequently, when the law is defined and understood against this static conception of creation, it is something that operates either to condemn the sinner in order to bring him/her to Christ (Elert) or to liberate, set the sinner free for a covenant fellowship with God (Barth).

The creature, as we have already suggested, is understood as a complete product of some past actions, but one which needs salvation. Seeing that, for them, God is primarily active in the salvation of sinners, it became logical for both Barth and Elert to lodge their understanding of the divine law within the context of human justification — because only there can an activity of the Creator through the law be understood. That is, the law as the divine activity has little room in the doctrine of creation which is seen as a past action.

Against such a static conception of creation, one which is finished and done away within its continued preservation by the mighty hand of the Deity, it is our contention — which will be maintained in this and the following chapters — that the divine law is correctly understood when it is grounded in the dynamic, on-going or continuous creative will of God, and that this continuous creativity is one which is not in competition with the salvational dynamics of God through the gospel but rather one which is supplemented and complemented by this redemptive act, as creation is carried to its completion in the *eschaton*. Therefore, it is of fundamental significance to realize that the dynamic, positive and continuous creative activity of God through the law cannot be adequately understood or done justice to when the law is not grounded in the creative dynamics of God but is based on the fact of fall, sin, condemnation or the need of law by governments to act as bulwarks or dykes against violence or spread of sin on the part of completed creation (Elert).

Neither will the law be adequately understood when it is based on the fact of salvation, election and liberation in need of which the creature (understood statically as a finished entity) stands when God decides to enter into a covenant partnership with it, thereby giving the law of the covenant to such an elected partner as a part of this rescue mission. We now proceed to demonstrate the nature of this static conception of law in the theologies of Barth and Elert and to show why such notions of law within the context of a static notion of creation are of such serious magnitude that we cannot follow either of the two theologians.

6.1 ELERT'S UNDERSTANDING OF THE LAW AS AN ORDER BUT WITHOUT CREATION

We have already pointed out in our exposition of his theology that, in opposition to Barth, Elert contends that a proper theological response to modern secularism and lawlessness should be one which roots its conceptions of law in the first article of the creed, namely, the doctrine of the living, creative and gubernatorial activity of God, when the law is used as a qualitative judgment on the human life. Elert's instincts at this point are correct and must be applauded. But the way he carries out his program is highly problematical and must be rejected. To be sure, Elert is rightly anxious to overcome what, to him at least, appear to be non-biblical and deistic views of God's relation to the world with their resultant thrust towards relativism, immanentism and the "crisis" of law.[2]

In order to overcome and circumvent these problems, he feels it necessary to anchor the concept of law on something "eternal and unalterable" rather on shifting sands of historical developments.[3] This leads him to talk about *lex creationis* by which God brought things into existence, namely, the *orders* of creation, or what he calls (interchangeably) conditions, structures, and categories of existence *(Schöpfungsordnungen, Seinsordnungen),* all of which flow forth from the hand of the Deity. As we have already shown, the problem becomes one of defining just what these *"Seinsordnungen" mean and consist of.* His elaborate definition of them is taken up in his discussion of an order, *nomos,* or nomological existence, which is the same thing as an ordered existence by God's mighty hand. We have seen that it is in the sense of this ordered existence that he understands law as security.

Consequently, Elert polemicizes against those Lutherans who, in his opinion, misinterpret Luther's thought on law by suggesting that what he meant by it refers to a body of commands, regulations or prescriptions *(Sollgefüge, Vorschriften).* By contrast, he contends that by law Luther referred to a wonderfully ordered cosmos, controlled categories of existence of interpersonal relationships into which each and every person is assigned by God at birth. He prefers to call them structures or facts of existence *(Seinsgefüge, Tatbestände),* the opposite of which is disorder or chaos *(Unordnung, Chaos).* This ordered nomological existence is not arbitrary but purposeful providence that relates all humans to God and others in society.

We need not enter into details of the types of structures in which facts of existence *(Tatbestände)* are believed to take their forms, because we have discussed them in full in the expository chapter. What is important to note here is the fact that these orders of creation or structures of existence are said to come directly from the creative will and governance of God. As such they are *sober facts* that transcend our wishes or choices, for they are God-given realities, structuralizations which are characteristic of all spheres of life and relationships, and as such they cannot be understood as attempts by humans to order their natural and social environment.[4] Rather, categories of existence are an order established long before we, as individual humans, appear on the scene without regard to whether we honour or despise them. It is for this reason that they are real even for the so-called atheists.[5] They belong to the realm of creation as such, and it is to them that God declared his creative satisfaction and approval as the Scriptures testify: "And God saw everything he had made, and behold, it was very good" (Gen. 1:31).

The upshot of Elert's understanding of the law in terms of an ordered cosmos or nomological *fact* means that God created in the beginning, and what was created has a reality of its own with which we have to contend either in our exhibition of obedience or disobedience in relation to it (divine order of existence). Indeed, the existence of God's ordered reality precedes our birth because the giving of the Decalogue at Sinai presupposes it. All this means that Elert has presented us with a correlation of creation with the concept of law both of which are understood as static, finished structures of existence. That is, now the law is portrayed in a way that it refers to a *thing, a state of being or affairs,* or an order which God has completed its creation but which is merely to be protected against all destructive forces of evil. In other words, the law is transmuted into a *noun, a thing* out there rather than an activity, and as such it is believed to be identical with God's order or nomological existence.

It is beyond the scope of the present discussion to investigate whether Elert is correct in claiming that law, for Luther, meant a structure of existence, things out there, or sober facts of existence *(Seinsgefüge, Tatbestände),* or even categories of existence *(Seinsordnungen)* and should, therefore be understood as referring to "orders of creation" *(Schöpfungsordnungen).*[6] What is incontrovertible is that Elert has here correlated notions of law with "ordered categories of existence" which he believes are implied by the theological conception of creation. As a consequence the notions of both creation and law have become highly static. A few more examples would help to clarify further how static the notion of law with which Elert's theology operates, is.

As we have seen, Elert believes that human life under the law is a product of creation. That is, the God-given realities or facts of existential life are of the nature that humans do not bring them about.[7] Furthermore, human history as one of sinful revolt against God is a product of irresponsibility which lacks progress; it fails to bring about a betterment for human life despite the fact that history is a human attempt to liberate mankind from fear. Instead, terror reigns, and the only thing humans are capable of doing in these divinely ordered structures of existence is to disturb them or inject disorder into them. And because human autonomy can disrupt these categories of existence, we must defend them against chaos through the civil use of law whose power is entrusted to governments.[8] Elert is quick to remind us that the *human defense of these orders does not at all imply that we create anything in this nomological existence into which we are assigned at birth; for it is God's order that is fixed before any of us is born.*[9] Rather, our responsibility toward these orders of creation is merely one of upholding them in the knowledge that they are divine mechanisms by which life is protected, that is, they are instruments of God's governing activity.

It is for this reason that Elert reminds us again and again that this order of existence is "not a product of the creative but regulative activity of God, it is an existential situation. As a product of his governing activity, it is a process in time."[10] Consequently, as realities that are in time, they are subject to the laws of becoming and ceasing. But, and this is important, as an ordered process in time these laws (viz., nomological structures) or orders of creation cannot be set aside. No, *"we cannot change them,"* for humans can only use them or misuse them.[11] Elert is willing to allow exceptions to his rule of unchangeable orders only with regard to what he calls "temporary orders," such as the neighbour-neighbour relationships of an occasional type (e.g., the Good Samaritan and his protégé).

By contrast, most of the lasting orders antedating our assignment into them are pretty much unchangeable, however. The clearest example of this type is the state, which serves God's administrative activity by maintaining law and order as willing citizens participate in its functions to oppose evil. To be sure, the state as one of good orders is vulnerable to demonization like every other order. But, even here, Elert cautions us against revolutionary overthrow of demonic regimes, unless one dares to do so in faith and in anticipation of God's judment on such a state. Otherwise, citizens have no right to destroy any government because:

> ...... what God has joined together man must not put asunder. That applies to matrimony as it does to the relationship existing between the power invested in the state and the citizens.[12]

But — and this is an important exception — because the state does not exist for its own sake but for the people, and also because a marraige can be severed if one partner is an adulterer, when those who are in authority abdicate their responsibility then the broken order must be replaced by a new one.[13] Even here, however, every law-abiding citizen will be slow to resort to drastic measures such as revolution, because no revolution is good insofar as it always destroys something good.[14]

The problem regarding the static notion with which Elert works, is compounded further when he correlates the Fall with the retributive function of the law by which God judges us. There is, for him, no time that life under the law does not exist in the history of total depravity and therefore under God's judgment. This is true for all cultural activities in which humans are involved. The upshot of the correlation of Fall and sin with the activity of death-dealing law of God means that, for Elert, tragedies of life, political imperfections, wars and other destructive forces could easily be endured as God's punishments on human life, which is characterized by its revolt from God.[15] For the same reason, even a demonic state can be endured as long as one does not anticipate — in faith — God's judgment on it, thereby overthrowing it.

When the element of retribution is added to the static notions of creation and law, it becomes very difficult to contemplate about changes, replacements or transformations of the structures existing in the world because they are directly believed to be God-given "orders of creations" *(Schöpfungsordnungen).* It is, therefore, not without some justification that in theology, such as the one Elert professes, a little room is left for real contact between salvation and transformation of social structures in the world.[16] Because this theology (of orders of creation) places too much emphasis on endurance and one's accommodation to the existing conditions, or on obedience in one's assigned place in the *"Seinsordnungen,"* salvation becomes a momentary release from bodily suffering; for no changes are plausible in history except in the future world. Indeed, as Schuurman's insightful observation rightly points out, faith in this kind of a conservative theology is understood as an escape "from the terror exercised by the creator-God, in a kind of *salto."*[17]

It is regrettable that Elert had to make a blunder where his theology is the strongest, namely, in his wish to anchor the understanding of the law on the doctrine of creation. The reason for this mistake lies in Elert's complete failure to inject verbs and dynamism into his theological conception of both law and creation. He is, therefore, unable to accommodate ongoing creative activities of God in the present. That is, had Elert used verbs, he would have been able to talk about past, present and future creations, and thus been able to bring some motion and dynamism which God's continuous creativity entails. Instead, he desired to ground his notions of law and creation on some inflexible order or something unalterable.

In doing so, he sought for fixed, lasting structures existing in society and wrongly identified them directly with God's instituted *"Tatbestände."* It is for this reason that he construes these structures of existence as somehow unhistorical, transcendent and timeless. In other words, Elert goes about deducing certain "orders" and structures which he hopes are to be found in the Genesis or in some past creation – orders such as family and nation or state, forgetting that all of them have emerged in a historical and cultural process, and that as such they are human creations that cannot be directly attributable to the "hand" of the God. Strangely enough, Elert is aware that marriage, in particular, reflects the socio-economic and cultural changes of particular epochs in human history. For this reason, monogamy, though ideally preferred by churches, has not always been there.[18] By a strange twist of logic, he exempts other orders, such as state, economy, family, et cetera.

The question is: How do we know that God has created free-enterprise economy rather than a state controlled economy? Or, can we really attribute democratic, socialistic, monarchic, aristocratic or dictatorial states directly to God's creativity? Which of these regimes are God's direct creation?[19] As we have already indicated, we are of the opinion that Törnvall is more correct in his rejection of the theology of "orders of creation" because it wrongly implies that God created some "orders" while other are not created by our Creator. It is simply wrong to freeze God's creativity at a certain point in the past when, in fact, most structures reflect ever expanding innovations and creations which humans – through the help of God, if you will – have brought about with remarkable success in our century.[20] Also, it is wrong to pick up and choose few structures which are preferable to or are liked by us as the ones which derive forth from the hand of the Deity while the rest are locked out from the sphere of the active and creative dynamics of the Creator.

We conclude our reflections by citing Gustafson's very insightful observation in which he writes:

> One of the mistakes of those who define "orders" of creation and preservation is that *they often find a kind of revealed positive sociology in the fact that man exists within family and state,* as if there is a clear pattern for these institutions ordained by God ..... *This, as has often been seen, leads to false identification of existing historical patterns or forms with the divine order, and thus to an uncritical, conservative acceptance of a status quo.*[21]

The best way to get out of this impasse, it seems, would be for Elert to learn to speak in verbs, not nouns – as we have argued all along. Instead of talking about orders, he needs to learn to talk about ordering, structuring, if he is to avoid past errors of directly identifying existing conditions of social life with divine creations, an error which leads to an uncritical acceptance and divinization of the *status quo.* He needs to realize that all these structures are human creations *par excellence* that have emerged in the historical process and that none of them can be deducible from Genesis.

Of course, equally important is the realization that creation is not only an ongoing process, but also that God continues to create in and through human culture and activity here and now as creation moves towards its completion in the *eschaton.* That is, God does not merely preserve what has been created; rather creations in the present are what must be understood as divine preservation. But this need not imply a direct creation of structures by God, as we have already warned. Finally, it seems that we look in vain for a dynamic and positive understanding of both creation and law in Elert's theology because he failed to use verbs which could have adequately expressed God's present creations.

6.2 BARTH'S VIEW OF THE LAW AS A FORM OF THE GOSPEL BUT NOT OF CREATION

As we have already suggested, Barth's understanding of creation, against whose background law as the form of the gospel is understood, is also static but in a different sense than that of Elert. Barth dismisses as untenable Elert's idea that the conception of "orders of creation" is the reliable and safest way to anchor a theological understanding of the law, one which could effectively counter the secularism, immanentism or lawlessness of modern times.[22] Instead, Barth sought to ground this understanding of the law in the only one Eternal Word of God, Jesus Christ, who is the ground, basis and content of the law and the goal of creation.[23] By making Jesus Christ the axis, the Archimedian point around which God and divine works (creation, covenant, law, gospel, etc.) turn, Barth wanted to acquire the greatest certainty possible concerning the ways of God with creation, because it is in Christ (the incarnation) that God has spoken the most decisive word.

By bringing creation and law into a close correlation with God's redemption in Christ, however, he has so concentrated on the latter that the two former realities are almost swallowed up, because not enough breathing space is left between them.[24] That is, creation and law serve merely as a prologue to the great event that took place in Christ. The upshot of this, unfortunately, is that creation is now seen almost as a past activity, an activity which sets the stage for the salvational acts that God now actively brings about. Also, the law almost loses its distinctive characteristics; for it now functions in pretty much the same way as the gospel: it sets free, it elects and invites sinners for fellowship, joy and glory with God. Moreover, by correlating these three realities too closely, Barth injects an understanding of creation, law and the gospel that can only become the absolute monopoly of God's work in which humans play no decisive role.

For this reason, creation – as we shall see – remains a past event which is not continuous with modern human innovations and scientific break-throughs in culture and civilization about which Barth is so pessimisitic.[25] As a consequence, Barth comes closest to identifying human creativity, achievements and history with man's Fall and therefore with life under sin.[26] Barth's presentation of his static views of a past creation is very complex, elaborate and does not become readily evident to his readers.[27] Unfortunately, a full examination of this conception of creation is beyond the scope of the present work; we shall give only the central thrust of his argument to illustrate the point we are trying to establish.

Barth's discussion of both creation and law are couched in verbs — unlike Elert who uses nouns — but the pastness of God's action still remains. Accordingly creation is a reality, a non-divine reality that is a gift or act of love, and it signifies the world which is elected, posited and limited by God's love. It is a reality that precedes and prepares the ground for the second work of God, namely, God's gracious dealings with creation in a covenant history that mirrors the eternal fellowship between the Father and the Son. Because the covenant fellowhsip between God and man is the goal of creation, a goal consummated in the true man, Jesus Christ, creation is the external basis of the covenant, while the covenant — or the envisaged goal of fellowship between the Cretor and creation — is the internal basis of creation.

The upshot of this claim is that creation and the covenant belong together, as external and internal basis of God's eternal decision to elect and to be for man. Concretely, this means that God is the subject who is active in choosing man for fellowship, and He remains the subject who takes action — after the Fall — to accept man in grace by initiating two counterparts of histories: one is the covenant history over against the secular or world history, and the other is the history of salvation constituted by God's own presence in Jesus Christ.[28] That is, with the coming of Jesus Christ, we are again given the time of grace — in the place of our lost time — in which our lost time is transformed and renewed.

It is important to note that grace is the connecting link between these three acts of God: creation, the history of the covenant, and the history of salvation in the person of Christ. In all cases it is the love of God that moved to create, to enter into covenant partnership with the creature, and to save it in Christ. But, Barth is quick to warn us, the three acts should not be collapsed into each other simply because they are all acts of grace. Rather they occur one after another. In the creation of man, the totality of creation was complete; creation was good and pleasing to God, and God entered Sabbath. God invited man to enter Sabbath, for man was created for freedom, not for work and toil. That is, he was created to be satisfied with what God had created and, therefore, to enjoy God's rest, freedom and glory in his participation in a common history with God.[29]

Barth does not tire to stress the fact that man was invited to enter Sabbath before he has done any work, before he engages himself with creative eagerness and zeal to do something, before and apart from all work of conflict, irrespective of any merit of his, and before he had anything behind him that he could count as a work.[30] This invitation to rest with God before any work should be emphasized even if this might annoy many readers and expositors, who do not take displeasure at the fact that God did not invite man to do at least some little work before he could enter rest with God.[31] Barth contends further that this invitation to rest was necessary to demonstrate the fact God wants man to be a grateful recipient of grace, a being who should become thankful to this beneficent Creator who has done everything to pour blessings on man.[32] This is because the gospel comes before the law that, without demanding any work, God should spread his goodness, compassion and beneficence all over man.[33]

By underlining the primacy of Sabbath over other days of toil and trouble, Barth kills two birds with one stone. First, he makes creation wholly and totally God's act, not human product. Humans must be on the receptive side merely enjoying the outpouring of God's love and blessings. Secondly, Barth wants to stress the fact that, by entering Sabbath, God looks back upon *what he had created,* which He finds pleasing. Consequently, Barth speaks at this point primarily in the *past tenses;* creation is something that is *done* and *finished* with. More importantly, also, Barth speaks about creation as though it were salvation in the past event which had now taken place. That is, in choosing the *ordered world,* God *rejected* chaos; God *pushed* away curse, misery, or anything hostile to what He *had willed* and *determined* as godly. Therefore, God *had* pity on His creation. Indeed, Barth goes on to say, creation was an eruption of compassion because once and for all God's World *rejected* and *went* against a reality that He had not willed or chosen. It is an act of mercy in which the creature *is* totally *allied* and *is met* by God's Word of grace and kindness without which it could not be.[34]

Barth uses allegories to demonstrate that, by choosing light over darkness, the earth over water, God chose life and salvation for the creature because darkness and water symbolize death and chaos. However, by entering Sabbath God was now looking back upon what He *had accomplished.* Hence Barth writes: "..... it must be clearly understood that the fact that God ended or 'completed' His work is expressly described as the work of His rest on Sabbath."[35] That is, with the creation of man, creation was now *done, concluded* and *terminated* on the sixth day. Of course, this does not mean that God stopped working but only ceased to create anything different from what *had been previously created.*[36] He goes on to say that everything that was created was good in so far as they were adapted to God's purposes. Therefore, there can be no complaint because God has declared His creation good; there is only room for thanksgiving and praise. After all, who is there to critique what God has created and found good to the extent of entering into fellowship with it?[37]

To underscore the pastness of creation, Barth discusses the problem of providence, preservation and divine accompanying that are further acts of God. Unlike creation, they are couched in verbs in the present tense. For, as we have seen, creation is something that is complete, a once-and-for-all or an unrepeatable act with a beginning and end in time. The very fact that we speak about the creature, according to Barth, means that it is a *"finished act in all its temporal developments, extensions, and relationships ..... in its individual forms of creaturely world and historical manifestations and modifications"* of this existing being.[38] If this were not the case, it would mean that creation is not well done, done perfectly and concluded. Therefore, providence is merely a guaranteeing and confirming, surrounding and sustaining creation in the history of the covenant.

To make sure that this pastness of creating is not misunderstood, Barth uses two Latin expressions: Providence is not *continuata creatio* but *continuatio creationis.* The play with Latin words and what they mean is very important here. The former implies a continuous and unbroken series of creations or elections without interruptions, while the letter means a series of elections, which is the same thing as continuing confirmation of what God has chosen but now merely surrounds and sustains continually. Again, Barth reminds us about the meaning of Sabbath, which is a sign of a break and thus incompatible with *continuata creatio;* for it points to a beginning of history of co-existence between God and creation after creation was completed.[39] To be sure, creation and providence are connected acts because an independent creature that needs no sustaining and confirming would be no creature but a second little god.

Another distinction between creation and providence, or God's faithfulness which Barth makes is this: in the former, God alone is active while in the latter God acts mediately rather than immediately. That is, God acts indirectly instead of directly, employing the creature as His instrument.[40] In doing this, God allows a meaningful role to be played by the creature. But, human service remains one of an instrument in the hand of its Creator, which neither knows the purpose for which it is used nor can in any degree effect God's work of grace, the subject of the work of preserving and sustaining creation. For the creature has no capacity to initiate or bring about God's preserving work except when it is given an opportunity by the Creator, and it is by grace alone that historical events and creaturely acts are authorized and qualified to co-operate with God.

Even here, the actions of the creature to be actual and possible at all must be preceded by God's work; and always and everywhere God must be understood as there and as the One who has already loved, saved, and already worked — even before the creature itself begins to work.[40] This is because God is

> ..... present, accompanies the creature in such a way that no collapse of the two is implied but rather He is so present in the activity of the creature, present with such sovereignty and almighty power, that His own activity takes place in and with and over the activity of the creature. It is He who does what Moses and David do. He as Jahweh thunders out of Sion when the prophet speaks.[41]

The elimination of an independent human activity reaches its climax when Barth claims that, in fact, "creaturely events take place as God Himself acts — in the slightest movement of the leaf in the wind ..... His will is accompanied directly and His decisions are made and fulfilled in all creaturely occurences both great and small."[42] Barth adds to this elimination of creativity on the part of humans not only when he rejects representatives who may act on God's behalf and thereby become second gods,[43] but also by employing metaphors of mirror and reflection. Lest we confuse creaturely participation in the preservative work with creation, Barth adds that human history should be understood as merely a "mirror which adds nothing" to the "original, primary God's working" — in the divinely ruled history of the covenant.[44] The mirror plays no role in creation but can reflect on this original creativity. For, were creativity of the original possible, it would mean that what has been created was not well created, and that it needs continually dissolution and re-election; the creature would be living in perpetual fluctuation between life and death.[45] Rather, what is not is that which God has not elected, has passed over and left behind as chaos. Therefore, there is nothing that humans can bring about which was not already elected because what is created (elected) is complete in all its temporal developments as well as in its "individual forms of creaturely world and historical manifestations and modifications."[46]

Barth nails down human incapacity to create even more when he discusses the creation of woman and the incarnation of Jesus. It is important to note that Eve was created later after the completion of creation, and after some work had been done, such as looking after the garden and tilling it, or naming the other living creatures (Gen. 2:15–16, 19–20). In order to remain consistent with his view that man contributes nothing to God's creation – despite the fact that his rib is used as material for the creation of the woman – Barth focuses his attention on the fact that man was made to sleep. In this unconscious state, man was neither a witness of this creation which follows Sabbath nor able to contribute to it. Barth tries to minimize the passivity to which Adam is consigned by saying that he terminated the "whole process" when he began to confess and confirm his humanity "with his unequivocal Yes to the woman given to him."[47] The praise is the maximum role man is allowed to play. Otherwise, an impression would be created that Adam shared in the work of creation.

It is the incarnation which provides an occasion for Barth to underline the passivity of man in the creative works of God. He discusses in some detail the role man is assigned and discovers something fascinating, namely, that God makes man the participant by excluding the male human. Instead, God involves man only in the form of *virgo Maria* which, according to Barth, signifies God's judgment over man, a judgment whose significance is that the Creator uses the human instrument that is "not God's co-worker." That is, God does not use man "in his independence" and therefore "not certainly as the one who controls what is to happen" in the incarnation, but rather only in that form which man is ready for God. Put differently, God's involvement in the human through *virgo Maria,* the female, means that He can co-operate with man not as the creature that has the capacity to act and create, but only with man

> ..... in the form of non-willing, non-achieving, non-creative, non-sovereign man who can merely receive, merely be ready, merely let something be done to and with himself.[48]

Also, Barth points out that human history has been male-dominated in arts, founding of states and nations, the sciences and economics, because this history is largely patriarchal and gives little role to females. He blames the Fall for male supremacy, which made man the lord of history and over the woman. But precisely because of man's wicked lordship over history from which nothing is left of a good human being that is worthy of communion with God, it is proper that –

because man is what he does, namely a disobedient creature — God should exclude the male father of Jesus Christ. This means that God has little reagrd for "willing, creative, and sovereign man," who "as such can be considered as a participant in God's work. For as such he is the man of disobedience" who must be set aside if God's grace is to meet him.[49] Consequently, Joseph as a male symbol is set aside completely — as God takes his place and functions not in the creative role of the human father but as God performs a miracle, creating something new.[50]

To be sure, the virgin's qualification to participate in this holy work does not lie in her merits consisting in virtues of non-willing and non-achieving behaviour, but lies in God's pure grace. This notwithstanding, it remains true that it is to *virgo Maria* that the form of human receptivity, readiness to receive, and letting something be done to her belongs, for she represents human possibility of being a participant in God's work.

Both in the creation of the woman and in the event of the incarnation, God was directly involved in creating life, something new that was not included in the six-day creature. So Barth does his best to exclude man from these divine works, for such a participation is out of character with the necessary requirement of being the obedient creature that is characterized by receiving rather than willing and achieving. That is, it is only when man is the recipient of God's gifts and love that his human activity does not collide with the work of grace, which requires him to be the object of the electing grace rather than the initiator, creator, and therefore a second and independent god.

Barth's affirmations here, that lead him to see human creativity and achieving as sinful attempt to be independent of God, as a rejection of creatureliness characterized by being the object of God's love and mercy, stem from a number of assumptions that are based on his static view of creation. Because, for him, creation is complete and concluded in all its individual developments and manifestations in history, it seems logical to conclude that divine preservation and providential accompaniment — in which God employs human agency and mediation — never mean a continuation of divine creativity in the present. As in the case of Elert, it seems that until Barth learns to use verbs in the present tense, neither the full dimensions of God's creativity nor the dynamic and positive use of the law — as the continuing creative act of God — will not be fully articulated. Indeed, he not only fails to appreciate the fact that God does not merely preserve some static, perfect and finished product from some distant past — though this is done too — but also that this divine preservation is God's creativity in the present.

As we have already pointed out, another problem lies in the content that Barth gives to the concepts: creation and law, after he has defined them in a tight and close correlation with the God's recemptive dynamics through the gospel. For, as it turns out, now creation, law, and the gospel come to mean the same thing: they are acts of God's mercy and compassion on the creature; through them God elects man and chooses life as death and chaos are passed over; through them God accepts, justifies us and invites us for fellowship. When creation, la law and gospel are given the content Barth has given them, it is logical to see them as exclusive tools by God whose use by humans either rivals God's graciousness toward them or is an attempt by humans to distort or misuse God's good gifts. Hence, Barth sees human willing and creating as enemies of grace. Moreover, the law becomes superfluous. That is, the law loses its independent status because its meaning is partly swallowed up by that of creation which is a past election of man, and also law is displaced by the gospel which in the present is the veritable means by which our election, our sonship is proclaimed.

Consequently, both creation and the establishment of freedom and obligation through the law are solely God's work and initiative, which are transcendent of human or cultural creativity. Hence, to tamper with either the law or creation is to try to be like God, who alone creates and establishes the law. That is, just as humans have no capacity to bring about their own salvation and sanctification which God alone through the gospel brings about, humans have no capacity to create nor to establish the true law, which is identical with Jesus Christ who is the law of the Kingdom.

To be sure, it may be true that humans are not capable of creating anything *ex nihilo,* as God is capable, and that humans cannot bring their own salvation. But is it necessary to correlate creation, law, and gospel in this tight manner so that their meaning are almost identical for no other reason than to ensure the total exclusion of human participation in any of them, as Barth does? Is it really true that human willing, achieving and creating somehow come into conflict with the grace of God? Is it true that God uses humans only in the preservation of the created reality? If so, *whose laws are operative* in the preservation of creation? Are the human attempts to devise ways and means to prohibit the extermination of animal species, to prevent soil erosion and protect the natural habitat not divine involvement of the human creative activity that Barth wants to exclude by making creativity the sole monopoly of God? Even in matters of salvation, it seems to be an error to exclude human creativity altogether. For without human mediation or creativity that brought about elaborate church structures, missions, and other evangelization structures, it seems doubtful that God would have brought the gospel to many parts of the world single-handedly.

Is it not true that human service, work and ingenuity in mass-media evangelization, in fact, do contribute or co-operate with God to bring about salvation? In the area of creation, human work appears to be more visible than Barth is willing to admit. As we have already argued (in our discussion of culture, personality and language) it seems hardly reasonable to exclude God's involvement of human agency in the dynamics of God's ongoing creativity. Indeed, human creativity is discernible in culture and history where great acts are being performed: either in the creation of social structures or laws that try to promote a healthy environment for the continuation and nourishment of life, the preservation of other species, or in cultural role-systems wherein individuals are moulded so that they function as helpful and contributory members of society.

Therefore, unless one is willing to claim that God is responsible for each and every thing that happens, it seems human ability to create cannot be denied altogether. Indeed, were God believed to cause everything that happens, the divine self would be a demon, a notion Barth is not willing to endorse. For such a God would be a colonial, a Nazist, or a racist murderer because the Creator would have created slavery and other forms of human exploitation and genocide. It seems hardly responsible to attribute these demonic acts to the Christian God. Yet, these demonic aberrations were not in existence in the six-day creation of the past but are distortions that have emerged in human history and, therefore, are all human creations or systems that can be changed.

Barth needs to allow much more room for human creativity which God has generously granted humanity. There can be no running away from the fact that humans have a great capacity to create. Creativity is a gracious gift that has brought awesome responsibility with it. Humans have the creative powers to name animals (they continue to do this in the scientific community) and to exercise this creative capacity as a trust from God, who in divine freedom gave it to them. Consequently, humans are responsible for what they create both before God and before their fellow humans. It is certainly to be regretted that humans have not always been responsible in the use of powers entrusted to them. But an abuse of this creative gift cannot be enough reason to deny its existence. It is there, for cultural and technological breakthroughs bear witness to it. To argue for a static and past creation can result only in denying the continuity of creation in the present and in lodging science and culture outside the realm of God's activities.

Against Barth, it should be argued that God in the divine freedom has limited the divine self by giving humans powers to create, thereby choosing to accompany them in their earthly creativities, standing behind their works, and committing the divine self to enterprises humans undertake. Of course, God does not do all this in a passive way nor as a mute spectator. Rather, the Creator is also actively involved in these human enterprises, inspiring creative thinking, modifying human hearts, and acting thereby at the level where humans are, namely, in culture. In one of his illuminating statements, Ellul rightly says that God acts in concert with human action, taking part "in the most hazardous and ridiculous situations that they can invent. He makes history with us."[51]

If God does all these things in concert with human creative activity then, surely, it is wrong to think that the Creator is less gracious — merely because limitations have been imposed on the divine self so as to make history with and through the creature. Indeed, what more can God do to show the divine loving kindness than to grant us creative ability? If our creative acts are permissions of God's grace, is it not strange to think that willing, achieving, thinking and creating are hostile to this grace (except for those who believe that "grace cannot share power")?[52] Against Barth, it should be contended that, by acting in concert with us and making us co-workers and co-creators with the divine self, God invites neither competition nor conflict. Instead God underlines human freedom to create and supports this creativity.

What is to be remembered is that human creativity does not occur in a vacuum but takes place within the context of God's grace, God's reality or given environment that conditions, limits and allows or modifies the creaturely creativities. That is, God's reality, with its fulness of grace that supports rather than thwarts human creative deeds, is the context within which our striving, willing, achieving and creating manifest themselves. As Leslie Dewart correctly points out, history is created by humans, but this creation does not occur as a result of sheer human will bursting forth from human subjectivity alone. Rather, he says, "history is made by man, but in the presence of God. God and man are mutually present and active in the creation of the world."[53]

It is because God and humans both actively create the world that Christian faith has come to affirm responsibility for scientific research, technological inventions and medical discoveries as helpful means to sustain and nourish life and, consequently, as tools not antithetical to God's creative purposes but supportive of them. Paul Schilling, who has reflected soberly on this mutual creativity, makes an important point, when he observes

> ..... it is in and through the uniting of his efforts with those of God that he and the world can become what his Creator intends them to be. Man's relationship to God thus involves not suffocation of human energies, but their emancipation.[54]

It is important to underline the futurity of what creation would be, as Schilling's statement suggests, because creation is on its way toward completion. The road toward this completion is a long, painful and tortuous one. Along this road, human creativity can obstruct or facilitate the move toward the goal of the Creator's creation. Distortions, like the demonic destruction of life, its oppression and choking, in the forms of slavery, colonial or Nazist as well as racist annihilations of human race, and other demonic ways of destroying life such as conventional wars or nuclear destruction of human and/or natural life are obstructions. But other ingenious acts, such as the development of hybrid corn and wheat, production of food or meat, protection of the environment or technological discoveries of medical operations, the correction of defective human organs through transplanting of healthy ones, attempts to wrestle with social, economic or political rights for many and the discovery of DNA (deoxyribonucleic acid) with its promise of correcting birth defects and thereby affecting the future evolution of human species through genetic control — all of which aim at the enrichment of life — could be understood as contributing to divine creative efforts and activity.[55]

Lest God be locked out of the scientific sphere, these modern scientific discoveries and creations — which may change the course of nature and human life — must be seen as the continuing divine creativity through human instrumentality in the present. Therefore, when a patient receives a healthy organ to replace the defective one that was given at birth, it is only proper that such a person should, in faith, see God at work and give praise that miracles are being performed through human hands. For such a person with a defective organ, creation is not a past and completed thing but continues here and now.

To be sure, the permission that God has granted humans to create history and the world with the divine self has potential hazards, as we have seen. But the Creator in the divine freedom chose to risk these dangers rather than deny humans the freedom to create; and despite repeated errors and failures, we are to be thankful that God has chosen to use our instrumentality, thereby allowing us to try again and again. But, then, God's continuous creative acts, or the continuity of creation in the past, present and future, would not have been maintained – had the Creator chosen to exercise monopoly of creating so as to deny the human contribution in the divine creative dynamics. Instead, the Creator chose to incorporate human contribution when God entrusted the earth to them to till and care for and to name animals.

Humans exercise this delegated authority when they labour to bring about new creations through scientific discoveries, when they try their best to discover laws of nature in order to care for the earth effectively, or when rules are constructed to regulate human relationships in order to bring about justice and social righteousness. All these are human creations *par excellence* that the Creator has not disclaimed but has accepted as good work. As human role-linguist and conceptual-intellectual creations, these activities do not rival that of God; they have a limited place and are supported and sided by divine grace and power that actively involve humans in the dynamics of love in an ongoing creativity.

Barth and Elert needed to work on and develop this kind of dynamic notion of creation upon which, and against whose context, God's dynamic and positive use of the law could be understood correctly – when through the law the Creator engages humans in the creative process. But this would have required the use of verbs in the present tense, so that preservation is not merely conceived as a past act in some distant past, but as itself the continuing work of creation in the present. Until dynamism is injected into their (Barth's and Elert's) notion of creation, we look in vain for a positive and dynamic conception of law – rooted in the dynamics of the creative will of God in whose continuing creativity humans are not merely dormant and passive spectators but are active participants and co-creators.

In addition to an injection of dynamism into the notion of creation, it is necessary – as we have argued in the preceding chapters – that definitions of law be broadened and made comprehensive enough to do justice to the positive and creative elements of the law that have to do with God's involvement of human beings in creative works for the purpose of bringing about healthy human relationships in the community here and now. In order to do this, it is essential that one-sided formulations of the law are abandoned because they give a false impression that the content of obedience to the divine will consists only of works that have to, and must always, be specified with reference to religious justification before God. While this is partly true, it is not the whole story because God is very much concerned with the penultimate and relative good and love that humans can show to others. For only when it is realized that there is a second component of human obedience to the divine command – one that must be specified with reference to attainment of social and political righteousness – that it is possible at all to move beyond the positions of Barth and Elert, thus correcting their imbalanced and inadequate views that often neglect the creative aspects of the divine law in its relation to life of the community.

A move beyond the positions of these two theologians becomes even more imperative when it is appreciated that the divine command is not an authoritarian injunction that has to be obeyed without further qualification. Indeed, its utterance by God does not demand servile obedience, as we are often misled to believe, but rather involves our mature manhood by making us creative participants in the dynamics of divine creativity which have to do with the ordering and transformation of the natural and social environment so that life is made possible, thereby making us servants of divine goodness and love. For it is in our willing participation in these divine works of love, which promote and sustain life, that one can speak rightly about fulfillment of the demands of the divine command, a command which has no other goal than to express God's creative will of love. This creative love, as it shall become clear in the following chapters, is the soul and inspiration for human striving after social justice and righteousness through which the divine will of love is served and institutionalized.

Finally, it is our contention that the heavy accent on human obedience to some divine law that we must submit to and yet cannot be fulfilled – in the theologies of Barth and Elert – is misleading. For such views lead to idolatrous and servile obedience to some authoritarian law that has as its content something other than God's creative will, a will that is essentially creative for the well-being of finite creatures here and now. These views of the law need a radical operation, an operation that can be performed by emphasizing the participatory theme that leads to responsible actions toward the human community when God involves us in the dynamics of creation, actions which can be understood as a fulfillment of the demands of this divine law that involes us in its creativity. This participatory theme, rather than servile obedience in relation to God's command, will be our main focus of attention in the constructive part of this book. We allude to it here because Luther's theology, which is the bone of contention in the dispute between Barth and Elert, provides resources for it.

Hence, it strikes us as rather strangely notorious that Barth who, on one hand, tries to correct Luther by grounding the law in the gospel, and Elert who, on the other, does his best to defend Luther's formulations, never appear interested in the examination of the participatory themes in Luther with their emphases on the positive and creative possibilities of the law in society, where the divine law requires that justice and political righteousness be done in God's name and therefore love. Yet, these resources are precisely the ones which would have been helpful not only in the development of the positive understanding of the law, but also in the overcoming of the negative emphases inherent in the "obedience motif" dominating discussions of the law in the theologies of Barth and Elert. We shall be tapping these resources from time to time as we move beyond the theological positions of these two theologians and attempt to construct, outline and offer a much more adequate and comprehensive understanding of the law that is both dynamic and positive.

Notes

1 Dr. Gordon D. Kaufman has pointed out to me, in one of his comments, that the problem may also be traceable to the Reformation's rejection of the natural law theory. His suggestion is well taken and is discussed in the next chapter where alternative conceptions of law are examined in detail.

2 *The Christian Ethos,* pp. 3, 6–9, 10–16, 40, 50, 70–71, 141–142.

3 Ibid., pp. 18, 40, 78, 142, and especially *The Structure of Lutheranism,* p. 37.

4 Ibid., pp. 17f, 23–25f, 46, 67–69, 96–101.

5 Ibid., pp. 37–41.

6 Gustaf Törnvall has registered his objection to the theology of "orders of creation," and correctly argues that this concept misleadingly gives the impression that some orders are created while others are not. Also, he is persuaded, against theology of "orders of creation," that Luther never uses *"Schöpfungsordnung."* For elaborate discussion of this issue cf. Martin J. Heinecken "Luther and 'the Orders of Creation' in Relation to the Doctrine of Work and Vocation" in *The Lutheran Quarterly* (Vol. IV, November 1952, No. 4), p. 396.

7 *The Christian Ethos,* pp. 17–18.

8 Ibid., pp. 40–41, 52–53, 68–70, 73–76, 81, 103–123.
9 Ibid., pp. 37–41, 50–52, 56, 78.
10 Ibid., p. 78.
11 Ibid. (Italics added)
12 Ibid., pp. 122–123.
13 Ibid., pp. 99–100, 104–111.
14 Ibid., p. 123.
15 Ibid., pp. 51–52, 70, 108, 113, 141f, 294.
16 Cf. H.R. Niebuhr, *Christ and Culture,* pp. 150–59, 191–96.
17 Lambert Schuurman, "Some Observations on the Relevance of Luther's Theology of the Two Realms for the Theological Task in Latin America," in *The Lutheran Quarterly* (Vol. XXII, February 1970, No. 1), p. 83. Elert incidentally confirms Schuurman's contention that in this theology believers live under constant terror of their God, when he writes: *"We can only bear this anguish when we believe in God's kingdom of forgiveness and freedom, in fact that we already transfered into it. But that is really only the beginning of the invisible struggle because we must believe against the God of wrath and condemnation.* As long as we live on this earth we live in both realms, the realm of law and the realm of grace" *(The Christian Ethos,* p. 294). (Italics added) There is no sense in this kind of theology of ultimate victory in this world, no triumphant hope that God will transform social structures, and there is little confidence in the creative possibilities of the Creator in whom one now believes. There is only resignation to an inevitable suffering. Indeed, the dynamics of the coming kingdom are not inspiring revolutionary zeal in the hearts of humans, thereby involving them in the transformation of the existing *Seinsgefüge* in this world. There is little hope here that historical process is a means by which God ushers in the new world, because humans must simply "bear anguish."
18 *The Christian Ethos,* p. 90. Why should monogamy reflect the growth of human civilization while the state and economic systems do not? Answers which Elert gives here are less persuasive.
19 Elert, in *Law and Gospel,* pp. 35, 45–46, says he does not know, and our suspicion is that he does not know because none of them is God's direct creation after all.
20 Should modern technological revolutions be understood as God's creations or not? Elert's static view would exclude them, we are afraid.
21 James Gustafson, *The Church as Moral Decision-Maker* (Boston: Pilgrim Press, 1970), pp. 69–70. (Italics added) Also, see insightful and pointed questions put to theology of "orders" by Pannenberg, cited by Carl Braaten in "Reflexions on the Lutheran Doctrine of Law," in *The Lutheran Quarterly* (Vol. XVIII, February 1966, No. 1), p. 74. Pannenberg concludes that no uniformity is discernible in social forms or patterns which arose in history, and we agree.
22 Cf. *Church Dogmatics* III/4, pp. 19–21, 29, 36–38, 45, 52, 288–289, 348, where Barth polemicizes against those who anchor the law, state and human relationships on "orders or creation" because these orders may claim to be a second revelation outside Christ.

23 *Church Dogmatics* II/2, pp. 568–571, 606, 632; IV/1, pp. 9, 36.

24 Cf. Von Balthasar, *The Theology of Karl Barth,* p. 184; Willis, *The Ethics of Karl Barth,* p. 430; Zahrnt, *The Question of God,* pp. 105–107; Niebuhr, *Christ and Culture,* pp. 191–192. It remains a mystery to us why Niebuhr has not included Barth among his "Christ and Culture in Paradox" representative types, because creation in Barth is a kind of "prologue to the one mighty deed of atonement."

25 Gustaf Wingren, in his *Theology in Conflict* (Philadelphia: Muhlenberg Press, 1958), p. 116, believes that Barth's pessimism about creation and possibilities in of human culture is a product of the "emotional position of a cultural epoch" following the shattering experience of World War I, and that this explains the acceptance of his commentary on *The Epistle to the Romans* in which God's positive relation to the world and humanity is negated. Since he made this judgment, Wingren has devoted some of his books and articles to trying to show that Barth has no doctrine of creation. A. Richardson, *The Bible and the Age of Science* (Philadelphia: The Westminster Press, 1961), pp. 92–93, also charges Barth with an atheistic anthropology. Are these charges totally unfounded in the light of Barth's own estimation of culture? Cf. *The Humanity of God,* pp. 15–17, 56–57.

26 Cf. *Church Dogmatics* I/2, pp. 194f.

27 See note 25 above. It is incorrect to confuse Barth's static conception of creation with a rejection of creation by him.

28 *Church Dogmatics* III/1, pp. 15, 43–46, 48–50, 59, 71–73.

29 Ibid., pp. 63–67, 98–99, 178–227.

30 Ibid., pp. 98–99. Barth is highly suspicious of any human labour at this point and, consequently, working is associated with conflict, self-sufficiency, and a rejection of creaturely dependence on God's grace. This is clearer in *Church Dogmatics* I/2, pp. 194ff.

31 *Church Dogmatics* III/1, pp. 98, 217–218, 225.

32 Ibid., pp. 110, 213, 219.

33 Barth eloquently argues that God's history does not begin with workday but with Sabbath, "..... it begins with the Gospel and not the Law, it begins with the freedom of man and not with his commitment; with a holiday and not with an imposed task; with joy and not with toil and trouble" (Ibid., pp. 219, 225).

34 Ibid., p. 110.

35 Ibid., p. 181.

36 Barth further adds that: *"In every new creation it will be partly a question of gracious preservation and confirmation, and partly a question of the gracious renewal, of the creation which is ready and finished"* (Ibid., p. 182). (Italics added). We wish to draw the reader's attention to the tenses of the verbs in the whole discussion, i.e., past or past perfect tenses. They have been underlined in order to stress the pastness in which creation is here understood.

37 Ibid., pp. 213ff, 230. Barth is aware that not everything in creation is glorious, for there is also the dark side of creation, some imperfection, if you will. Thus, to say creation is good has nothing to do with human optimism, but this is based on God's justification of what He has created, accepted and elected as good. Consequently, even the dark side has its meaning and purpose. First, it gives the Creator the opportunity to fight against the imperfections of the creature, and this fight is the confirmation of life or the justification of creation. Second, the creature is not supposed to be self-sufficient but must be a suitable recipient of grace; for grace is given to it because the imperfections of the creature imply that it needs God's help in its threatened existence. Therefore, in the light of the future and God's coming salvation, the fact that problems of good and evil, life and death, are God's concern and not human concern, the Creator rightly justifies what has been created, because both the imperfections and the threat the creatures will face shall be finally overcome. It is for this reason that God has bound "creation to the covenant, His willingness to help and save man." Hence, in view of this glorious future, the creature is not nothing but something that is loved, and the creature must say yes with God and say no with Him in covenant fellowship (Ibid., pp. 368–388). Barth, exuberant with joy at his treatment of the justifiability of the creature despite its imperfections, compares his reflection to the theodicy of Leibniz because of the common affirmation of the positive Yes in spite of weakness, temptation, and nearness to the edge of the abyss and nothingness in which the creature stands (Ibid., p. 388).

38 *Church Dogmatics* III/3, p. 6. (Italics added)

39 Ibid., p. 8.

40 Ibid., pp. 19, 21–25, 45–50, 64–67, 94, 107, 110–119.

41 Ibid., p. 132. In order to preclude any independent creativity by humans, Barth takes issue with the views of Lutherans, Catholics and Arminians which claim that God works through masks or representatives. He retorts that God has no time for "representatives or vice-regents" because God is neither creation ..... in detail nor as a whole" and thus it can never be his "face" (pp. 19, 131).

42 Ibid., p. 133.

43 Barth cannot think about human creativity without also attributing to it the status of God (Ibid., 131ff, 157; III/1, p. 187)

44 *Church Dogmatics* III/3, p. 50.

45 Ibid., pp. 68–73.

46 Ibid., p. 6. Barth here is claiming quite a bit, for he seems to be saying that God so created that He foresaw all future expansions and the developments of every individual creature that was created in the six-day creation. But does Barth mean to suggest that God foresaw that technology would come up with new synthetic materials, or biological or botanical cross-breedings, such as mules from horses and donkeys, or hybridization of corn and other botanical species? Are these not new creations by humans in our century which might not have been foreseen nor anticipated in the six-day creation?

47 Ibid., p. 294. There are two points which must be noted here. First, the reason for the praise lies in the fact that man – on his own – could not find a fitting mate in the entire creation. Graciously, however, God decided to end man's solitude by creating a mate for him, a mate above the animals who man can recognize as a gift and an equal. Second, man neither initiated the act of creating the woman nor did he know what he needed and why he was so unsatified – all of which are implied in the word "sleep." So he should praise God who allows him to utter an active yes by affirming his humanity, thereby having man's needs met and loneliness ended.

48 *Church Dogmatics* I/2, p. 191. It is important to note that passivity is regarded as a rightful human conduct before God.

49 Ibid., p. 194. It may be true that a sovereign creature, independent of God, is sinful. But does it follow from this that grace is against achieving willing and creativity of humans, as Barth suggests? Should humans merely receive and not create? Does not the naming of animals involve human creativity (Gen. 2:19f)?

50 Ibid., pp. 192, 194.

51 Jacques Ellul, *The Ethics of Freedom* (Grand Rapids, Michigan: Wm. B Eerdmans Publishing Company, 1976), p. 121.

52 *Church Dogmatics* II/2, pp. 531–532, 517.

53 Cited by S. Paul Schilling in *God in an Age of Atheism* (New York Abingdon Press, 1969), p. 154.

54 Ibid., p. 155.

55 Ibid., p. 157. Schilling's notion that humans are God's "fellow work-men" in scientific exploration is illuminating here.

PART THREE

The law as agent of creative possibilities (process): a constructive statement

Chapter seven

God's creative activity through the law

In the critique, a number of objections were raised against the theologies of both Barth and Elert. It was pointed out that because their understanding of law was not grounded in the idea of a dynamic and creative will of God, their conceptions of the law tended to be negative. Law, in their theologies, appears to be an authoritarian word which intrudes from outside, either to judge a sinner (Elert) or to set a sinner free from self-incurred enslavement to distortions of laws (Barth). Because the law is construed as something that intrudes, an impression is given that it functions only to disturb the flow of events in life.

More often than not, Barth and Elert tend to talk about law within a framework of human justification before God, and the positive ordering and structuring of life-situations in a continuing creation by God are ignored. Yet the divine law, when it is properly understood, cannot be viewed as a foreign instrument or something that is external to human community and cultural activities. For God, as the Creator, brings about structures through the law and thereby creates life for the community here and now. In order for these positive and creative aspects of the law to be given full expression, it becomes necessary to pay attention to the social, political and other cosmic creative activities of God where law functions to enhance both the natural and the social life. This also means that law and the divine creative will should be closely correlated, so that each is not understood separately from the other.

In the following sections, we will try to outline a broad and comprehensive exposition of the meaning of law with a view to overcoming weaknesses that have been pointed out in the critique. Our discussion of these positive and creative elements is not intended to give all answers, but to construe a balanced and adequate theological understanding of law.

7.1 THE COMMAND OF GOD AS AN INSTRUMENT OF THE DIVINE CREATIVE LOGOS

The problems facing any theologian who tries to spell out the place of law and its positive relation to human community are enormous primarily because, unlike the gospel whose relation to the dynamics of God's redemptive activity is relatively clear, the relation between the Creator's dynamics of creativity and the divine command (law) remains ambiguous.[1] Not only do theologians differ as to whether the command should be grounded in the Christology or in the "orders of creation," but also some theologians appear unwilling to recognize that the command is the ground and the instrument of God's creative will of love both in originating and in sustaining creation in its historical development. They fail to see, therefore, that creation and the command must be correlated in such a way that God's use of law (creative command) should be understood as nothing else but the divine creation from the point of view of the present. For in sustaining creativity, the Creator does not use any command (creative word) that is different from the one that brought finite creatures into existence; rather, in both it is the same creative word (command) that is at work. Thus creation and the divine command (law) belong together.

Before we proceed to a detailed exposition of the divine command, which is grounded on the dynamics of the creative will of God and embraces both originating and sustaining creativity, it is necessary to challenge and dispose of two factors that have muddied most theological discussions of the law in the past. The first concerns the understanding of the divine law. While Barth and Elert do not directly identify God's law with the Decalogue, in the past theologians tended to do so, especially Protestants since the time of the Reformation. To this day, some biblicists and catechisms give a central place to this idea.[2]

In addition, the theory of natural law has often been used to explain the existence of laws in the areas of life that are not fully covered by the Decalogue. This theory assumes that there is a constant, immutable law that is somehow deducible from and based on the general rule of God, and that this law is pretty much available or accessible to human reason. Because the awareness of these universally valid principles of moral order is given potentially to all people, it is the human duty to apply reason, seek after, find and reduce these principles to legal enactments such as civil and ethical rules of behaviour.

The assumption that such a universal and immutable natural law exists, outside the chosen people of Israel, provided rather strong evidence for God's universal rule. For it was upon this natural law that the existence of governments and civil and moral laws was premised. The Christian Church came to regard this immutable law of nature and her special law of the covenant (Mosaic-Christian law of revelation) as the material content of the divine law. The Reformers accepted this traditional view of the immutable order of moral law to varying degrees. Luther qualified his acceptance by recognizing the validity of cultural conditioning of all laws of different nations.[3] Hence he rejected the enforcement of the Decalogue on non-Jewish people who had their own laws. Luther argued that the content and function of all laws, such as the *Sachsenspiegel* or the Decalogue, were the same and that differences were matters of divergent interpretations of the natural law which is "written in our hearts."[4]

Despite differences and no matter how law is conceived, that is, whether the material content of the divine will is believed to be the Decalogue or the natural law, or a combination of both, the underlying assumption is one that regards this posited, immutable or eternal order of moral law (principle) as *something God has given* to the fallen creation. In other words, the preservative will of God is believed to be embodied in some revealed or natural law, one that is waiting to be discovered by us and applied. Our thesis is that such static notions of the law of God should be rejected, because they ignore the fact that the law is always a historical production. Therefore, any conception of law that construes it as somehow above historical happenings, something that hovers above events in time and space and thus is static and removed from activities that transform the world, must be regarded as sheer abstraction. For, as we argued in the critique, laws truly understood are human and historical productions.

Moreover, our rejection of abstractions of law (which is thus understood as a nonhistorical and eternal gift from the Deity) is based on our fundamental contention that human beings are not objects of some abstract and eternal ideals, but are historical subjects with God, a God who *does not produce* the world and humanity *according to some past model.* Indeed, God's creative activity through the law or command, as it will become clear in this chapter, does not mean a return to some lost "Paradise" or "Golden Age," but rather a dynamic involvement in a creative process in which creation is carried towards its completion. In this dynamic creativity laws are never abstractions, but are historical, relative and conditioned culturally. For laws are linguistic and conceptual constructions made by human beings as they try to order their environment. The historicity of all laws en equally true of the Decalogue.[5]

Consequently, theologians must be grateful for the historical consciousness of the nineteenth and twentieth centuries, which has successfully rendered untenable the assumption that there is an immutable law, either revealed or natural, "out there," which has been given once-and-for-all for the conservation of the fallen creation. As it becomes clear that all laws are not abstractions that hover above the historical, it becomes even more imperative that the divine law should be understood historically and be grounded in the dynamics of God's creative activity. Apart from the God who is engaged in either originating or sustaining creative works, God's creative will or law is not accessible to us. Nor is it something that is given and is "out there." We shall return to this point in some detail later on.

The second major problem that has caused enormous difficulties in the construction of a theologically adequate conception of law is related directly to the first. Not only do theologians assume that there is an immutably given law that expresses the divine will, but it is often argued that this divine law has to do with the preservation, conservation and sustenance of the world. As we have pointed out in our discussion of Barth and Elert, theologians believe that God employs this gift to produce order and justice, to act as a dyke against sin or evil forces. Even Barth, who believes that the divine law ultimately sets free, as we have shown, appealed to governments to uphold law and justice, and to churches to help found true and just laws.

There is nothing objectionable about the assertion that God employs the divine command to sustain and to care for creatures out of pure Creator's love. The problem is that theologians tend to correlate the function of law at this point with a providential preservation, conservation and protection of the creature against some alleged threat of chaos. What is troublesome, as we have observed already, is that the finite creatures who are thus to be protected are understood as finished products. What is needed is merely a defense, confirmation, or conservation. God's activity, that is, the sustaining creativity, often is not understood as creation in the present, but merely as a conservation of a finished product that was created "once upon a time." The underlying assumption is that, were it not for evil forces, creation would be on its own, without sustenance from moment to moment. Yet creatureliness, properly understood, means that we are continually dependent upon God's creativity:

> ..... in every hour and every aspect ..... to give us our being and sustain us in our freedom. We would literally (not merely figuratively) *be nothing* without him, for he is the indispensable source and continuing ground of our existence.[6]

Indeed, with Kaufman we must reject any static conceptions that suggest creation was established "once-and-for-all," because it was not completed in a momentary six days. Also, to correlate law (by which the creature is preserved) with a static view of creation does violence to the understanding that God's providential caring is itself creativity, as the Creator continues to work on and in this world so that creation may be completed.

As Schleiermacher observed long ago, creation and preservation belong together since they express fully the divine creative activity. We contend, in agreement with Schleiermacher, that it is important that God's active involvement through the command (law) – traditionally understood as preservation and the providential rule of God – should be understood as a complementary creative work in the historical development of finite creatures. Creation and law should never be construed as separate units that must be juxtaposed as if different things are meant; rather, together they constitute the totality of God's originating and sustaining creativity through the word (command).

The two activities, to be sure, must be distinguished, but it should be remembered that it is the same creative commanding of the Creator's word that both originates and sustains finite creatures. Moreover, historical existence always involves continuity in time, for creation is only the beginning, which does not exclude development. This continuity or development in time is what is meant by the sustaining or preserving creativity, which is the same thing as the Creator's continuous molding of finite beings. What ties the work of creation (origination) and that of the law (preservation, or preferably the sustaining creativity) is the working of the same formative forces that exist through God, who is the source of all. That is, since all finite creatures are not self-sufficient, but are absolutely dependent upon the source of their being, the Creator, it follows that God's creative command (word) is involved in the continuity of creation as much as it was involved in its inception.[7]

We agree with Schleiermacher that both originating and ongoing dynamics of creativity are what theological talk intends to express through the conceptions of creation and law (the latter functioning to preserve creation). We wish to contend, further, that the divine command (law), properly understood as God's sustaining creativity, and creation are not only two sides of the same act, but imply each other. When theology talks about preservation (through law, command) it really means creation continues and nothing else. Wingren eloquently expresses our contention when he says that any theology that fails to bring out this continuing creativity in the present more forcefully, but merely thinks of creation as a result of a past and momentary act, destroys "the assurance that God is actively creating *now,* and that life itself is the other side of God's continuing creative activity."[8]

Paul Tillich, also, warns of dangers that arise when the sustaining activity of God is correlated with static notions of creation which needs only preservation. He points out, for instance, that when preservation or providence is not itself understood as God's creation viewed from the present, the result can be only an opening of all doors:

> ..... through which deistic concepts easily creep into the theological system. The world is conceived as an independent structure which moves according to *its laws.* God certainly created the world "in beginning" and *gave it the laws of nature.* But after its beginning he either does not interfere at all (consistent deism) or he acts occasionally through miracles and revelation (theistic deism), or he acts in a continual interrelationship (consistent theism).[9]

Tillich adds that to speak of sustaining creativity is improper for all these cases; rather because God creates things and time together, the Creator should always be understood as continually creative "in every moment of the temporal existence, giving the power of being to everything that has being out of the creative ground of the divine life."[10] God is thus always involved in originating, sustaining and directing creativity, not only momentarily but continually.

In order to overcome dangers that may result from either a partial or a total deistic understanding of the Creator's relation to the world, it is very necessary to ground our conception of God's creative command (word) more adequately in the ongoing dynamics of divine creative will, which is essentially creative and is highly charged with a sense of an active and continuous interrelationship between finite creatures and the divine self upon whom they absolutely depend. In addition, as we have argued already, it becomes necessary that conceptions of a given immutable law that hovers above history should be abandoned, so that creation and law (divine creative command)[11] might be understood historically, dynamically and always as activities that are never understood independently from the life-giving and active involvement of God in temporal existence. We now shall analyze this correlation of the conceptions of creation and the creative command (word) in some detail.

7.2 THE COMMAND AS A PRESUPPOSITION OF CREATIVITY IS A FAITH-STATEMENT

It was our thesis that the command of God has to be understood in a continuing interrelationship of creative acts of the Creator and finite creation. Also, we argued that God's originating and sustaining creativity through the creative command (word), though distinguishable, should be understood as complementary works of the Creator in the historical development of creatures. Finally, it was suggested that the creative command of God not only should be correlated with creation, but also that, because creation is incomplete, God's use of the law (traditionally understood as a providential preservation) must itself be understood as (sustaining) creation in the present. That is, the creative command (law) and sustaining creativity must be seen as implying each other, because God's command is essentially creative. We shall return to this idea and demonstrate that theological talk about God's command means essentially that God is actively creating here and now.

We also rejected any suggestion that God's law is something that is "given," either in an immutable natural law or in the Decalogue. For laws, as much as creation is, are historical productions rather than nonhistorical abstractions. The question that follows from all this becomes: If there is no immutable law that God has "given" to the fallen creation for its preservation, a law which is universally accessible and upon which governments are based, what is involved when theologians talk about the command of the Creator? The answer to this question is not an obvious one, nor is it simple; yet it must be given because it defines what is and what is not meant by a theological understanding of the law. Our answer is neither novel nor final; it has been given, or rather recognized, with varying degrees of clarity. Like most theological answers it remains tentative, and yet it is an answer that cannot be strongly overemphasized.

The Christian affirmation about the acting God, who is in charge and is creatively sustaining finite life, life which has been created and which is continually being recreated, should be understood for what it is – namely, a statement of faith. Therefore, theological talk about the law of preservation, or preferably God's sustaining and directing creative command, does not mean that God's work, acting, or rule is directly deducible from the general nature of this rule, or from a general and immutable natural or moral law that "is there to be discovered and applied." Nor does it refer to a fixed collection of laws such as the Decalogue. Rather, it is a creedal affirmation of believers' assurance that God is presently creative now, giving life and sustaining it. Because a creedal statement is tied closely to personal involvement and is coloured by believers' experiences, it remains an expression of thanksgiving and praise to God who stands behind human life, showering on it blessings, love and divine goodness. To remove these religious statements from the level of personal faith in the acting God, who originates and creatively sustains one's being, is to reduce them to the vapour of general theories or speculative ideas which are both abstractions with no confirmation in fact and are as misleading as the positing of immutable laws, which in reality do not exist.[12]

It is important to stress that reality as we experience it never points to some kind-hearted and loving Creator as its source.[13] There is a lot of suffering and sometimes needless destruction in the world. Hence, experienced reality, or facts, can be interpreted differently outside the sphere of faith, and one may conclude that the source of reality is demonic. It is for this reason that a theological talk about the acting God who creates and rules can never be supported by the facts of the world, for divine actions are not always transparent even to those who believe. Therefore, as a religious statement the Christian belief in the God who is a merciful and gracious father remains a belief in spite of experience – the existential experience of injustice and of the brokenness of human community.[14] It was for this reason that Luther confessed that a belief in God the Creator is perhaps the most difficult article of the Creed. Thus he exhorted pastors to keep this belief alive because Christians may doubt God's goodness.[15]

However, even though a theological talk about the Creator who is creatively sustaining us never implies that these divine acts can be demonstrated to neutral observers, Christians have always maintained that there are grounds for their affirmations. They hold, for instance, that these divine acts are not entirely dependent upon the psychological or subjective feelings of individual believers. It is contended that the basis for this creedal affirmation is derivative from their encounter with the saving and healing dynamics of God who, in Jesus Christ, has demonstrated His goodness and willingness to give. That is, the encounter with God through the redemptive dynamics of the gospel, which promises them an ultimate salvation, leads to the conclusion that this loving and saving God can be no other than the God who already was and is their Creator and Sustainer.

Consequently, being grasped, accepted and involved in the salvational love of God through the message of the gospel believers begin to reach back beyond the ambiguities of experienced reality to see God at work in everything around and within their world, that is, they begin to interpret daily events in their lives either as blessings or chastisement from their Creator, who has at last found them in Christ *(Deus revelatus).*[16] This belief is a projection into the beginnings of things and an affirmation that the source of the present life was the source of all finite reality. As a projection, or a movement of faith[17] from a personal involvement in such redemptive dynamics of a healing love, it moves from the particular to the universal claim that this God who gives me life and saves it, despite the questionableness of my life and sin, has been and now is actively creative in the entire cosmos. God's creativity is not dependent on our ability to believe, for, as the creator, God has been giving and sustaining life before our birth and shall continue to do so after we have ceased to live.

The upshot of all this is that faith understands the existence of life and its continuance in time as correlates of God's willingness to create, that is, faith sees God as the other side of life. Consequently, even though divine acts are not transparent, the believer, in faith, still sees a birth of a child, a healing of illness, an escape from an accident, or a loaf of bread on the table as blessings from the hand of the Creator and Sustainer. All these result from the peculiarity of faith itself, which sees and interprets most events in the life of the believer in the light of God's continuing life-giving activity, whose clarity, climax and revelatory heights were unequivocally demonstrated in Christ.

Finally, it is important to note that a creedal belief in the originating and sustaining creativity of God — one who creates me, other finite creatures and the entire cosmos — is never neutral, but is highly valuative, once it is personalized. It holds that the world in which I live is not a hostile place because it is under the control and rule of God who is my father and Creator. Also, creation is understood as something that is good, or a blessing by the Creator. As a reliable place, the world provides home and security by affording me and others psychological, emotional and social comfort through human fellowship. Also, it provides physical comfort by providing bread, fruits, and everything that is necessary for this life. Furthermore, because all of created existence comes from the hand of God, who alone is the Creator and Sustainer, creation is neither divine nor an object of worship. Rather, it is a place where I must exercise responsibility, care for it, explore it, and relate to it freely. Because my life depends on the supportive health of the world, my relationship with it must be positive rather than abusive.[18]

In conclusion, we must return where we began: Because all the above assertions in the end are but creedal statements of thanksgiving, or affirmations of assurance that God is actively creative now, it must not be forgotten that they remain conclusions of faith, drawn from the encounter with the redemptive dynamics of God's healing love. Because they are projections or inferences of faith in the beginnings of things, and they mean to express the faith that God who created still creates today, it is a mistake to think of creating as an "event" that is complete and finished. Creation is not a past *thing* but God's activity, which goes on all the time. It is also a mistake to construe sustaining creativity (traditionally understood as providential rule and preservation of fallen creation through the use of the law)[19] as if it were an existent or given thing.

To do so is to ignore that these creedal affirmations are but conclusions of faith, which are statements of thanksgiving to the Creator who is the present source of comfort, hope and assurance. Therefore, it is an error both to conceive of either creation or sustaining creativity apart from the active God of faith and to reify these faith-statements into static things. Indeed, if this reification is allowed to occur, it is bound to have a distorting effect on our theological understanding of the creative dynamics of God in an ongoing creative process; one in which either the originating or the sustaining creativity does not refer to "things out there," but to an active involvement of the Creator through deeds and acts in the past, present and future development of finite creation, as it is being carried toward its *telos* and, therefore, completion.

7.3 THE DIVINE COMMANDING (WORD) AS ITSELF A CREATIVE ACTIVITY

One important claim made in the previous section is this: Because the creedal belief in the originating God who also creatively sustains now is a conclusion of faith, it is a mistake to construe these affirmations as if they referred to static things rather than God's deeds and acts. They are inseparably tied to the dynamics of God's ongoing creative and life-giving work in the world of humans and other finite creatures, for there is never a time when creatures are independent of their Creator, who actively and creatively gives them life and being.

More importantly, one of our theses was that it is an error to suppose that the God who issues commands does so merely to interrupt or interfere with a flow of life, for the divine self is already involved creatively in the dynamics of life-giving activities. That is, the originating as well as the complementary creative acts (sustaining creativity of the creatures in temporal existence) are what theological talk is all about, or intends to express, when the concept of the divine command (creative word) is used.

It is, therefore, our contention that in issuing or uttering the command (creative word) God does not interrupt from outside, as it were, threatening to punish the human creature, because the Creator has always been involved in the ordering, structuring and life-giving processes of the historical existence, giving being and time to finite creatures who, without God's continuous presence or nourishing creativity, would cease to be. This continuous interrelationship between the divine self and the recipients of the divine life-giving activity becomes even more evident when the Creator's commanding (law, creative word) is adequately grounded in God's ongoing creative dynamics in which the creature is given being (originating creativity) and is being re-created (sustaining creativity) from moment to moment.

The upshot of these claims led us to further observations that were made briefly, namely, that the originating and sustaining creative acts (traditionally understood as creation and law) should be seen as implying each other. On the one hand, the two activities must be closely correlated in such a way that no doubt is left that in both it is the same creative word (commanding) of God that is involved. For life itself, both in its origination and continuance in time, is the manifestation of God, or implies the Creator who gives it. On the other hand, because they are the creative acts of the divine command (word), theological discourse must make it clear that they cannot be comprehended independently from God's active involvement, who thus creates being and time together. For God's use of the command (law, creative word) in the sustaining creativity of the finite beings does not aim at a goal other than creation. The only difference is that it is not creation *ex nihilo* but a molding of the creature in the continuing work of creation.

These observations lead us to another thesis: It is our contention that the divine commanding (command, fiat, creative word, or law)[20] should be understood as itself a creative activity. As we have argued and shall demonstrate, it is by the same creative word (command) that created "in the beginning" that God continues to create now. When it is understood that it is the same creative command (word) that is involved, it becomes possible to express the positive and creative functions of the divine command, functions that express the divine will of love. It is the creative will of love that is characterized by the divine goodness and willingness to give life in the past, present and future.

The significance of our thesis that the divine command(ing) is itself God's creative activity lies in its close correlation between creation and the creative word of God, and also in its attempt to ground our conceptual understanding of the divine law (command, creative word) directly in the creative will of God in action (rather than in the fact of sin, fall or retribution, as Elert does, or in the sanctification of man, as Barth does). As a consequence of this grounding of law (creative commanding or word) in the dynamics of creativity, the other positive aspects of the command can be expressed because law is not forced in advance into a "strait-jacket" of the framework of justification of the sinner before God.

Before we proceed to explore the implications of our claims here, it should be borne in mind that the command (creative word, fiat, law) as it will be used in this chapter is largely purged from moralistic connotations, which often go together with a discussion of the law. The moral implication of the creedal belief in the creative God, which has been already alluded to, will have its place and be made explicit later.[21] For the moment we wish to focus attention on the peculiar manner in which the divine commanding is being understood as itself a creativity — an understanding that not only emphasizes the divine creative activity but also tries to offer and outline a more adequate and comprehensive expression of the Creator's ongoing, dynamic and positive use of law.

The non-legalistic understanding of the divine command, which, as we have contended, should be understood as itself creativity, is not entirely novel. It is found in biblical literature. In the Psalms, for instance, it is pointed out again and again that creation came into being through the instrumentality of the divine commanding, speaking or the creative word. By this command (creative word) the heavens were made, and through the divine breath, or the word of his mouth, the waters of the sea were gathered up, "for he spoke, and it came to be; and he commanded and it stood forth" (Ps. 33:6–9). God thundered in the heavens and "uttered his voice," thereby effecting some actions (Ps. 18:13ff). The voice of the Lord is upon the waters, is powerful, breaks cedars and shakes the wilderness or makes the oaks to whirl (Ps. 29: 3–9).

When God sends a command to earth, or sends a word, certain creativities result, such as the giving of snow, scattering of frost, melting of ice, blowing of wind and flow of water (Ps. 147:15–18). The Psalmist also urges all creatures in heaven and on earth to praise the Lord because "he commanded and they were created and he established them" and fixed the bounds of heavens, earth, and oceans (Ps. 148: 5–6).[22] In the book of Job we are told that God's voice roars and thunders wondrously, thereby doing "great things which we cannot comprehend." To the "snow he says, 'Fall on the earth'; and to the showers of rain, 'Be strong.' " By the breath of God ice is given, and the broad waters are frozen fast. He loads the clouds with moisture and turns them around and around to "accomplish all that he commands them on the face of the habitable earth" (Job 37:2–12). In all these usages the command or the sending of God's creative word, breath or voice is clearly understood as itself a creative activity (or power).

The prophet Isaiah also understands the word of the command of God as a creative activity. Consequently, because this word (command) is itself creative, it never goes from the mouth of God without accomplishing or doing that which God has intended. That is, God's uttering of commands is never an empty exercise, but results in creative and sustaining acts in which the creatures prosper (Is. 55:11). The earth and man upon it were created by God, and so were the heavens and their hosts (Is. 45:12, 18–19).

Luther, taking his cue from Genesis where God brings creation into existence through the utterance of the command or creative word, has followed the tradition of the Psalmists, Isaiah and Job when he declares that *for God to command is to create* because the Creator creates through the word (fiat).[23] Because Luther's contention, namely, that the divine command is itself creative activity, comes closest to the position we are going to develop, we shall often draw from his insights. By doing so, we shall be limiting the data to be discussed, as we outline and construct an alternative understanding of the divine command, one that is not only positive and dynamic but that also will overcome problems inherent in the positions of Barth and Elert.

The most important characteristic of the divine command is that it is a function of and is inseparable from the creative will of God. More concretely, it is identical with an attribute in the being of the Creator. It is that quality in the innermost being of God which expresses itself in the creative works of love. Therefore, it exists from the very beginning and functions – as it did with the inception of creation and history – apart from historical enactments and interpretations of laws in biblical passages or secular codes. For the latter are but a part of the manifestation of the finite existence of the divine uncreated Word, which has now assumed concrete forms and is involved in the dynamics of the historical process of ongoing creativity.

This uncreated Word (about which we shall say more later on) which at the inception of creation took a historical form, is not something that is jealously guarded by the Creator in eternity and therefore is above time and space.[24] Rather, it is the divine creative power of the Word (command) that is being uttered in divine essence so that it may effect activities in the world. That is, as the creative Word is directed outside the Creator, its power creates out of nothing while it also involves the finite creatures in its dynamics of creativity, a creativity that is charged with services between existing creatures who become beneficiaries of this creative process.

To elucidate what is being claimed here, we wish to utilize Luther's vocabulary, which is very illuminating and insightful regarding the manner in which the divine command is itself a creative power. Luther's understanding of the Hebrew noun is extraordinarily rich. In a slow and painful struggle to understand the biblical meaning of the "righteousness of God," as this relates to the sinner, Luther discovered that the Hebrew noun is highly dynamic – just as much as its verb is.[25] He, for instance, points out to us the difference between a Greek and a Hebrew understanding of "the knowledge of God." For the Greek, this term is understood in an abstract sense, that is, it refers to the "known things of God," or "what is known" about God in Himself.[26] But in Hebrew it means much more. It can mean an attribute in God, that is, a quality that distinguishes God from human knowing. Also, it might mean the knowledge of God that "comes to us from Him and is in us."[27] Such a knowledge becomes a power of the wisdom of God by which "He makes us wise and strong before Himself."[28]

Even though it took several years for Luther's theology to mature, it is generally accepted that even in the early years, he was aware that a Hebrew noun is dynamic and has several meanings. For instance, in his lectures on the Psalm 71:19 during 1514, Luther began to distinguish between the active and the passive righteousness of God. In its active or formal sense, it refers to an attribute of God, while its passive meaning is that power by which God justifies us. It is a given righteousness. Luther writes:

> ..... anyone who wants to understand the Apostle and the rest of the Scripture aright should understand all these things tropologically: truth, wisdom, power, salvation, justice – namely the means by which God makes us strong, saved, just, wise, etc. So also the works of God, the ways of God; Christ is all these things literally, and morally they are all the faith of Christ.[29]

When he began to lecture on Romans (1515–1516), Luther continued to speak of these several meanings of a Hebrew noun, that is, the active and passive righteousness of God. The citations above are indicative of this. In addition to them, he discusses such nouns as *iustitia dei.* He argues that this righteousness of God is that which distinguishes God's from human righteousness, which comes from works.[30] The latter is attained or earned, while God's righteousness is a divine attribute. Luther further points out that *iustitia dei,* which is proclaimed by the gospel, is not God's own eternal justice but rather is the power by which God justifies us.[31] That is, God's righteousness is revealed when He justifies us without any merit on our part.

He also discusses the power of God and says that this *virtus dei (Möglichkeit,* in German) should not be understood as the "power by which according to His essence He is powerful but by virtue of which He makes us powerful and strong."[32] It is also true that *virtus dei* may mean a quality in the being of God "in distinction from the 'power of men.' "[33] However, as an action it means a power that comes from God. In this sense, it is no different from such sayings as "the gift of God," "the creature of God," or "the things of God."[34] For it refers to something that comes from God and is given to humans, such as we read from Acts 1:18 where it is written: "But you shall receive the power when the Holy Spirit has come upon you."[35] Furthermore, Luther argues that the gospel is called the power of God, or the power of the Spirit in the same sense. As God's power, the gospel comes to us as riches, weapons and adornments on us. It is something good that comes from God and we receive it from Him.[36] For if God is not directing the activities of the gospel toward us, "the power of God will not be in us."[37]

One year later, in his exposition of the Hebrews (1517), Luther continued to argue that in Scripture the words "peace" and "justice" everywhere refer to the divine justice and peace. But it is the justice by which God justifies us. Consequently, it would be wrong to understand justice as referring to "that justice of God by which he himself is just."[38]

Even after his theology had undergone refinement and conceptions of law and gospel as well as the alien justification had begun to overshadow a notion of passive *iustitia dei,* Luther did not give up his dynamic meaning of the Hebrew noun. For instance, in his commentary on Psalm 118:2, Luther calls our attention to the difference between the Greek and the Hebrew understanding of the "mercy of God." Consequently, he translates the Hebrew *ḥesed*(חסד)as God's " 'goodness in action,' such as God grants us and we, in turn, should show towards others,"[39] That is, the "mercy" or "goodness" here does not refer to the attribute of God in Himself, but to an action directed toward us and transforming our actions.

Also, in his *Lectures on Galatians* (1535), Luther calls our attention to the function of a Hebrew noun, when Paul talks about the "Gospel of the circumcision." He says this may be understood in a passive sense as well as in the active sense.[40] He holds that there are many other examples throughout the Scripture, such as the "glory of God," which may mean the glory God has in Himself, but in the passive sense means "the glory in which we glory in God."[41] Therefore, Luther concludes, "the Gospel of God" in the active sense is that which only God has, gives and sends to the world. In the passive sense, however, it means the gospel that has been sent and is accepted. Put differently, it is the gospel that has been "entrusted" to either Jews or Gentiles.[42]

Finally, in his autobiographical *Preface* of 1545, Luther makes a point that it was by the way of Hebrew nouns that he finally discovered the content of the gospel. He says he was meditating night and day, trying to understand Paul's phrase, "in the gospel the justice of God is revealed," when the context became clear. He began to understand that *iustitia dei* referred to the justice by which God makes us just. It is a passive justice, revealed through the gospel, and is received in faith. He felt himself born again and entering the gates of paradise. The whole of the Scripture also opened itself to him. He ran through memory looking for analogies such as: the "work of God, that is, what God does in us, the power of God, with which he makes us strong, the wisdom of God, with which he makes us wise,....."[43]

To sum up: in this discovery Luther found that the Hebrew noun can stand for several things: (i) A quality or an attribute in the being of God, which God has in the divine self, and which distinguishes the Creator from creatures. (ii) An activity of God, or that power by which God comes to creatures and does divine works, e.g., God may justify, make wise, make strong, cause things to be, and make them creative and fruitful. (iii) A noun may stand for the result of God's activity in us, that is, that divine power in us which transforms us; for example, God may transform us through the divine love or mercy so that we in turn may become loving and merciful, etc.[44] Because it is God who thus works in us, or it is the power of God's Spirit that makes us perform these helpful works of love and mercy, often thanks is given to the Creator when something that is good is done through human hands — as, for instance, when a doctor restores health to an ailing person.

Following Luther's understanding of the dynamic nature of the Hebrew noun, I wish to examine the concept of the command (creative word) of God. In doing this, I hope to make explicit my basic thesis that for God to command is to create. By extension of Luther's analogy, it will be my contention that the command of God must be understood in a threefold sense: First, the command (creative word) of God is that distinctive divine quality, and attribute, in the being of God as the Creator. As the creative power that God has in the divine self, it distinguishes the Creator from finite creatures. This distinction will be discussed later under the title: "God, the Creative Speaker." Second, the command (creative word) of God is that power by which God creates us. As an activity, it translates the divine speaking or word into concrete realities, by giving being and time to finite creatures and by sustaining them in their existence. Third, the command (creative word) is that power of God in us that transforms, empowers and enables us to become creative agents with God. It is the result of God's work in us with which the Creator continues the creative process.

7.3.1 God, the Creative Speaker Through the Command (Creative Word)

In the preceeding discussion, a number of examples were given in which we demonstrated how the Hebrew noun in Luther has several meanings. Those examples were intended to prepare us for this later discussion about the command of God and to underscore the fact that this usage is an important aspect of Luther's theology. Indeed, Luther distinguishes various senses of God's speech (command, creative word, fiat). As we have observed, the command (creative word), as the power that God has in divine majesty, signifies an attribute in God, that is, it refers to that distinctive quality of the Creator with the power to create *ex nihilo* and sustain creation in its temporal development. As such, the creative Word (commanding or utterance) is the power that inheres eternally in God and is, therefore, inseparable from the divine will of love, which is essentially creative.

Luther, wanting to underscore this qualitative difference between the Creator and finite humans, says: "we must realize that this Word of God is entirely different from my word or yours. For we, too, have a word, especially a 'word of the heart.' "[45] This difference does not lie in utterances because every word must be spoken in order to be heard by others. Rather, the command (word) of God differs from every human word qualitatively by its power to effect, create or bring about what the Creator wills or commands.[46] That is, God's utterance is intended to bring into a concrete existence what the Creator wills in his divine majesty. For this reason God alone has the absolute freedom of the will, because what is willed is caused to exist, while humans can only propose without the power of effecting what they will. God alone disposes.

The divine Word is therefore the instrument of creation through which God performs divine works and relates to the world either creatively or redemptively. One other qualitative difference between the creative command of God and human words is that the divine command (word) is with God eternally. It is the uncreated Word.[47] In his *Sermons on the Gospel of St. John* (1537–1539), Luther argues that it is not only characteristic of God to want to speak, but God is Himself the eternal Word. This is what John affirms by saying that the Word was with God, and the Word is God from the beginning of the universe. Because God is the Word, or the creative Speaker, the biblical God cannot be understood apart from the divine speech. For there is never a time when God does not have the Word.[48]

Further, Luther concedes that because God does not have a mouth, like us, all analogies are inadequate and vague. Indeed, the creative Word of God, the Creative Speaker and Lord of all creatures, is:

> ..... immeasurably superior to poor, miserable man, who is earth and dust, so there is no analogy between the word of man and the Word of the eternal and almighty God. There is a wide gulf between thoughts, discussions, and words of the human heart and those of God.[49]

Nonetheless, because we, too, have thoughts and words, the inadequate analogies give us a faint idea of God's thoughts and the Son as the Word. Luther points to human words that carry with them creative weight, especially those of the prince when they are heeded and acted upon. In view of this, it follows that "heaven and earth, all creatures, both the visible and invisible, come into being when the eternal, almighty, and the divine majesty speaks to Himself or carries on a conversation with Himself, as it is written in Ps. 33:6."[50]

Carrying his analogies further, Luther says that when humans have thoughts or think about something, they also have words and carry on conversations with themselves. But what is in their thoughts is never known until it is translated into action. Similarly God, the Creative Speaker, has a speech and a conversation with Himself from eternity. His thoughts are not known to us until they are acted upon. It was, therefore, after this divine conversation had taken place that God "through this Word resolved to create the earth and heaven."[51]

The qualitative difference between divine command (creative word) and human utterance, as we have already observed, lies in the power to call into existence things that do not exist. As Pelikan rightly points out, however, the command of God that interested Luther above all was the uttered and historical sense of the word. That is, the category of Luther's doctrine of the word (command) was not the category of "being" but the category of "deed."[52] Consequently, the creative word of God in its historical sense is that divine quality whose power is manifested in concrete actions and creative deeds. Therefore, when the command is uttered at the inception of creation, it reveals the nature of God, as the creative Speaker of word, whose speaking is equivalent to a creative action. That is, what the creative command (word) expresses is nothing other than what the Creator has willed, and which in time becomes extended outside the divine self in order to be translated into a reality, namely, creation.

Luther expresses this eloquently when he writes:

> *What else is the entire creation than the Word of God uttered by God, or extended to the outside?* But the uncreated Word is the divine thought, an *inner command* which abides in God ..... Thus God reveals Himself as the Speaker who has with Him the uncreated Word, through whom He created the world and all things with the greatest ease, namely, speaking.[53]

Pelikan's comments about Luther's understanding of the Word of God are both illuminating and insightful. He points out that the Word of

God, for Luther, is something that both reveals God, either as a Creator or a Redeemer, and is a deed or an action.[54] As a deed or concrete action (we would prefer creativity), the command (creative word) of God is therefore the basis and the essential element of the created reality. In other words, the creative Word of God is constitutive of all finite existence.[55] For all the finite creatures are but the uttered words of God, the words that, when extended outside the divine self, assume concrete and historical forms. Furthermore, by ascribing the origin and sustenance of finite creatures to the creative command of God, not only has Luther (and indeed the Scripture as well) construed the Word (divine utterance) as the constitutive element of all finite beings, but also as the instrument of all relationships between the Creator and all creatures.[56] That is, the creative Word of God, the Speaker, is both an activity with a power to give being to all of finite reality and a means by which the Creator is known and relates to creatures.[57]

Luther continues to underscore the qualitative difference between the Word of God, which is essentially creative, and human commanding, which is ineffective rhetoric. He says God says a simple word (command) and all things are made, and by the same word they are sustained (Rom. 4:17, Heb. 1:2–3). In his commentary of Psalm 147:15 this qualitative difference becomes even more glaring. He writes: "it takes one word from Him and that is *fiat*, as in Gen. 1:3." God, Luther continues, does not need a forge, a hammer, and tongs to make gates fast. Nor does He need the help of women, merchants or manufacturers of coins to make "His children rich and happy. He needs neither plow nor harrow to satisfy us with wheat; but He needs only say to the bars: 'Be fast,' and they are fast. And to the populace: 'Be rich and happy,' and they are rich and happy."

God needs only to say to the earth: "Bring forth wheat," and there it is. He heals through the command, and raises the dead by calling them into existence, because "His command or speech is equivalent to creation."[58] In one of his strongest metaphors, Luther makes this qualitative difference between the creative command of God and the human word:

> ..... everything that God wills happens quickly, instantly. And as soon as He speaks, there it is ..... His Word is not a rotten, sickly, or dead word, like the words and commandments of men. Let them order and command as they will; nothing happens, or at least very little. For even the words and commands of the king or of our masters are done piecemeal and slowly ..... if God's Word is not added, saying: "What you, king or prince, have ordered, let that be done," nothing will happen. His Word must be added in order to give force to the ruler's command .....[59]

There is little doubt that here Luther has overstated his case. For through his verbal overkill he wants to claim that God creates instantaneously without human help and difficulty. This view will have to be radically qualified because creation is a long and painful process, a process that has taken the Creator thousands of years and that is not yet complete. Luther at times recognizes human cooperation, as it will be demonstrated later. Despite these exaggerations, the point he is making is still valid, namely, that human willing and commanding have limited effect, for they do not have the creative efficacy of divine commanding. Were the opposite true, the finite creatures would, in fact, be no different from God their Creator in their creative capacity and self-sufficiency. However, creatureliness implies dependence on the creative God, who is the Speaker and Giver of being and time to finite beings through the divine utterance. Because this creaturely dependency continues, the accompaniment of the divine command (creative word) in the lives of creatures is as necessary as the air they breathe.

Luther persuasively points to the birth of children as the clearest place where, without God's command (word or blessing), even the most suitable and healthy couples often fail to have children,[60] no matter how they try. Of course, unbelievers may explain such infertility as the result of some accident or misfortune; but believers may not be persuaded by such explanations, for such explanations may not be *the only truth*. Indeed, believers also know that children are a creation and a gift from God, the creative Speaker, who ultimately is the one who creates. Therefore, religious men and women acknowledge that unless God stands behind human work and activities, they are likely to be fruitless. Consequently, they often commend their plans and works to the Almighty God whose Word (command) alone is powerful enough to bring forth what it commands. And as God adds a divine command (word, blessing), men and women are enabled to become creative agents with God.[61]

In conclusion, it is interesting to note that our understanding of the divine command, which is itself a creative activity, is (incidentally) close to the meaning of commands in the gospel with reference to the activities of Jesus. Through commands Jesus demonstrated a qualitative divine power that creates (or heals). As a result, those who lived around him were led to the conclusion that they were not dealing with a mere human being, but rather with the creative Lord and God *(Kurios)*. It is reported that even the Devil acknowledged this creative ability by asking Jesus to command the stones so that they should become bread (Mt. 4:3). By a command Jesus healed a man full of leprosy (Mt. 3:3; Lk. 5:13). He healed the servant of the centurion by uttering a command that he be well (Mt. 8:13; Lk. 7:8ff). By issuing a command, Jesus cast out evil spirits and healed the sick (Mt. 8:26). He healed the paralytic by commanding him to rise, take his bed, and go home (Mt. 9:2–8).[62]

These and many other great works that Jesus performed by means of uttering a command led many, as we already observed, to conclude that Jesus was no other than Jahweh *(Kurios),* the creative Speaker, because Jesus could bring into existence – as the Creator did in the beginning through the creative command (utterance, word) – things which did not exist, such as the restoration of life, and the raising from the dead. All these were actions that no ordinary human being could effect.

Because Jesus' command was creative, Peter – as the representative of those who believe in the qualitative Word of God with a power to create and give life – rightly asked: "Lord, to whom shall we go? You have the words of eternal life; and we have believed, and have come to know, that you are the Holy One of God" (Jn. 6:68f). Peter's confession sums up very eloquently the point we have been trying to establish, namely, the commanding word of God, the creative Speaker, differs qualitatively from human speaking because for God to command is to create.[63] Indeed, a conclusion had to be drawn that Jesus the Messiah was, in fact, the Lord and God, the creative Speaker. For as God speaks or commands, something is created *ex nihilo* and sustained in temporal existence; and, as we have argued all along, the divine command (creative word) is nothing else than God's creative activity and therefore the word of life.

7.3.2 The Uttered Command as a Reality Creating Activity

Any discussion about the command of God, that is, that distinctive quality in the being of God with the power both to create *ex nihilo* and to sustain finite existence, will be incomplete without also discussing the *what* of that which this creative command (word, utterance) brings forth. Because this divine command is uttered so that the Creator's thoughts and words could be translated into realities, as the word assumes historical forms it is necessary to discuss these created realities in their own right.

From the preceding exposition, it is obvious that, in fact, God's creative utterance (word, command) – as the power of the activity of God and therefore the instrument of creation – cannot be understood separately from that which it creates, effects, or causes to be. As we have already observed elsewhere, God, the creative Speaker of the creative word, and the manifestation of life or finite existence in temporal development imply each other. Consequently, it was not completely accidental that a discussion of the creative command of God should have led us automatically to a discussion, though only sketchy, of the realities that are brought forth into existence as God commands. Seeing that some of the realities that came to be, as the power of the originating and sustaining Word (command) was being translated into deeds (creative actions), have already been mentioned, the exposition will be brief.

The biblical witness and the Christian confessions make it abundantly clear that the totality of finite existence constitutes the realities that God's creative speaking (word, command) has called forth into existence from nothing. That is, all of the finite creatures owe their being to the divine creative power and activity, which in the beginning created and continues to sustain creation in the ongoing interrelationships between God and all creatures. This totality of finite realities includes all things both in heaven and on earth. They are continually being created and acted upon by the creative word, which gives them power to be and to continue, as the Creator carries on the work of creation towards its future goal.

The creative activity of God through the power of the command (word) is not limited to the origination of creation *ex nihilo.* Rather, as we have seen in Luther's understanding of *iustitia dei, notitia dei, virtus dei,* etc., as both a means and an activity by which God justifies, makes wise and makes strong, the command of God may signify the power that comes from the Creator to the creatures. The creative Word then becomes the divine power that enables or causes the created media to be creative, productive or fruitful. This means God does not always create *ex nihilo* but very often uses the existing material to further the divine purposes of creation. Consequently, the earth can be commanded to give forth vegetation, fruits, corn, wheat, and other necessities that provide food and sustain life. The earth may, through the power of the creative Word, bring forth such things as silk, cotton, gold, silver, and many more minerals.

In this way, the Creator continues to translate the creative Word into divine blessings, or good deeds, which are continually being showered upon the creatures for their sustenance. It was in this connection that

Luther rightly suggested that human labour would be futile, had God not placed gold, silver, and diamonds in the mountains through the divine creative Word, the word that originates, sustains and is constitutive of all of reality itself.[64] Human labour, therefore, is but a collection of what God has first bestowed. For if God did not create, uphold and sustain, the earth would produce nothing, since human labour and the earth are unable by themselves to create or preserve these blessings.

Also, through the activity of the creative word, God causes living creatures to give birth to their offspring. In this way, creation does not always begin afresh, but continues. The cattle are commanded to give milk, butter and meat. The sheep are commanded to give wool, etc. Human beings, too, are commanded to multiply and fill the earth. While other creatures provide all the necessities of life for humans, the latter are commanded to provide services to creation and to care for it.[65]

Finally, the creative efficacy of the word (command) is still in force to this day, for creation is not complete but continues in the present. It is because the command is creatively active that life continues and children are born. Therefore, with Luther, we can acknowledge our own birth today as God's creative act and confess: "It is he who gives us body, life, food, drink, nourishment, health, protection ..... and all temporal blessings."[66] To underscore this continuity of creation, Luther suggests that the heat by which hens keep their eggs warm "is the result of the divine word."[67] He adds that "because all things grow, multiply, and are preserved and governed until now in the same manner as from the beginning of the world, it is obvious that the Word still continues in force and is not dead," and so we continue to increase "without end."[68]

To sum up: It has been one of our theses that the creative command (word) of God is nothing else than the divine creativity itself. The other was that creation is nothing but the divine word (creative command) as it is being translated into reality. That is, as God speaks existence is brought about because the divine command is inseparable from that divine creative will of love, which is characterized by the Creator's willingness to give, to help, to do good and to shower blessings on creatures daily. Because God's creative Word is not only the ground or the basis of creation but also the constitutive element of finite reality, creation and the creative Word of the Creator belong together. Expressed negatively, for God to stop commanding means life would cease – because life is inseparable from the divine Giver who both originates life and relates to us through the Word.

Two consequences follow from the claims made above. First, not only is it important to ground our understanding of the creative command of God in the dynamics of God's ongoing creativity, but also it is an error to think of divine commands as foreign intrusions into life from the outside, as it were. For God was and is already involved in each and every phase of the temporal or historical development of finite creatures: ordering, creating, surrounding, upholding and creatively sustaining all creatures through the word that gives being and time to creatures.

Second, there is never a time when the Creator is not related to creatures through the creative Word, giving them the power to be. For this reason, we argued that creation is nothing but wholly the words of God uttered in divine essence. That is, the creative Word is not only constitutive of all finite reality but God is so present in all creatures that they are indissolubly related to their Creator, from whom they receive life daily through the power of the creative Word.God is present in all creatures, as that power which moves, quickens, and dispenses life. That is, God is immanent through transcendent, so as to effect and preserve all things.

To be sure, God is "immeasurable, beyond and above all that is or may be,"[69] but through the power and activity of the Word, the Creator participates in the creative acts that structure and order the universe. We conclude by quoting Luther, who eloquently sums up the ongoing creativity of God through the Word among creatures:

> If he is to create or preserve it, however, he must be present and must make and preserve his creation both in its innermost and outermost aspects. Therefore, indeed, he himself must be present in every single creature in its innermost and outermost being, on all sides, through and through, below and above, before and behind, so that nothing can be more truly present and within all creatures than God himself with his power.[70]

Notes

1 "Law" and "command" will be used interchangeably in this chapter. We will often prefer to use "command," which has less legalistic overtones.

2 Cf. Alex R. Adler, *Christ's Strange Work* (London: Longmans & Co., 1945), p. 32. For him the Decalogue is the eternal law. Hence governments that deviate from it deserve to be overthrown.

3 Luther holds the view that no law can encapsulate God's creative will of love. All laws are imperfect and human constructions that must be revised again and again because they are a patchwork (LW. 13, pp. 164, 198f). Human beings cannot maintain themselves without laws, says Luther, but these laws remain tools that "every country and city can observe or change" (LW. 14, p. 14). Because all laws are relative, Mosaic law is relevant for Jews only and does not concern Christians who have Christ and the New Testament (LW. 14, pp. 19ff; LW. 20, p. 90; LW. 35, pp. 158f, 164–169; LW. 40, p. 92). He did not dismiss the Decalogue but doubts whether there is any universal law to which all nations should be subject. What matters is the Golden Rule, that is, "do unto others what you would like them to do to you." It is love that must be served. Moreover, Luther contends, when we have Christ (and the gospel) we are free to make new Decalogues, as Paul and other Apostles did. In fact, these Decalogues, may be better than the Mosaic Decalogue (LW. 34, pp. 112–113). For him, we keep the Decalogue because it agrees with the law of reason and because it contains God's promises (LW. 35, pp. 164–169ff).

4 For an exhaustive treatment of the emergence of natural law theories, their influence on Roman jurists and the early Church and their adoptions by various Christian groups, see: Ernst Troeltsch, *The Social Teachings of the Christian Churches* (New York: Harper Torchbooks, 1960), pp. 41, 65–68, 258–261f, 306, 464–505, 525–572, 602–617; Paul Tillich, *Morality and Beyond* (New York: Harper Torchbooks, 1963), pp. 33–36. These authors agree that the theory of natural law was developed by the Stoic School, which believed in the existence of a universally valid moral law. Men are part of it, and it has its origin in the divine *logos,* who creatively is present in the moral laws of human inventors and in the natural or physical laws. This divine principle controls the universe, assures everyone a place in the world and uplifts men toward a spiritual good in which virtue can be attained by intense moral cultivation and knowledge. As one becomes in tune with it, this divine principle

is then embodied as the law of reason, a reason that both knows and is one with God. Both Tillich and Troeltsch agree that this theory of natural law is a static, immutable and unchanging "First Cause." Not only does it place people in society, but also people must accommodate themselves to their allotted limitations in society. Therefore, even though the Stoics advocated equality and freedom for women, children and slaves, society was never transformed. For the ideal the Stoics sought through the natural law was premised on the belief that the purest state or "Golden Age" had been realized in remote antiquity and is now lost irrevocably. Its ideal remained a possibility for upper classes. Troeltsch also points out that because natural law theory is correlated with sin and human weakness, which is characterized by a fallen state of humanity, so people are supposed to endure existing conditions. Moreover, this divine principle was viewed as nonhistorical, hovering above all events in space and time. Yet men were supposed to discern it and be guided by it. Regrettably, the Roman jurists adopted this theory, while its abstractness, nonhistoricity, and immutable nature remained intact. Positive enactments of laws were believed to have been done under the guidance of this abstract and immutable principle. Social and historical laws were believed to be interpretations of this nonhistorical law, according to which society must develop and conform. *Man was thus believed to be an object of eternal principles rather than a subject who acts and creates laws.* According to Troeltsch, the early Church made no changes either. Rather, its universality confirmed her belief in God's rule over the cosmos. Also, the Stoic idea of a lost "Golden Age" was understood as a confirmation of the doctrine of the Fall. The Church merely distinguished between absolute and relative or positive laws of nature. The Mosaic-Christian law of revelation was the former, by which the latter was to be illumined. Law was correlated with sin and viewed as a remedy for sin. Also, states were seen as products of sin that needed purification, a role the Church willingly played as a dispenser of grace. Hence, legal enactments were placed under the tutelage of the Church. This step was necessary because natural law antedates all states, and their duty was merely a working out of this law. But because humans err, the Church was to be an arbiter of what a correct interpretation of natural law is, because she possessed a supernatural insight. Basically, the law remained static, and improvements in laws were supposed to be only a further insight into this immutable natural law. For everything that is necessary is believed to have been already given through this nonhistorical and eternal law. Law under the Church thus was neither revolutionary nor world-transforming, but remained conservative, static and patriarchal. Troeltsch believes Reformers did little to change the static nature of natural law theory. They were suspicious of reason, so the idea of spiritual gradualism of the natural realm was removed. But law remained *remedium peccati.* Calvin moved further to make the Decalogue central, but in doing so he conceived of it as an eternal rule of life, which is non-historical and unchanging.

5 I do not mean to imply that the Ten Commandments are not a unique heritage for which the Church must be thankful. To be sure, the Decalogue was molded under special divine dispensation with the Jewish people. But I want to argue that it, too, has not completely escaped influences of its cultural milieu. For studies by archaeologists have shown that there are certain similarities between the Hammurabi code and our Decalogue. Nonetheless, these similarities do not nullify its uniqueness nor the authority it has gained in the Judaeo-Christian tradition.

6 Gordon Kaufman, *Systematic Theology,* pp. 144–145.

7 Cf. Friederich Schleiermacher, *The Christian Faith* (Edinburgh: T. & T. Clark, 1968), pp. 142–148.

8 Gustaf Wingren, *Creation and Law* (Philadelphia: Muhlenberg Press, 1961), p. 46. Also see pp. 22, 30–46, and Gustaf Aulen, *The Faith of the Christian Church* (Philadelphia: Muhlenberg Press, 1960), pp. 160f.

9 Paul Tillich, *Systematic Theology,* Vol. 1 (Chicago: The University of Chicago Press, 1971), pp. 261f. (Italics added) Cited hereafter as *Systematic Theology.* Kaufman in *Systematic Theology,* p. 144, makes a similar point.

10 Tillich, *Systematic Theology,* Vol. 1, p. 262.

11 Since for us creation and the preservative activity of God through the law are not sharply separated, law is understood here as nothing else than God's sustaining creativity.

12 Barth's observation is very insightful at this point, when he writes: "The truth that God rules, and that the history of existent creation in its time is also a history of His glory, is no less inaccessible and inconceivable, no less hard for man to grasp, than the truth of the origin of creation in the will and power of the Creator ..... In both we find ourselves in the sphere of the confessions" possible "in faith or not at all" (*Church Dogmatics* III/3, p. 15).

13 Cf. James Cone, *The Spirituals and the Blues* (New York: The Seabury Press, 1972), pp. 37, 66–69; John Macquarrie, *Principles of Christian Theology* (New York: Charles Scribner's Sons, 1966), pp. 222f.

14 Cf. Barth, *Church Dogmatics* III/3, pp. 15, 44; Tillich, *Systematic Theology,* Vol. 1, pp. 264–267; Bultmann, *Jesus Christ and Mythology* (New York: Charles Scribner's Sons, 1958), pp. 65–85.

15 LW. 33, pp. 28f, 61ff, 105f, 139f, 145f, 189f; LW. 40, p. 308; LW. 45, pp. 324–333; Luther's "Large Catechism," in *The Book of Concord,* trans. Theodore Tappert (Philadelphia: Fortress Press, 1959), pp. 369–374; 413.

16 Cf. Nürnberger, *Dogmatics* I, pp. 97–106; Harold Ditmanson, "The Call for a Theology of Creation," in *Dialog* (No. 3, Autumn 1964), pp. 269–271. Ditmanson's discussion of Gilkey's *The Maker of Heaven and Earth* (New York: Doubleday & Co., 1958), pp. 1–28, 37ff, comes closest to that of Nürnberger. Both of them persuasively demonstrate how belief in the Creator and creation is derived from the message of salvation (e.g., redemption from Egypt and in Jesus Christ in the Old Testament and New Testament respectively). Another book very illuminating on how faith

goes about creating a world by both a retrospective and prospective projection is that of Edward Farley, entitled *Ecclesial Man* (Philadelphia: Fortress Press, 1975), pp. 87, 150–233.

17 Faith is used here in the broadest sense of a basic trust in the meaningfulness of life, a trust in the ground or source of life, or a trust that God stands behind the finite life. It is, therefore, a fundamental stance or posture, a perspective or attitude that orients one's thought and life as well as one's actions. Also see Kaufman, *Systematic Theology*, pp. 20–23.

18 This dynamic relationship between human beings and the rest of creation, which is valuative, or moral, and therefore of mutual caring, will be taken up later when we discuss human responsibility for, rather than merely a utilization of, the created environment.

19 This is the mistake of those who think about God's law of preservation in terms of immutable, unchanging and eternal law (either natural or revealed) that is given "once-and-for-all." By contrast, the law should be understood as a historical production in the continuing creation of God, and therefore as something never separable from the God who creates in the present through finite agents.

20 The concept of law is loaded with legalistic connotations, and we prefer to use the concept "command" which, as used by Barth and Althaus, has less legalistic meaning. The problem is that this concept "command" can be misused or misunderstood in the sense that it is conceived as a thing, or reified as Barth does by equating the command with the ruling grace (Jesus Christ who is the law's form and content). In order to avoid this reification, we will often use "commanding" because the verb preserves the dynamic and active nature of God's work in the life-giving process. Also, we will use "creative word," "creative speaking," "creative fiat" to construe God's creative activity. However, even though "fait" is used, we do not mean to imply instantaneous or immediate creating. At any rate, when one or the other is used, what we are trying to express is the dynamism of God's creative activity in a *long* and *continuous* creative process.

21 Cf. note 18 and an extended exposition in chapter eight, subsection 8.2, where we argue that humans are accountable to God, who has entrusted them with creative powers as stewards. It is there that ethical questions are taken up.

22 In these cited passages the word of God, the command, the voice of God or his speaking are used almost interchangeably as instruments of creating. The Latin text of Jerome (*Biblia Vulgata*) uses related expressions such as: "Verbo Domini," "spiritu oris," "ipse dixit," "ipse mandavit (iussit) et creata sunt (facta, facti sunt)," and "qui emittit (emittet) eloquium (verbum) suum."

23 Convinced that in ordinary life-situations commands are given through words, such as the prince may give commands to his subjects, Luther arrives at a startling assertion that God creates through commands (speaking). He writes: "*Denn Schaffen heisst gebieten, und ordnung is ein creatur der menschen*" (WA. 12, 328:16f). He also adds: "Hie zeiget er an

die gülden kunst, durch welche Gott alle solche wohlthat ausrichtet und gibt, spricht: Es koste Gott nicht mehr denn ein wort, das heist 'Fiat', Gene. 1., ... *Sein reden odder sprechen ist so viel als schaffen,* wie wir lesen Gene. 1. Das er die welt geschaffen hat durch sein sprechen" (WA. 13/1, 445:3–5, 21–23). (Italics added)

24 The difference between the uncreated and eternal Word of God, which God has in Himself from eternity, and the historical word, which became constitutive of created reality and by means of which God communicates with the world, is borrowed from Luther. He advises us to distinguish the word of the divine person, which was with God before creation and in time became an instrument of creativity, from any human or created word. For instance, Luther writes: "Atque hic fecerunt discrimen verbi increati a verbo creato. Verbum creatum est factum per Verbum increatum" (WA. 42, 17:24f).

25 By referring to a "discovery" of the dynamic nature of the Hebrew noun in Luther's attempt to understand the meaning of the "righteousness of God," we do not wish to enter into the difficult and controversial discussion about the so-called "tower experience" of Luther. Scholars have tried to date this without much success. Thus, an attempt to date the birth of Reformation theology is beyond the scope of this study, and the examples we shall give will range from the earliest to Luther's later writings. For it is his peculiar understanding of the Hebrew nouns that is of interest to us. Regarding a comprehensive discussion of the "tower experience" controversies, the most recent publications known to me are those of Ian D.K. Siggins, *Martin Luther's Doctrine of Christ* (New Haven: Yale University Press, 1970), pp. 3–20, and also his edited work entitled *Luther* (New York: Barnes & Noble Books, 1972), pp. 75–86, 177–189. In the latter book, Siggins examines a wide range of publications and Luther's works. For anyone interested in the debate regarding the dating of the Reformation, Siggins provides an excellent bibliography to date, which need not be reproduced here.

26 Cf. Luther's *Lectures on Romans* in LW. 25, pp. 153f. To underline the abstractness of the Greek noun, it is interesting to take note of the footnote where *notitia dei* is translated by the neuter το γνωστον τοῦ θεοῦ and of the comment that accompanies it.

27 LW. 25, p. 153.

28 Ibid.

29 The citation and translation come from Siggins, *Luther* (New York: Barnes & Noble Books, 1972), p. 78. (Latin text in WA. 3, 457:38.) Cited hereafter as *Luther.*

30 LW. 25, p. 152.

31 Ibid., pp. 30–33, 151–153, 249. Luther holds that the passive righteousness of God is *imparted to us* so as to make us righteous. That is, it is God's action that comes to us, and has as its goal our lives (p. 151). Not only does it justify us, but also, the gospel is the divine wisdom and power in which we live (pp. 153, 249).

32 Ibid., p. 149.
33 Ibid.
34 Ibid.
35 Ibid.,
36 Ibid., p. 150.
37 Ibid.
38 Cf. Siggins, *Luther,* pp. 80–81.
39 LW. 14, p. 50 (WA. 31, 75–76).
40 LW. 26, p. 101 (WA, 40/1, 185f).
41 Ibid., p. 102.
42 Ibid.
43 LW. 34, pp. 337. Also read an excellent translation of the Latin text (WA. 54, 179–187) in Siggins, *Luther,* p. 77.
44 I am indebted to Warren Quanbeck (St. Paul, Minnesota: Luther Seminary, Fall 1973), who, in his course entitled "Luther as a Catholic Theologian," pointed out the threefold meanings of the Hebrew noun in Luther. However, the implications of such an understanding of Hebrew nouns for a theological exposition of the command of God became clear recently, as I struggled to outline a dynamic and positive understanding of the concept of the command (word). So the conclusions that shall be drawn are mine and I am answerable for them as they are expounded here.
45 LW. 22, p. 8.
46 LW. 1, p. 21. Luther adds that what God commands is experienced with such a "force and effectiveness of that divine command as he will not find in the oration of any orator, either of Demosthenes or of Cicero" (LW. 4, p. 104). While human rhetoric is ineffective and does not create what humans always command or wish, this cannot be said of the command of God: "Deus enim vocat ea, quae non sunt ut sint, et loquitor non grammatica vocabula, sed veras et subsistentes res, ut quod aput nos vox sonat, id apud Deus rest est. Sic Sol, Luna, Coelum, terra, Patrus, Paulus, Ego, tu, etc. sumus vocabula Dei" (WA. 42, 17:16–19).
47 LW. 22, pp. 12–14. Also in his *Lectures on Genesis* (1535–1536), Luther is at pains to explain the difference between God's created and uncreated words: "verbum creatum est factum per Verbum increatum." The latter is "divina cogitatio, iussio interna, manes in Deo, et idem cum Deo ..... per quod mundum et omnia creavit facilimo opere, dicendo scilicet" (WA. 42, 17:27-30). The former is the uttered word, an agent or an external word that reveals God with the Uncreated Word (Christ): "quod simpliciter et proprie significat prolatum verbum, ut sit verbum quiddam distinctum ab eo, qui dicit, sicut distinctio est inter dicentem et id, quid dicit" (WA. 42, 13:27–29). Luther's semantic analysis is very interesting. For God has a "(דבר)" in himself and the uttered word "(אמר)".
48 LW. 22, pp. 12–14; LW. 1, pp. 16–19, 21–22, etc.
49 LW. 22, p. 12.
50 Ibid.
51 Ibid., pp. 9–14. Pelikan in his *Luther the Expositor: Introduction to the Reformer's Exegetical Writings,* a companion volume to LW., (St. Louis:

Concordia Publishing House, 1959), discusses these texts in dramatic metaphors. He says Luther's portrayal of God is like a man who walks along the street, holding conversation with himself. All of a sudden he stops and shouts and everyone is startled to hear him speak. Yet what he shouts is what he had been saying to himself all along, but now he says it for others to hear (p. 52).

52 Pelikan, *Luther the Expositor,* p. 54.

53 LW. 1, p. 22. (Italics added) Also, see pp. 16ff, 21, 25–41; LW. 13, p. 92; LW. 14, pp. 123f.

54 Pelikan, *Luther the Expositor,* pp. 54–55.

55 Hence Luther writes: "God calls into existence things which do not exist (Rom. 4:17). He does not speak grammatical words; He speaks true and existent realities ..... Thus the sun, moon, heaven, earth, Peter, Paul, I, you, etc. – we are all words of God, in fact only one single syllable or letter by comparison with the entire creation" (LW. 1, p. 22).

56 See note 53 above. Also, Luther adds that because all things are made through the Word, they seem more to be truly born: "The creation of the world was for God a kind of begetting ..... a kind of birth which took place at the command of God" (LW. 13, p. 92). The metaphor of birth suggests that, as human birth does, one owes one's existence to parents. Human material or element becomes constitutive of one's being.

57 LW. 1, pp. 11–13, 21–22; LW. 37, pp. 57–58; WA. 24: 37, etc. God is not known outside the dynamics of the creative or redemptive word. Nor is there any other medium by which God deals with us other than the word.

58 LW. 14, pp. 123f. The German reads: "Sein reden odder sprechen ist so viel als schaffen" (WA. 31/1, 445:21f). We cannot agree with Luther's suggestion that "fiat" must mean an instantaneous creation. In reality, creation is a long and painful work, as it will become clear. The important thing is that it is the divine word (command) that has the power to create, not a magical word that creates "at the snap of a finger."

59 LW. 14, p. 124. The German text has single rather than plural nouns both with regard to God's and human word and command: "Wie Gene. 1: Gott sprach, und es geschah. Es ist nicht so ein faul, kranck, tod wort, wie der menschen wort und gebot ist" (WA. 31/1, 445:26ff). We prefer the German text here because it is the quality rather than the quantity of the command that is being compared and differentiated.

60 LW. 2, pp. 131–132; LW. 4, pp. 5, 120f, 136, 291, 355. This conviction led Luther to a startling declaration that: "even if the whole world were to combine forces, they could not bring about the conception of a single child in any woman's womb nor cause it to be born; that is wholly the work of God alone" (LW. 45, p. 333).

61 In order to emphasize the inseparability of finite existence form the creative word of God, which is creative, Luther writes: "Sein wort und heissen schaffet alles, das ir habt" (WA. 31/1, 446:22f). He adds: "..... hoc verbum tamdiu in creaturis est, quamdiu Deus loguitur: quando non loquitur, id est, cum vim verbi sui aufert, nullam vim habent. Terra

nihil producit, ignis non ardet, coelum non lucet, sicut et miracula quandoque prodiderunt" (WA. 24, 38f).

62 To these examples may be added the healing of the blind, the deaf, and the dumb through Jesus' command that they should see, hear and speak (Mt. 9:28f, 32–24; Mk. 7:32). Furthermore, Jesus restored a withered hand by commanding, or saying: "Stretch your hand" (Mt. 12:23; Mk. 3:5). A daughter of a Canaanite woman was healed when Jesus willed it so (Mt. 15:28). He raised a girl from the dead by commanding her to arise (Mk. 6:41; Lk. 8:52–56). People were amazed also when Jesus restored to life a boy of the widow by commanding: "Young man, I say to you, arise" (Lk. 7:14ff). A similar praise to God was given when Jesus raised Lazarus from the dead after many days in the grave (Jn. 11:34f). Some of these actions led many to believe in Him as the Messiah.

63 Cf. Luther's expressions such as: "Denn schaffen heisst gebieten" (WA. 12:328:16). "Sein reden odder sprechen ist so viel als schaffen ..... Sein word und heissen schaffet alles ....." (WA. 31/1, 445:21–22).

64 LW. 45, p. 327. Also, see notes 51, 53, 54 and 59 in this chapter.

65 Human creative responsibility for the earth and other creatures will be taken up later. For God involves them as co-agents of ongoing creativity.

66 LW. 2, p. 131ff; LW. 4.4., pp. 5, 68, 119, 355; *The Book of Concord,* p. 367.

67 LW. 1, pp. 53f.

68 Ibid., pp. 75–76.

69 LW. 37, pp. 57f.

70 Ibid., p. 58. This quotation expresses the creative activity of God through the power of the creative word *(logos),* which is the means of relationship between the Creator and the creatures. But, like the concept *fiat*, it needs to be qualified because God does not always act immediately or directly. This qualification will be made even more explicit in the following chapter in which the instruments that God employs are discussed.

Chapter eight

The empowering activity of the creative logos in an ongoing creativity through human agents

One major criticism that was levelled against theologies of Barth and Elert hinged around the contention that their notion of creation with which the divine command was correlated is highly static. Hence this static notion of creation fails to accommodate God's ongoing creative acts that are occurring all the time in all ages. To overcome this weakness, we argued that these theologians needed to have realized that creation (both in its originating and sustaining aspects) is an ongoing process; for the world which is in the making is open to new and future creations, or breakthroughs, as it moves through all historical developments to its completion in the *eschaton.*

Put differently, theologians need to be aware that all structures (which are attempts to order the world) are but products of historical developments and reflect stages of these creative processes in the history of humankind; for none of them is identical with a past creation "in the beginning" which, as such, can be deducible from the Genesis story of creation. More importantly, it is compellingly necessary to appreciate not only that creation is an ongoing, continuous and open process on its way towards a *telos,* but also that God's creative activity is going on right now and is being carried out through human agents, without whose contribution the world might not become what the Creator wants it to be.

This appreciation enables us to maintain continuities between divine and human creative activities in this ongoing, unfinished creation of the world because history, or the creation of the world (not to be confused with heaven and earth), is not the sole monopoly of a jealous God but is also the creation of human work; for humans are co-agents, co-workers and co-creators with, in the presence of and through the help of God. The continuity between the divine and human creativity cannot be maintained when creation is frozen into some distant past and the sustaining work of God is not itself understood as creative activity from the point of view of the present. Indeed, a similar charge could have been made against our exposition, had we concluded this study with the preceding section. For it was argued there that the divine command is itself a creative act when it is uttered, and that the command must be understood as the divine power, that is, that distinctive quality in the being of God with the power both to create *ex nihilo* and to empower creatures in the world to produce what they are commanded by their Creator. (For example, the earth is commanded to bring forth fruits, vegetables and other necessities of life.)

The portrayal of God as the One for whom to command is to create may have given an impression that the Creator is the sole agent and creative source of history and the world, because little was said concerning God's involvement of the human agency in the dynamics of a slow but continuing creative process. This impression must now be corrected. For, as we have argued in the critique, it is an error to believe that God causes and is responsible for everything that happens in the world. Such a God would be demonic and the source of distortions and sufferings which humans experience in the world. Rather, God employs agents who are free in the creative use of their power, and some of the destructive aberrations are directly caused by them. Indeed, as we shall see, much more than God's instantaneous creativity is involved. God does involve finite creatures in the creation, nourishing and protection of new life, most particularly in the union between man and woman. And because God does not create everything immediately or at the "snap of a finger," creation is not a once-and-for-all "event" but a long and painful process until it reaches its completion in the *eschaton.*

This broad involvement of human agents, who very often misuse the God-given power to resist and frustrate the creative divine will, shall now be discussed in some detail, as we take up the third aspect of the meaning of the divine command.

As it was pointed out above, this command signifies a result of God's creative activity through the uttered command in and with us, an activity that grants human beings creative capability by transforming, engaging and involving them in the dynamics of divine creativity as instruments, vehicles, agents or channels of the creative goodness and love of God in relation to other creatures.[1] A further exposition of this aspect of the meaning of the command shall now be made with specific reference to human and cultural creative undertakings in society in which the human victory over, and transformation of, nature is clearly visible – as human beings exercise their entrusted creative power in their role of agents, co-creators, co-workers, bearers and makers of history with and under the guidance of the creative God.

8.1 GOD'S FAITH IN HUMAN BEINGS AS INSTRUMENTS OF CREATIVITY

It has been stated more than once that God's originating creative activity through the Word (uttered command, fiat) continues in the present through the sustaining and directing creativities. Though heaven and earth were created *ex nihilo* through the power of the divine speaking, it does not follow that an inception of history "in the beginning" was *the whole* of history. Rather, the actual making of the world, which God continued to develop in the subsequent long historical process, means that even at the beginning there was, there is, and shall still be *the history* yet to be made – at the end of which the world will be complete (at the coming of the new world) and God's purposes for creation will have been realized.

In this long, tortuous and often painful unfolding of history, as the biblical God produces the world and what is in it, it has become clear that another historical creature, the human being, does play a significant role in the production of human history, in a manner that carries divine history further.[2] Human history is not a second history alongside God's but falls within the larger context of cosmic history which God's ongoing creativity brings about. Human activity which is creative, however, continues alongside God's creativity and has its meaning in the mutual production of the world within the over-all sustaining creativity of God that surrounds, supports, modifies, permits and limits the human acting.

The fact that human beings stand before God as free and creative agents of the ongoing creation of the history of the world points to the unique position they occupy in contradistinction to other creatures. This uniqueness lies in the ability of humans to create culture which, though often rich and beautiful, is also marred by sin and even the danger that someday human beings may actually destroy life, civilization and the world — something which has become frighteningly clear with the creation of atomic weapons.

That human beings do possess enormous creative power second only to God, and that they alone can do what no lower creatures can do, is not debatable. However, it is not agreed just how, or why, humans are unique, and how they came not only to possess the power to be co-creators of history but also to pose a threat of self-destruction. Theories have been advanced by theologians and philosophers to account for why human beings alone are makers of history and transformers of their natural environment, social structures and, therefore, themselves. A detailed discussion of these theories is beyond the scope of this work. However, we shall mention briefly those that throw some light on the positions that shall be taken that form the context of our argument.

Theological theories have tried to explain the uniqueness of man's contribution in the ongoing creativity in the light of the concept of *imago Dei.* It is argued that human beings are unique creators by virtue of their being created in the image of God, and by virtue of their capability to rise above the other animals over which they have dominion; for history is not only a conquest of the natural in the historical process but also the attainment of full human destiny as men and women transform rather than accommodate themselves to their social conditions. But in what this image of God consists has been a matter of debate. The traditional view argued that humans possess this image of God or uniqueness among creatures because they are endowed with reason, the power of will, religiosity or a supposed spark of immortality and other related intelligence which enable them to transform the animal state and realize their purpose in history.[3] In the meantime, however, it has become clear that to define *imago Dei* in terms of some "divine spark" inherent in human nature is misleading.

One of the theologians who has rejected the traditional definition of *imago Dei* is Brunner who rejects it because to define man as some substance of the divine "spark" deifies him.[4] He also rejects any suggestion that this likeness to God be understood as creative freedom or a gift that enables human beings to be creators of civilizations and culture. For him, human beings are appointed to this unique position of being *Homo faber* and creators of history because they already have *imago Dei.*[5] Creation of history and civilization do not make humans into the image of God but their creativity presupposes *imago Dei* which must precede cultural and historical achievements.[6] That is, only when man in anchored in a truly human relation to God and realizes his destiny of being-in-the-love and eternal life of God does human participation in the creation of civilization and history cease to be an end in itself. The priority of the *imago Dei,* according to Brunner, is meant to counteract those germs of inhumanity and destructive intoxication that are sown when culture is absolutized into a god rather than understood as a means to actualize a human victory over the forces of the natural environment.[7]

Brunner's understanding of *imago Dei* as primarily relational responsibility to the God of love is insightful. Equally correct in his view that human beings are unique by virtue of divine appointment rather than because of some divine spark or quality in them. But just how this uniqueness relates to the human agency in the creative process remains unclear because he rules out creative freedom as having anything to do with the true meaning of *imago Dei.*[8] He also rules out human creative transcendence over the brute status of nature as signifying uniqueness or *imago Dei.* Transformations of nature imply instead that *imago Dei* already exists. But when *imago Dei* is disconnected from creative undertakings in civilization, and when the uniqueness of the human does not lie in his unique transformation of nature, one wonders whether Brunner's formulations are not abstractions. Also, it remains unclear, apart from creative participation, just how unique human beings are if this does not mean that they are so by virtue of being divine instruments in the creative process. Moreover, it remains unclear how these powers came to exist if the *imago Dei* does not, in a sense, imply divine empowerment of humans to be co-creators.

If humans are not empowered by God, are then these powers inherent in their nature as humans? If these powers are not bestowed in this relational context of divine creativity, is it not reasonable to assume that human creative acts occur outside the sphere of God and are, therefore, not dependent upon God's creative power? But if humans create independently from the context of God's creativity, this destroys the assurance that God is actively creating now in the present revolutionary and technological age in concert with and through the human actions, in their role as co-creator, to produce history and the world; for if human beings are not creators secondarily within the context of God's creativity then surely the existence of life and creative power is now implied to exist outside the overall context of the Creator's activity because they appear to be independent of the divine self.

Fortunately, other theologians argue that *imago Dei* should be understood as referring to the human ability to create and to further the history God is producing. Franklin Sherman, for instance, succinctly observes that

> ..... the meaning of the image and likeness — or at least one meaning of it — is that man shall be *like God in his creativity.* Be creative as your Father in heaven is creative! ..... could be seen as a form of *imitatio dei* ..... Every man is called to be creative.[9]

He further adds that he speaks of the human creative use of freedom not *in loco justificationis* but *in loco vocationis* where we should use our freedom to mold raw materials in our lives and environment for our authentic and meaningful existence.[10] In acting creatively in our vocation, Sherman argues, we shall be imitatingly learning God's own activity as a cosmic creative artist. An evaluation of his position will be made later.

A much more rigorous interpretation of *imago Dei* in the light of the human creative agency in the production of the world and history is supplied by Gordon Kaufman. He, like Brunner, rejects traditional meanings of *imago Dei,* for they imply that human beings possess powers that lift them above the realities of finite existence. Rather, contends Kaufman over against Brunner, the uniqueness of human beings lies in their historicalness, their historicity.[11] This historicity is what should be understood by *imago Dei,* and this means that humans are thoroughly historical but also respond to God creatively and freely.[12]

The views of Sherman and Kaufman on the meaning of *imago Dei* are persuasive and illuminating. Kaufman's position is the one we agree with because it stresses the totality of human immersion in historicity in all of his/her parts; a person is a being-in-process of an ongoing production of the world. Kaufman does not split up the human being into two parts, as Brunner does. Still, there are problems with these views. Both Sherman and Kaufman agree that *imago Dei* is a reflection (imitation) of the divine being, who is immensely creative, and that it does not refer to a human attribute. But they fail to state whether this human possibility of imitation implies that there is a latent (inherent) power in humans to create; that is, does an ability to imitate imply that we can or are capable of creating? If these creative powers are not inherent — seeing that Kaufman's thesis is that our historicity does not refer to an element that has been added to an otherwise animal nature because historicity is the form of human existence itself — then should we assume that humans became historical by accident because nothing was added to their nature? If nothing is added to human beings specifically to make them sharply distinguishable from other animals that are also finite then why is it that humans, and they only, are participants in the dynamics of the creative activity? Why is it that only humans have these creative powers, though, like all finite creatures, they were created in an ongoing historical process? Did human beings become historical by their own self-appointment, or were they appointed, empowered, to be co-creators only by God?

Sherman does not say whether our imitative creativity is part of the ongoing divine production of the world in whose dynamics we are thus involved. Kaufman clearly holds that we are co-creators of God's world and history, but he, too, tells us little about how human beings, and they only, came to acquire such enormously creative powers.[13] It seems something is missing in the positions of these theologians. They talk about human creativity without also saying that, as humans are absolutely dependent upon their Creator for life and continued existence, so their creative ability is not independent from the context of God's creative energy or power. That is, they create because God's creative power surrounds them, and is made available to them; for they continue to create only because God has not withdrawn this creative power.

It is when this human dependence upon God's creative power is maintained that human beings can further God's creation. On their own merits, they cannot produce God's world, at least not the coming new world. But as repositories of the creative power they can, as divine instruments, contribute towards the realization of the coming Kingdom.

Unlike Marxists and other existential humanists who tell us that humans are transformers of history and the world by sheer reason of being masters of their destiny, Sherman's and Kaufman's positions tell us little about why and how humans, and they only among finite creatures, became continuing vehicles of the divine production of history. Therefore, their positions fail us, just as those of the humanists do, when they do not go further to establish the reasons why we became co-creators despite the fact that we, like all finite reality, are absolutely dependent upon God. This is what we intend to avoid by suggesting here two important theological reasons for this creative role of humans.

Brunner's assertion that we become partners in the mutual production of the world with God by divine appointment is correct. For we are co-opted into this role of being co-creators and bearers of history not because we somehow accidentally deserve this, merely because we developed a language or because of some latent powers in us that, in time, burst forth with creative powers, powers that are not derivative from the divine creative power itself. Rather, the gracious God has reasons known only to the divine self why human beings were elevated to such a unique position of being fellow workmen with their Creator.

The main theological reason, which is also our first *thesis,* is this: *God has appointed us to this unique position because of the faith our Creator has in us.* And the second important reason is this: Because God has faith in human beings, the divine self has been continually willing to empower them with creative ability without which no finite creature can, on its own, produce the world. For we have no inherent power to make the world (at least the coming new world which is being awaited with hope) and history into what God wants them to be, just as we have no inherent powers to inspire ourselves to become prophets, and just as no water has any power of its own to bring about a re-birth without the divine word in baptism, nor any bread the power to become the Lord's supper.

What we have proposed here is quite a lot and some of it needs unpacking. For one thing, it is very uncommon for theologians to talk about *the faith* God the Creator has in human beings, the faith that has actually been demonstrated when humans were involved in the dynamics of divine creative acts by being made co-agents in the making of the world and history. Most common among theologians is talk about the human fath in God by which alone we are justified. Or they talk about the faithfulness or constancy of God in His promise or in the covenant which is made with us despite our unfaithfulness as partners of the covenant.

For a theologian who has been and is being nurtured in the Paul-Augustine-Luther line of tradition – a tradition which frequently makes redemption the central theme by stressing the graciousness of an all powerful God in the midst of human helplessness in sin – to talk about the faith God has in human beings, as the above argument and subtitle of this chapter suggest, is to introduce a novel language[14] that requires clarification because it may be misinterpreted. This misunderstanding may arise because this tradition, as Brueggemann succinctly states, has not trusted human beings. Rather it had

> ..... spoken primarily of fallen man, one who has had all his powers and abilities crippled so that he is unable to act in his humanness. This theology affirms that man is unable to choose. Even if he tries to choose ..... he will without fail choose death rather than life. Indeed, he has no real option.[15]

At the risk of being misunderstood by this tradition, it must be asserted that Brueggemann is correct in his contention that human beings are trusted; for God has faith in them, a faith that has led the Creator to co-opt them in the ongoing dynamics of divine creativity. Indeed, human beings have been elevated to this unique position of being bearers and makers of history because they are valued beings in the eyes of God, who sees nothing wrong in the involvement of humans in the creative process — despite the repeated errors and mistakes they continually make. The only thing remaining is that human beings should take themselves as seriously as God does,[16] so that they may become boldly creative in this co-operative production of the world with their God. The concept of faith is here used in the sense of a basic trust that God has shown in human beings by entrusting to them a mature and meaningful role in the making of history.[17]

What immediately surprises us, when we read about the originating and sustaining creativity at the inception of history in which the world is continually being made, is that at this very dawn of history, God did demonstrate an indescribable faith (graciousness, if you will) in human beings by a willingness "to share His power with man and to grant him power,"[18] enabling and empowering human beings to create the world and history with their Creator. This act of granting power and the ability to create -- with the awesome and disastrous consequences that are involved in the granting of such creative ability to finite and imperfect creatures — does demonstrate, in our view, the considerable faith God has in human beings, a faith that risked imperfections and distortions rather than deny humans the ability to create freely.

God's faith in humans, as capable and responsible agents in the on-going creativity of history yet to be made, is even more startling when it is kept in mind that, by involving human agents at this dawn of history, potential hazards were multiplied by the fact that the production of this history and the world was not a fore-ordained or mapped out course where everything was ordered to occur in a particular and predictable way "before the foundation of the world." Indeed, as Tillich rightly observes, the actual making of history which is partly a human production is not, and should not be understood as, "nothing more than the execution of a ..... suprahistorical plan," or a replay of predetermined history in which human beings are not free agents who play meaningful roles but are "cogs in a machine."[19] In an open future of ongoing creativity, it required extraordinary faith on the part of God to "share power" (to borrow Luther's expression) which transforms human beings into agents of divine creativity.

The biblical narrative portrays this faith God has in us, and the divine empowerment of human beings that goes together with our appointment to the role of being instruments of continuous creativity, in a very moving and dramatic narrative. First, it makes it abundantly clear that human cooperation, contribution, and co-creativity is not something that rivals God's creativity, nor are the two creativities to be equated. God creates *ex nihilo* while human beings are entrusted with the creative power to transform their social surroundings and environment as well as shaping and naming what is given as secondary and existential creators in this mutual production of the world.[20] Secondly, the originating and sustaining creative power of the uttered Word (fiat) remains, however, the relational context which energizes, empowers, enables and transforms human actions by giving humans the capacity to create as they place themselves within its overall and embracing dynamic creativity. This fiat of the Creator continues to involve, engage, condition and modify human actions as the production of history and the world is being carried out.[21]

The creative production of the world is a historical victory yet to be won because the world is in the making, but as we have already indicated, the power to create has already been demonstrated by achievements that are being made. The biblical narration of the actualization of the creative empowerment of human beings by God is highly impressive. It states that, within the overall context of God's faith in us, and the relational context of the creative power of the Word which gives human beings the capacity to create, the Creator has entrusted Adam with the power to name the other finite creatures. Indeed, that this naming actually took place and continues to take place is a testimony that the creative empowerment has been efficacious.[22]

Cox, in an exuberant tone, describes the creative ability of human beings as subjects who create when he writes:

> It is both fascinating and signifcant that God did not name the creatures himself ..... God does not give names to the objects of the physical universe, to the things that we find around us. It is to man that God has assigned this responsibility. So God brought the giraffe, the pterodactyl, and the microorganism to Adam, for he wanted to see what man would name them. The Bible says that "whatever the man called every living creature, that was its name." God did not have any secret names he was getting ready to give these animals, which he put in the mind of man. He gave man the responsibility. It continues to be our responsibility to give meaning and significance to the things that we find in our universe.[23]

Indeed, the fact that human beings could name all things in the world, without God's paternal intervention or suggestion of what to call them, is the clearest indication that God's empowerment has successfully transformed a finite creature into a creative subject, and that we are free agents and trusted creatures to whom the Creator could entrust so much. As long as we remain in the relational context of divine creativity, we are capable of being co-creators, co-agents and co-producers of history in the freest and most responsible manner possible with God. The success story of the human creative ability to produce the world by virtue of God's trustful empowerment through the creative command-in-action began at the inception of history and still continues today.

The empowering and enabling creativity of the command-in-action which transformed human beings into creators was not limited to the naming of all other finite creatures (Gen. 2:19–20). Human beings were also exalted to this unique position when they were commanded (empowered and invited) to "be fruitful and multiply," to "fill the earth and subdue it," to have "dominion ..... over every living thing that moves upon the earth" (Gen. 1:28). Furthermore, human beings were given fruits and meat for food and use (Gen. 1:29f; 2:9, 16). More importantly, they were commanded to till the garden and look after it (Gen. 2:15). The same mandate was repeated to Noah after the deluge (Gen. 9:1–3, 7, 19ff).

Human beings have been trying to actualize this empowering and enabling creative command through their history by transforming their environment and by creating civilizations and their world, culture and history. Indeed, as Cox points out, neither the finding nor the naming of the things in the universe is yet complete, because "nowadays we find a lot more of them than our forefathers did," and therefore "this naming is a much larger task, perhaps, than our forefathers had, but it is the same task."[24] The creative ability to find and name, which has been increased by modern revolutionary and technological knowhow, has not only enabled human beings to discover laws of nature and varieties of mineral resources and foods but also to discover and explore an ever-expanding universe, planets with a whole range of microcosmic and macrocosmic realities yet to be named.[25] The creative victory over the tyranny of nature occurs because the empowerment of human beings, through the creative command (word), to dominate and use the created order is gradually being realized or actualized as humans become involved in the dynamics of the ongoing production of history.

In addition to discoveries and naming, human beings have been exercising their entrusted lordship and ability to create by transforming the natural order, by creating ever-emerging structures, by ordering their world and by a variety of social relationships in society and culture. To the degree that human beings have been involved in creative works in the ongoing creativity, they have been able to prosper on earth, to develop civilizations, traditions, all kinds of socio-economic, legal and political institutions, laws and customs, judicial and governmental administrations, all of which seek to establish and enhance healthy human relationships in a community or society, or between nations.[26] And these creative acts that continue creation in the present as the world is being made have been achieved by the labour and deliberate transformative creativity of human beings in their attempt to till and care for the earth and to structure and order the social environment, thereby creating themselves (to use Kaufman's expression).

Also, creative acts were achieved because God stood behind them, making cultural and historical creativity meaningful and enriching productions through which human agents find their individual and communal self-fulfillment.[27] Consequently, by placing themselves within the overall context of God's cosmic activity, not only do human beings fulfill their task of solving problems of peace, justice and of transforming social structures for the well-being of others, but they also affirm themselves, their mature humanhood and dignity as unique beings in whom God has put faith. And because creation must continue through the human agency, the question is: How faithful have human beings been toward that faith of God upon which rests their share in the dynamics of divine creative power?

8.2 RESPONSIBLE CREATIVITY OF HUMAN BEINGS AS TRUSTEES OF GOD

If, as we have argued, human beings are co-creators in the production of history by virtue of divine appointment, by virtue of God's faith in them shown in the Creator's willingness to share the capacity to create and transform the world; and if they create, in the continuous unfolding of history, because they have been made repositories of the divine creative command (fiat, word); then one cannot escape the feeling that human actions are not fortuitous and accidental nor done for their own sake but, rather, that they have some ethical or moral and vocational implications.[28] Indeed, they carry with them a moral responsibility before the Creator who has appointed, empowered and enabled finite human beings to become co-workers in the production of the world. That is, God's elevation and transformation of humans into the status of being creative agents means that they are forever to be accountable to their Creator for what they do.

Consequently, neither can their acts be regarded as neutral before God nor can the Creator afford to remain indifferent toward their activities. For their activities can become irresponsible and obstruct God's creative purposes. Or they can promote and further God's continuing creation in what they do. There is no third alternative. This means, moreover, that human actions cannot be regarded as neutral either in relation to the natural habitat (garden), which has to be both tilled, used and cared for, or in relation to other finite creatures (human beings included) to whom these actions must prove to be a blessing. Not only do we stand before them (natural and social environment) as representatives of God through, in, with and under whose activities the Creator is understood to be creatively present in the ongoing creation, but also we remain forever accountable to the One who has ennobled, called and transformed us by the divine power, so that we, though finite like all other creatures, could still be co-creators of the world and humanity.

Our accountability follows from the fact that the Creator, by granting us creative ability in continuing creation, has goals and purposes which our willing obedience and active participation in the dynamics of divine creativity should achieve or serve. These purposes include the responsible and meaningful creative caring of the natural order, the responsible ordering and structuring of society and willing cooperation in the production of the world with our Creator as divinely delegated representatives. The fulfillment of these tasks, goals or purposes in our participatory involvement in the creative dynamics of God constitutes our vocation, mission or service as the trustees and stewards of the Creator[29] who has enlisted human service.

The recognition that our lordship over the natural and social environment is an entrusted, deputized and representational one can, as we have already contended, be understood only as carrying moral overtones, because we must justify our actions before God who has thus made us creative agents in the world. In order to create responsibly before our Creator, it then becomes necessary to realize that, in our actions, we must embody God's own way of acting in relation to the finite reality which was caused to be through divine creative commanding (speaking). This embodiment of the Creator's relationship to the created reality, which occurs as we act as trustees and stewards in God's place, brings with it thrilling challenges but also an awareness that we cannot do what we please with the created order over which we exercise entrusted lordship. While we may thankfully till, work and husband the earth, we are not free to idolize it because it is a finite creation. Indeed, it becomes irresponsible relationship to attribute divinity to the fields and culture which are but centres of human creative responsibility.[30]

The natural and social environment are, to be sure, good gifts to us from God: They provide nourishment for life, security or home for our bodies. But to see them as ends in themselves – ends that take the place of their Creator so that they become objects of worship[31] – is to forget that our relationship with them must embody God's way of acting, which rules out any need to worship finite creatures.

Therefore, it is certainly to be regretted that human beings have not always acted responsibly toward the finite order. Cox rightly contends that "man" has not always fulfilled his assignment or lived up to the "full stature of his manhood" because he "has abdicated his crucial place" in the world by refusing to become responsibly creative as a trustee and representative of God. He laments the fact that, instead of becoming a responsible co-creator through joyful participation in the dynamics of creativity and by exercising the divinely appointed lordship over the finite order, man "sells out" and permits one "of the animals to tell him what to do. He surrenders his position of privilege and responsibility,"[32] unlike Jesus Christ who takes up full responsibility and exercises the full prerogatives of his manhood, or assigned power.[33]

When human creative responsibility is here understood in terms of the divinely entrusted stewardship, and in terms of the representational role that must be played as humans embody God's own acting in relation to the finite creatures, Cox's suggestion that the abdication of the vocation and lordship given to trustees of God is sin makes sense.[34] We cannot agree more because it is clear that such an abdication violates the embodiment of God's own way of acting and is also a refusal to discharge the entrusted lordship.

Furthermore, the fact that we exercise an entrusted responsibility before God as deputies, stewards, trustees and messengers in the dynamics of ongoing creativity means that our freedom to rule over creation is highly qualified by the need to account for our actions before the Creator. That is, we cannot claim that what we do with the finite order is unlimited, uncontrolled and, therefore, absolute. Rather, as we till and exercise lordship over the earth, our rule must be accompanied by a creative and resonsible relation to the environment in which we live, a relation that is charged with moral concern and care for the earth. For the human relationship to the earth is also one of mutual caring and is not neutral. The earth provides food for this life. Because we depend on it for survival, any irresponsible use of the earth can result only in the abuse of humanity itself.[35]

For this reason, there cannot be unlimited industrial expansion, unfettered development — no matter how good in the short run — without the environment and the health of humanity itself being affected because, as Mbiti rightly points out, "the well-being of man is intimately connected with the well-being of the total creation. If man abuses nature or the environment, nature also will abuse man."[36] It is unfortunate that Mbiti's formulation of the issue gives the impression that nature is herself the subject which can, in fact, abuse human beings. Nonetheless, his point — that human abuse of the environment in turn affects the well-being of human beings — has been driven home by such health-related problems as pollution of air and water resources by chemicals, industry or oil-tankers. It has become clear that uncontrolled growth of industry, over-population, depletion of natural resources and mass-killing of certain animal species cannot be allowed to continue without causing imbalances in the natural order that will ultimately threaten the health and well-being of human agents as well.[37]

What has been said about creative responsibility toward our natural environment, a responsibility which comes along with our trusteeship, also applies in our relationship to our social sphere. There, too, we are expected to embody God's own way of acting in relation to others in the communities in which we live. And our vocation there, as we have already stated, consists in a creative and responsible ordering of social relationships for the well-being of our fellows and for meaningful human existence. It is our thesis that human involvement in the dynamics of creativity or the transformation of the natural order has no other end or purpose than that of translating all actions into services and good works for the benefit of other human beings, as an embodiment of God's own way of relating to human beings. For it is as we till the earth, gather food, produce culture and transform the environment in order to nourish and sustain life that possibilities arise for the building of a just, righteous and caring society in which life may yet become fully human in this world which is in the making.

Indeed, as Gutierrez succinctly points out, "to dominate the earth as Genesis prescribed, to continue creation, is worth nothing if it is not done for the good of man."[38] Therefore, to work and labour and to transform the natural environment are not ends in themselves but means both to fulfill our humanhood (which is the same thing as the dutiful discharge of our creative responsibility to which we are appointed as co-agents of the creative activity) in the mutual production of history and the world with God and to build healthy human community by placing ourselves at the service of other people so as to nourish life.[39] For human existence is a vocational, purposive and responsible existence, which is fully charged with mission. To be a true human agent, who acts as an entrusted steward and trustee of God, carries with it personal, social, political, judicial, economic, fraternal and many other moral and cultural initiatives and responsibilities.[40]

However, in order for this vocation or mission to be carried out in social and interpersonal relationships, it is necessary that those who act representatively in God's stead should become consciously aware that creation is not a "once for all event" which was done and completed "in the beginning" but that it continues even now. Indeed, there is an outstanding history, which is yet to be made by human beings in concert with and under God's creative and incessantly active and activating power that works in all and moves all. The awareness that the world is still being made should result in a realization that all socio-political, legal and economic orderings of personal and interpersonal relationships are relative, historical and culturally conditioned structures, and that none of them is "pre-ordained." For there is as yet no absolute and final stage in the unfolding of history, no unchanging God-given *status quo* to which human beings must accommodate themselves, that should be idolized as such. Indeed, there are no "eternal" structures and "orders of creation" because all the existing conditions have emerged through temporal development. As the productions of human beings in history, they must be built up but also pulled down when the need arises, in order that better structures (though never perfect or final ones) may be constructed for better service toward humanity, and in order that God's love, goodness, justice and righteousness may yet be radiated and channelled to other finite creatures.

All this can happen when, in our obedient and joyful participation in the creative dynamics of God, we realize the need to move beyond a point of merely protecting the *status quo* and innocent lives in order to do what is positively good, just, right, caring, loving and life-nourishing to our fellow humans. In doing this, we shall be fulfilling our *iustitia civilis* (civic righteousness), which our appointment and empowerment to become co-creators with God requires and involves.[41]

However, the constant recurrence of injustice and oppression, wars and fratricides, divisions and confrontations, greed and exploitation, uncaring and loveless interactions, that are experienced in all phases of human history make us wonder whether human beings have been any more responsible in their vocations within the social sphere than in their interactions with their natural environment. Despite great achievements in the transformation of their environment, human beings have *not fully* been able to translate it into blessings to others. Indeed, a naive optimism here is ruled out by the reality of suffering and destruction among human beings. Sin is still a problem,[42] a problem that is not on the decline but increases with cultural achievements and with the increasing power of human beings to destroy themselves. History shows us that human beings have failed as trustees of God because they have refused, and do refuse, to take themselves seriously, to create responsibly and to serve others willingly in those vocations that require them to embody God's love and creative goodness.[43]

We have to be really grateful to God that, up to the present, the world and humanity have not been totally destroyed through human irresponsibility before reaching their completion in the *eschaton.* This is because God has not become totally dependent on the human willingness to create history. Indeed, despite the enlistment of human beings as agents in the production of the world, God has not left the world to human whim and control.[44] God is still actively creative, and it is for this reason that culture and the world are not wholly evil but are interspersed with beauty and goodness, despite the taint of sin in all human productions. Because God is not totally dependent upon human goodness in order to show goodness and love to finite creatures, it must be argued that God uses even those who may not be willing to serve their neighbours and to acknowledge any divine overlordship.[45]

As Luther rightly observes, God cannot leave his instruments idle because of sin. Instead, the Creator employs them in such a way that divine goodness always comes through to his children.[46] Wingren agrees with Luther and insightfully comments that, because the creative power in whose dynamics human beings participate is God's power rather than a quality inherent in human nature, the very fact that rogues and sinners can do some useful work that nourishes life means that God's creative command is in action.[47]

He points to the fact that this power is not withdrawn when a child is born out of wedlock because of misuse of human instrumentality to bring forth new lives. He also points to doctors who may complain about sacrificing leisure to save life and contends that, here again, we see God's goodness which is not dependent on human goodness. Even where human beings act out of their egoistical interest, this does not prevent God's goodness from reaching us. Doctors may reap huge profits while they also help to heal and restore health. A farmer or industry may act out of sheer greed for profit, yet God uses them to enrich us. To sum up: God uses human beings in spite of themselves to continue the work of creation and to provide for services in the production of history and the world.[48]

However, if it is true that God does not fully depend on the whim of the human agency and, therefore, can still create and produce the world by using irresponsible human beings despite themselves and their sin, then the question becomes: Why must human beings be expected willingly to become involved in the mutual production of the world within God's embracing creative dynamics? The answer can be no other than that human beings were appointed to be repositories of the divine creative power when they were empowered to create responsibly with God as trustees and stewards in the Creator's plan. This responsibility should and ought not be avoided or neglected because God intends to use us as divine masks or media through, in and under which He may bestow all blessings to our fellow creatures and thereby enrich them.

By placing ourselves at the service of our fellows, we not only embody God's own way of acting toward finite creation but also fulfill a necessary purpose of our existence, namely, one of providing a cover the Creator can wear when divine works are done. As Luther pointed out long ago, God "creates and preserves us ..... that he might work in us and we might co-operate with him," to create and preserve other lives, to show mercy to the poor, to comfort the afflicted, and to preach.[49] Indeed, we must work and let the divine goodness and love go to others because it was for the purpose of acting and embodying God's own way of doing things that the Creator endowed us with creative ability so "that he might conceal his work under this guise"[50] or human work. It is as we cooperate and place ourselves within the cosmic context of God's creativity that we are able to do good and become a blessing to our fellows.

By doing all these things, we attain social righteousness *coram hominibus,* a social righteousness that should not, however, be confused with the righteousness of faith *coram Deo.* (The latter is freely given, administered through the gospel for the purpose of the granting of "eternal life," while the former, *civilis iustitia,* is human work, one in which God actively engages us as divine vehicles so that the Creator's love and goodness may pass from one person to another.) This social righteousness must be attained because it is a required content of our obedience or willing participation in the dynamics of divine creative activity, an obedience which, according to Luther, makes us "good and righteous in the eyes of the world."[51] This social righteousness is also said to be required because God therein is served "by administering this temporal righteousness."[52]

This righteousness is no less a holy work than spiritual righteousness – seeing that through our good and responsible creative use of stewardship God distributes "temporal blessings" to other human beings. And because this righteousness is attained when God works under the cover of a human mask in concert with the human agent, Luther suggests that it is the Creator's righteousness; for when God's own way of acting is embodied and radiated through us, God's honour is at stake, though we also get rewarded by maintaining our virtue, integrity, honesty and clean conscience before our fellows in acting justly and in proving our love to all.[53] And to underscore the fact that behind the human mask God is actively at work, because when we let our love go out to others it is as though this human acting is of God,[54] Luther adds that "God himself is the founder, lord, master, protector, and rewarder of both kinds of righteousness ..... each is a divine thing entirely."[55]

Consequently, because the attainment of *iustitia civilis* is possible through human work, culture and creative transformation of the environment, and because God is involved in our work through and through, empowering and enabling us to attain this social righteousness, there is no reason why we cannot discharge our appointed task as divine trustees faithfully and let our creative responsibility truly be affirmed by allowing God's power in us to burst forth with goodness, love and beneficial deeds to our fellows. Only in doing so will we be cooperating with God in the production of the world and taking God's faith in us as well as ourselves as seriously as God takes our trusteeship; for we can achieve penultimate good.

Finally, because it is possible, if we take our creative responsibility seriously, to become righteous and good *coram hominibus,* and therefore *in loco vocationis,* human dignity, uniqueness or elevation to the status of being co-creators or God's fellow workmen in the production of history has been defined in terms of human labour and work, namely, creative responsibility. Over against Brunner, who argues that human quality does not consist in the mastery of nature or the production of civilizations, it must be argued and asserted that the concretely human characteristic which sharply marks human dignity and nobility from all other creatures lies in nothing other than the responsible and creative use of human hands and labour by means of which this truly human element is fulfilled and mediated to other human beings, to oneself and to God.[56] Only in creation, in the transformation of the environment by humanizing it, do human beings realize themselves, their vocation and purpose for which they were created and appointed by God as trustees.[57]

Consequently, what constitutes human obedience to the divine command assumes a positive meaning. The utterance of the command (fiat, creative word) which is itself creative power is not an issuing of some authoritarian demand – alien to human dignity and nature – that aims at frightening, humiliating and suffocating human energies (this happens when the content of obedience is specified with reference to servile obedience). Rather, as we have tried to demonstrate, God's utterance of the command aims at involving, urging and realizing our creative energies so that we may become humanly responsible in our reciprocal relation to our fellows and the natural environment as God acts through us, and so that we may fulfill our humanity and thus our vocation as we become willingly and joyously involved in the creative dynamics in which God with and through us, as trustees, produces a world still in the making.

Notes

1 See note 39 in Chapter Seven. There we discuss Luther's translation of the Hebrew noun *hesed* (חסד) by "mercy" which, he goes on to suggest, should be understood as signifying "divine goodness in action." That is, the noun "mercy" does not here refer to an attribute or quality of God, but rather refers to the result of this mercy in us – as that active power which transforms in order to make us channels of divine goodness and love to others. By the same logic, it was suggested there that the creative command in this third sense of the Hebrew noun refers to a result of the creative power of the command in action as it transforms humans into creative vehicles of divine creative works. The command results in a certain creative responsiveness in us to our surroundings; it is, therefore, that inspiring, incessantly restive and creative urge which stirs but also enables human creativity by empowering them. In this way, the command as a result in us involves and makes us participants in the dynamics of creativity. And this creative urge is as old as the human phenomenon itself; for humanity has always been trying to transform and create the world, from the stone-age hunters to the present.

2 Kaufman, *Systematic Theology,* p. 329; Jose M. Bonino, *Doing Theology in a Revolutionary Situation* (Philadelphia: Fortress Press, 1975), p. 134. Henceforth cited as *Doing Theology in a Revolutionary Situation.*

3 For an elaborate treatment of traditional views and their shortcomings, see G.D. Kaufman, *Systematic Theology,* p. 329; Emil Brunner, *The Christian Doctrine of Creation and Redemption,* Vol. II (Philadelphia: The Westminster Press, 1952), pp. 59f. Henceforth cited as *Creation and Redemption.*

4 Brunner, *Creation and Redemption,* Vol. II, p. 60.

5 Ibid., pp. 67–68. Brunner understands *imago Dei* rightly not as a self-subsistent thing but rather as expressing that fundamental quality which makes man truly human, a quality that is neither a production of culture nor can it be lost through sin or fall. This image is fixed at creation and consists of a structurally relational form, namely, that man is created to be a responsible and answering creature to the Creator whereas other animals merely react. Responding to God is unlike re-action because it consists of relational responsibility to God's claims over us, answerability to the claims of the Word which in man finds its true reflex which can answer with free speaking. This human answerability before God is never lost (through sin or fall) in its formal sense even though materially it may not be actualized, except in the church through Christ who restores our true *imago Dei.* The *imago Dei* structurally (formally) remains simply because humans alone stand before God to whom they must give an answer, and they alone can sin before God because they must give this answer. The *imago Dei* is realized when man chooses rightly, when he believes and becomes a truly responsible human who realizes his destiny of being-in-the-love of God. When this material element of *imago Dei* is not realized, when man chooses unbelief, inhumanity or existence under the law or abdication of responsibility, the human being is the sinner by a negative response. But whether the choice is positive (faith and being-in-the-love and life of God) or negative (unbelief) there is residual (formal) *imago Dei* because by being responsible man is distinguished from other creatures.

6 Ibid., pp. 67f.

7 Ibid., pp. 67–68. Because the *imago Dei* is primarily the relational response of faith to God and existence under the gospel (being-in-the-love of God and the eternal life) which are both being restored in Christ, there is little connection between creativity as such and this likeness to God. Historical creativity does not constitute the true quality of man but rootedness in relation to God does. Yet creativity can take place outside this relational context, and it can, in fact, supplant God and put itself in God's place with all inhuman consequences that would ensue.

8 Ibid., p. 60.

9 Franklin Sherman, "God as Creative Artist," in *Dialog* (Vol. 3, Autumn 1964), p. 287.

10 Ibid. He admits that his thinking is inspired by Berdyaev's "ethics of creativeness" which transcends not only "ethics of law" but also "ethics of redemption."

11 Kaufman, *Systematic Theology,* pp. 330, 345. He rejects the traditional understandings of *imago Dei* because they define man one-sidedly by a dominant characteristic while historicity understands the human concretely but also gathers these other meanings unto itself (pp. 329, 344f).

12 Historicity for Kaufman refers to a full human immersion in history as a product of history, who is shaped by past decisions, who lives in the present which points to some yet undetermined and unknown future (p. 330). All finite reality, to be sure, is a product of history as man is, but, unlike them, man in created in an on-going movement of history which he deliberately also shapes and thereby carries history further. Man alone takes an active part in the creation of history, according to Kaufman; and that makes him unique. What is more, man, by acting as another being alongside God, makes history by producing himself. Humans make themselves and are made by history. They are produced or shaped by past decisions as well as by actions of themselves and of others. Kaufman goes to some length to show how human beings produce themselves and one another. An individual makes himself by taking certain decisions, or is produced by decisions of another, which determine what kind of person one would be in the future – such as a decision to become a doctor, or parents' decisions to emigrate to another country. He concludes by saying that human beings are *imago Dei,* which is the same thing as historicity, by their ability to produce themselves in a manner no other creature does. Like God who comes or proceeded from God-self and created Himself so humans also create themselves by coming from themselves, thereby imitating God's *aseity.* For a clear statement of historicity, cf. Kaufman, *Systematic Theology,* pp. 332-335, 337f, 341–347.

13 Kaufman drew my attention to his *Systematic Theology,* chaps. 19–20, where he discusses the creation of human beings and their purpose in life, as "laborers together with God." Therefore, my statement must be radically qualified, for he does suggest reasons why human beings became co-creators. In these two chapters, he discusses the evolution of humans from mammals to the present stage of their historicity, which began with the creation of language and other symbols by which past memories were preserved while the future could be projected imaginatively. He tells us that the first history began with evolution from "non-being" to "being" with *reproductive powers* or the capacity to organize and transform the environment according to human needs (p. 276). This took many years (pp. 266, 277). This is the second stage of historical development. The third stage is an appearance of another intrinsically historical being within history. The first two stages are historical but God alone was active; first in the evolution from non-being, and second in the creation of life, an emergence of being with reproductive powers. The third is different qualitatively because humans, like God, are able to set purposes for themselves, decide, act and achieve their goals, and transform themselves. Here relations begin to be complicated because humans further God's history only where their actions coincide with divine plans. But where this is not

the case, humans disrupt the divine plans, creating tensions (pp. 279f). Also, humans continue to depend upon God for life and sustenance without which they could not engage in works that either disrupt or continue creation. Their purpose must be to continue God's creation, and it was for the realization of the divine purpose that they were created (pp. 297f), namely, to contribute toward the historical process through which God's Kingdom comes. All this is fine and illuminating. It is unfortunate that Kaufman discusses the creation of man separately from his discussion of *imago Dei.* This creates tensions for, on the one hand, he wants to say humans depend upon the divine source for their being. But, on the other, he does not indicate that the human creative ability also depends upon that of God. In fact, he rules out the possibility that historicity itself (which for him is what constitutes our *imago Dei)* implies that *something special was added to an otherwise animal nature.* If *imago Dei* does not mean that human beings were somehow uniquely equipped, empowered, and granted creative ability, what else does? Was the emergence of human beings as historical beings *par excellence* within God's history something that could have happened naturally without divine empowerment? Does this mean that other species that evolved from mammals could very well become historical beings? Why is it that human beings, and they only, became historical, like their Creator? If other primates, such as chimpanzees and gorillas, could not become historical beings by virtue of latent powers that transform them in historical development, does this not suggest that much more is involved than a mere evolutionary process? One cannot avoid the conclusion that Kaufman did not ask these questions. For, as soon as they are asked, one cannot escape the feeling that somehow God's special favour was involved, and that this creative ability which humans have is derivative from divine empowerment; it is entrusted power that is not latent in us as such. But this leads us to all kinds of mythological language in which *imago Dei* will have to be specified with reference to God's empowerment of finite human beings so that they could become co-creators. Is Kaufman trying to avoid this mythological talk when he does not connect his view of *imago Dei* with the creation of man (pp. 276–279, 332–335ff, 341–347)? Yet, it seems to us that some form of mythological talk cannot be avoided if one is to give a satisfactory theological answer to these difficult questions.

14 Walter Brueggemann has inspired my formulation of the subtitle in this chapter by his invaluable booklet entitled: *In Man We Trust: The Neglected Side of Biblical Faith* (Richmond, Virginia: John Knox Press, 1972), pp. 24–47. There he talks about man as the trusted and noble creature. Cited henceforth as *In Man We Trust,* p. 21.

15 Brueggemann, *In Man We Trust,* p. 21.

16 Ibid., pp. 20, 23–26. Brueggemann states that people do not take themselves seriously enough because theology has encouraged dullness rather than creative responsibility and choices. It stresses that God is everything but man is nothing, and that human achievements are nothing. Theologians wrongly think that people need to be frightened off, scolded, belit-

tled, contained, reigned in and reprimanded, even though God values them highly (pp. 22, 25f). Barth and Elert do belong to this group which sees history and civilization as a revolt, a series of blunders of human attempts to run away from God's grace.

17 The analogy that comes to mind here is a parental decision to accept, at last, the fact that children are grown-ups and are capable of acting and making responsible decisions in their lives. This is a form of trust or faith.

18 LW. 2, p. 141. Luther knows of the creative God who is not jealous of human beings, but this God freely shares His creative power with them so as to enable them to be effective instruments of the divine creative will. Indeed, this God is unlike the One who, according to Barth, "cannot share power" nor tolerate little creators beside Him *(Church Dogmatics* II/2, pp. 517, 531f, 577–579 etc).

19 Tillich, *Systematic Theology,* Vol. I, p. 266.

20 Ibid., p. 256. Also see Bonino. *Doing Theology in a Revolutionary Situation,* pp. 109, 134; Kaufman, *Systematic Theology,* p. 333; Cox, *God's Revolution and Man's Responsibility* (Valley Forge: The Judson Press, 1965), pp. 19–44. Henceforth cited as *God's Revolution and Man's Responsibility.*

21 It cannot be stressed strongly enough that human creativity occurs because we act within the context of divine creativity which empowers, or entrusts these creative powers to us. Even though we are agents of creativity, it remains a fact that it is the creative command (fiat, word) in action which enables us to create. Just as we depend upon God to live and to exist, so, too, we depend upon God's creative power that is actively at work in the world. This means that we cannot, on our own, be creative outside the context of this creative power. It also means that, because it is an entrusted power that is not inherent in us, it can, in principle, be withdrawn by God when our mission as agents is no longer needed, just as God can freely withdraw the power to live. That this empowerment to create and become vehicles in the creation of history can be withdrawn is demonstrated clearly by the fall of Saul when David replaced him as God's co-creator of the history of the Jewish people. By extension of this logic, we can also understand the fall of the Jewish kingdoms in Samaria and Judea as a withdrawal of this entrusted power to be God's instruments in creating history. The same can be said about the fall of other empires, such as the Babylonia, Persian, Hellenistic, Roman, or modern British empire, when their mission in the history of the world was withdrawn and they ceased as communities and individuals to be co-creators of the world. Luther, who has understood this creative power as a trust, a borrowed power, speaks about God's "heroes" or "wondrous men" who are sent from time to time to carry history further by extraordinary acts. Their empowerment is more than the normal one and they do more, just as judges in Israel did more. But their power to act on God's behalf as co-creators of history is always an entrusted one. Hegel, too, speaks about heroes who are given extraordinary power to thrust history forward,

and they stand above the constraints of existing conventions; they are a law unto themselves. These people have a "special star before God" who empowers them to achieve great success (Luther), and they are "world-historical men" (Hegel) who serve the purposes of the Spirit and, like all human beings, they are at the disposal of the One who empowers them and can be subject to the "slaughter-bench" of history as soon as the goals of the Spirit (or God), for which they were appointed to do or create, are complete. See *Luther's Works,* Vol. 13, pp. 153–200; Hegel, as a good Lutheran, discusses the role of heroes in *Reason in History* (New York: The Bobbs-Merrill Company Inc., 1953), pp. 10ff, especially pp. 26f, 39–44. And Harvey Cox does not use the concept "heroes," but the choice of people who are empowered to create history bears resemblance to Luther's and Hegel's. Cf. *God's Revolution and Man's Responsibility,* pp. 21–22. Although some people are more creative than others, the creative command involves and empowers everyone who places himself within the divine creative context – as long as God grants this energizing power to those whom He co-opts into the ongoing creative activity of producing the world and history. In fact, non-creativity is inexcusable because God's creative Word (command, fiat) is addressed to and exists for all who are willing to be co-creators and God's fellow workmen (and women). And no one is too low or above the Word to be empowered, or used by it; for one's very life implies the ongoing creativity of the Word.

22 Just as the transforming power of the gospel is shown through conversions that occur, or its ability to transform natural elements into holy instruments, such as water (Baptism), bread (Communion), the transforming power of the creative command (uttered word, fiat) is shown by the ability of finite creatures to create history as instruments of divine creativity.

23 Cox, *God's Revolution and Man's Responsibility,* p. 20.

24 Ibid., p. 20.

25 A host of other creativities have been mentioned in Chapter Six of part two, especially the last five pages, where a brief response is made to Elert's and, primarily, Barth's views and estimation of the value of human participation in continuing creation.

26 Luther discusses these human attempts to order the natural and social environment for the well-being of the community here and now in numerous writings (cf. LW. 13, pp. 45–48, 154–200; LW. 14, pp. 50, 56, 114–123; LW. 15, pp. 35–39, 49–56, 70–74, LW. 26, p. 97; LW. 33, pp. 241ff; LW. 25, pp. 26–29, 109, 170f, 237; LW. 45, pp. 325–334; LW. 51, pp. 267–269).

27 John Wallhauser, "The Lordship of Christ and Social Change," in *Christian Hope and the Lordship of Christ* (ed.) Martin Heinecken (Minneapolis, Minnesota: Augsburg Publishing House, 1969), sees rapid social changes in the technological age as evidence that the natural order is amenable to the human transforming power given by God from hunters' community to the agricultural, from villages to urbanization and, finally,

from urbanization to the end of the historical process which, for him, refers to technological structures with their enormous potentialities (p. 62). Heinecken also suggests that creations of civilizations (including modern creativities that have resulted in the advent of the space age) in which humans are involved – as they try to work for more justice, equality, freedom and other means in order to meet human physical needs, as well as efforts of the United Nations towards peace and opportunities for all peoples – are indications that the divine creative law and its impulse toward creativity, through human hands, are at work. Despite the persistence of sin, the fact that creativity increases indicates that God's command, which itself is a power of creativity, is being obeyed, even if this is limited. Cf. "The Scope of the Lordship of Christ," in *Christian Hope and the Lordship of Christ,* pp. 80ff.

28 The moral implications of a creedal belief in the Creator who daily gives and nourishes life, who places me in interrelationships of mutual responsibility in a world which must be cared for and tilled, was suggested already in chapter seven (cf. note 65). Further suggestions will be made in the following pages with regard to the way in which the command could be understood as exposing human sinfulness, when we do not match up to the stature of the full humanhood God expects of us. Indeed, it cannot be stated strongly enough that God has graciously placed us within the context of divine creativity, one which empowers us to act responsibly and creatively towards other creatures and our world. Therefore, the Creator will find us unfaithful if we do not willingly become participants in this creative context which surrounds us and gives us power to be creative. For further statements on the ethical implications of the command of God, one which cannot be exhausted by interpretations of law within the categories of justification before God, read chapters four and five of the critique. There we argue that the obligations humans have toward their fellows should not be obscured or neglected, for God's command also requires penultimate goodness and righteousness which may result from the construction of just laws and structures that order life for the good of all. God inspires and empowers us for action *but we* must act and achieve this social righteousness before our fellows.

29 Cf. Brueggemann, *In Man We Trust,* p. 26f; Bonino, *Doing Theology in a Revolutionary Situation,* pp. 109, 134; Wingren, *Creation and Law,* pp. 93–106; Manas Buthelezi, "The Theological Meaning of True Humanity," in *The Challenge of Black Theology in South Africa,* (ed.) Basil Moore (Atlanta, Georgia; John Knox Press, 1974), pp. 94–97.

30 Brunner is justified in correlating irresponsibility with divinization of the finite order where inhumanity both replaces true humanity and puts the finite creatures in the place of God. Cf. *Creation and Redemption,* pp. 67f. Indeed, true humanity and responsibility before God are not mutually exclusive.

31 Luther concurs with Brunner and says that creatures must be seen as finite things given for our use rather than as gods to be worshipped, feared and respected, while God is forgotten. "Let us use bread, wine, clothing, gold, etc., but not worship them," adds Luther (cf. LW. 26, pp. 95–96).

32 Cox, *God's Revolution and Man's Responsibility,* pp. 39, 43–45.

33 Ibid., p. 44.

34 Ibid., pp. 39f, 43–44f.

35 This is Brunner's point who rightly points out that untrammelled intoxication with civilization and technology when it is not subject to a higher power and responsibility under God leads to perversion and inhumanity to humans. Cf. *Creation and Redemption,* Vol. II, pp. 67–68. Indeed, irresponsible use of creative ability leads to corruption and distortions through which "man, like a blind Samson, is, in the very strength of his historicity, pulling down the temple in which he stands ..... thus destroying himself." (Kaufman, *Systematic Theology,* pp. 343, 349). Kaufman also calls irresponsibility sin (p. 343).

36 John S. Mbiti, "Christianity and African Culture," in *Journal of Theology for Southern Africa* (No. 20, September 1977), p. 31.

37 Theologians should be grateful for the emergence of environmental and other groups concerned about the use of our environment, the need to curb industrial growth, the need to control population growth, the need to clean air and water pollutions, to care for earth and seas through soil conservation schemes and laws, such as the United Nations Law of the Sea, and institutions that try to protect endangered species among lower animals. Laws will force us at last to exercise our creative responsibility toward the earth, a task long overdue and neglected because theologians have restricted the "civil use of law" for too long to the social at the expense of the natural environment and an exposition of a theology of creation which embraces the two spheres.

38 Gustavo Gutierrez, *A Theology of Liberation* (New York; Orbis Books, 1973), p. 159.

39 This is at the heart of Luther's ethics on the basis of which he urges all people to work and to be channels of God's blessings and to shun laziness (such as running into monasteries instead of working) so that each may share with others.

40 Cox, *God's Revolution and Man's Responsibility,* pp. 47–48.

41 See note 26 for elaborate references to Luther's discussion of civic righteousness which we must attain in relation to our fellows.

42 Cf. Kaufman, *Systematic Theology,* pp. 343.

43 Wingren, *Creation and Law,* pp. 93–99. He strongly suggests that by not serving other human beings we *rob* them of God's goodness and blessings to which they are entitled.

44 LW. 33, pp. 119, 175–180, 241ff. Absolute creaturely dependence rules out this possibility, as we have argued before; for they create only as secondary creators with an entrusted power which can be withdrawn.

45 Cox, *God's Revolution and Man's Responsibility,* pp. 21–22.

46 LW. 33, pp. 175–180, 241ff.

47 Wingren,*Creation and Law,* p. 99.

48 Ibid., pp. 47–48, 94–99, 102–103. Wingren expresses the opinion that God would be completely paralized were he to depend upon the goodness of human beings. Rather, the fact that God still uses them in spite of

themselves to do good, to serve others even in their ignorance and blindness, proves that God is God because he is not powerless before sin and human irresponsibility. We could not agree more.

49 LW. 33, p. 234.

50 LW. 45, pp. 331–335. Luther's certainty that we embody God's own way of acting, by becoming divine guises or Christ's to others, leads him to say that all people can expect goodness from us because we are commanded to do them all kinds of good. But, when this is done, praise must go to God who, by acting through humans, is the ultimate giver of good things. For when God's love is radiated in human acts, a sharp line between where divine acts stop and where human acts take over cannot be neatly drawn. We find his observations very insightful.

51 LW. 46, pp. 99f.

52 Ibid., p. 100.

53 LW. 51, pp. 260–274, 299. Luther adds that if we were faithful in placing ourselves within God's overall creativity and power, and at the service of one another as God works through us as divine masks, the world would be full of services and of God.

54 Ibid., pp. 260–273, 299.

55 LW. 46, p. 100. Luther talks about two righteousnesses: faith-righteousness or Christian righteousness and social righteousness. How many know that their social righteousness is also God's righteousness? If we took this seriously, our actions would be revolutionary.

56 Cf. Bonino. *Doing Theology in a Revolutionary Situation*, p. 109.

57 The Psalmist sings a hymn to God for letting human beings embody God in their relation to other creatures; they are little gods (Ps. 8:4–9).

Chapter nine

Summary and prospect: law in the light of the coming kingdom

It is about time now to bring the discussion to an end by summing up the major aspects of this investigation. Our concern here has been to outline and construct an alternative theological understanding of the command of God. It is an understanding that, in our opinion, is much more comprehensive and broadly defined, more positive and well-grounded in the dynamics of the divine creative will itself. Not only does it promise to overcome major weaknesses and inadequacies that haunt the theological positions of Barth and Elert – as indicated in the critique and in several other places – but this understanding also does justice to the emphases of the theological use of law (which deal with human justification before God) by taking them up unto itself, while at the same time the positive elements of the social, or civic, uses of law (dealing with human righteousness before other humans) are also given their necessary expression and emphasis.

An attempt was made to ground this understanding of the command (understood as creative *logos)* in the essentially dynamic and creative holy will of sovereign love, that inner being or quality of the Creator which is characterized by a loving willingness to bestow life on finite creatures and to care for them with goodness, blessings, nourishment and everything necessary for their sustenance. In this attempt, we discovered that the divine command (fiat, Law which is no less God's word than the Gospel) is, in fact, the manifestation of God's creative power and activity in temporal existence. And we also found that this command gave, and continues to give, being and life to all of the finite reality, as the creative will of the Creator is directed outside the divine self and is thereby brought to an expression through the utterance of the creative Word. As a power and activity which embraces the totality of the creative process in history, the command is an instrument by which the Creator creates and causes all things to be; it also works in all, through all and over all creatures by involving them in the dynamics of the creative process wherein the world is being ordered, structures and produced as it moves towards its *telos*.

The other discovery was the fact that the divine command and its consequent creation must not be construed or understood as somehow independent from the life-giving activities and active involvement of God, the creative Speaker, in the historical development of finite reality. For when the command is viewed as independent from an active God who commands (speaks), the tendency is to reify the command and to construe it in such a way as to give the impression that it is "a thing out there" waiting to be discovered or applied by us. Moreover, creation may seem to be a finished product of some past event, and creation's absolute dependence upon the originating and sustaining creative activity of God in the ongoing creative process may not be given its due emphasis.

However, because creation is a historical production which, though it began with the inception of history, continues until *the whole* of history is completed; and because the world is a product of historical development in a dynamic, open creativity in which the command never functions separately from the active and creative will of God; it was necessary for us to take exception to static and reified notions of immutable laws (either natural law or revealed command).[1] By giving the impression that the function of the command (Law) is to restore the world to a "lost paradise" and to produce the world according to some past model (of what it should be), or to preserve a fallen (but finished) creation, these views tended to obscure the historical nature of an open process of divine creativity and the futurity of the world in the making.

Over against these views, it was contended that all creative productions of the world, both those by God "in the beginning," and those within an all-embracing context of sustaining creativity in which humans, as divine agents, transform their social and natural environment, must be understood somehow as an historical victory through and through. This victory is yet to be won, for it will be won only when the not-yet part of the world to be created arrives,[2] when the production of an undetermined future (of the outstanding history yet to be made) is complete and is what its Creator wants it to be. This leads us to an important prospect.

To talk about an uncompleted world, which is in the process of being made, and about its coming as an historical but future victory, that the power and activity of the divine command will bring about when the totality of the creative process of God and the divine agents reaches its goal, is to suggest that Law (command, fiat, creative word)[3] should be understood in the light of its *telos,* the completion of creation in the *eschaton* or the coming of the Kingdom of God. This, of course, requires some connection between this world and the next because God, the Creator, is the creative agent in both. Indeed, we must argue with Bring that "it is *this* world, the created order as we know it, which is to be changed and which is to be given new and imperishable form,"[4] because the world is destined for life, and this destiny "cannot be reversed even by sin." But to say just this goes against a reactionary theology which, in its rejection of the Social Gospel's suggestions regarding progress in humanity or an evolutionary progress of the natural order, so stresses the difference between this world and the next that no connection seems possible.

A clear representative of this dualism is Nürnberger, who argues that human beings must participate in changing structures but then turns around and tells us that we should not imagine that, by using our brains and imagination as partners in creating the world, we are building the coming Kingdom which God alone can bring. Further, he adds that the world is destined to "death and destruction" because it is a patient "that is going to die anyway."[5] If this view is correct, namely, that God is going to consign everything to fire when the new creation takes over from the old, then human beings have to be pitied that their Creator could involve them in the mutual production of the world and history only to waste their energies, labour and cultural strivings by discarding them. Indeed, this would be a cruel God, taxing human energies so much only to reward them by rejecting everything. It may be true that human beings do not build or bring about the coming Kingdom, and that sin cannot be wiped out from what they produce, but to suggest that no connection exists between what God is continually creating now and what comes with the Kingdom is untenable.

Over against this, we must argue that human labour is not entirely futile, not totally unnecessary and inconsequential to the production of the world and history yet to be made that comes with the Kingdom. Indeed, human victories, human achievements which try to embody God's love in order to bring about peace, justice, righteousness, caring love and meaningful co-existence between human beings – no matter how imperfect, partial, relative and impure – are significant. They come about as God involves humans in the production of the world. Human beings are invited by the content of the coming Kingdom from the future, so that they may strive for better and better structures that may serve their fellows best and approximate God's own way of acting now and in the coming righteousness.

Were this not the case, God would be totally indifferent to what human beings do, and there would be no moral implication in their vocation as God's entrusted stewards, who must produce history in concert with their Creator. Our discussion above shows that God is interested in our becoming responsibly creative. The coming of the Kingdom is not entirely divorced from the present creation when its future (the outstanding part which is yet to be produced) comes with the coming new age, when the totality of creativity reaches its goal, and when the historical production of the world and humanity becomes a realized victory. Indeed, it is the victory which, when it is won, must not be disconnected with the coming Kingdom itself, for the content of both the present and future world is God's love wherein justice and righteousness shall reign.

This is a victory in which the demonstration of God's willingness to give and love will be more clearly visible in its perfection. This constitutes a victory over sin and distortions, oppression and suffering, pain and groaning of the entire creation, and is a victory over lovelessness, injustice, mercilessness and unrighteousness, all of which are common experiences in the present structures.[6] It must be realized that these goals are partially being achieved in history through human actions, despite limitations and imperfections, because God is presently active and creating in order that the world may be complete in the coming Kingdom. For then it will be clear that it is the same God and the same justice and righteousness in the context of creative love that are at work in both because the goal is the same. The only difference is that, in the existing structures, sin is not eliminated nor has God's love, divine justice, or righteousness been fully embodied. The media used are themselves just as sinful, imperfect, relative, particular and limited. This is true of the human agency as well as of the structures humans produce.

However, the fact that human agents are imperfect, and that structures are still oppressive and sometimes demonic, should not be a cause for folding our hands and for giving up in total pessimism. Rather, because the command of God with its divine power and activity involves us as we anticipate the future victory which is to be won, and because the coming Kingdom is already breaking in with its content and qualities of perfection, righteousness and justice for the poor and oppressed, and with its promise of the ultimate actualization of God's sovereign love, we should become even more dissatisfied with the existing structures and productions and transformations thus far achieved. And this should give us enough reason to strive even harder to create better structures to serve the love of God best as we serve our fellow finite beings – structures that should supersede the particular, limited and imperfect ones.

Moreover, because there are no pre-ordained structures which, as such, must be identified with the will of God and, therefore, must be viewed as unchangeable, and because no structures and productions that have come to exist in the transformation of the world are absolute and divine, there should be no limits to the creative transformations of our natural and social environments. Indeed, because all structures are tainted with oppressive, sinful and destructive laws and forces of evil, there is no reason why human beings must be required to accommodate themselves to, rather than change and transform, them.

Indeed, in the light of the coming Kingdom, to which the totality of the creative process leads as this coming world invites us into its futurity, the content of divine righteousness, which is the enemy of the *status quo* (with its imperfect and destructive, loveless and unjust structures that are full of strife), should have a profoundly disturbing effect and transformative power which shatters and breaks down each and every thing that prevents the attainment of the victory that awaits us. When this happens, when all historical creativities are informed and influenced by the dynamics of the coming Kingdom and thereby drawn into its futurity, when the content of this coming Kingdom breaks gradually into the present strivings in which we are involved and allows us to participate in the coming victory – then, and only then, can it be expected that dynamic, positive, just, humane, meaningful and healthy social changes may be brought about here and now. And the result of such changes and creations of new structures would be actualizations of God's sovereign love, a love which, though embodied in penultimate, partial and incomplete victories in the human community through social justice, righteousness, caring concern and equality, may at last be channeled from one person to another, despite the limitations involved, in contrast to the final and universal victory in the coming Kingdom.

When the totality of the creative process, which is the sphere or scope of the activity of the command of God, is seen in the light of its vision, *telos*, the completion of creation, and the victory which comes along and, therefore, in the light of the coming Kingdom, God's creative command functions as no less than a prophetic mobilizing challenge to action, as a denunciation of the existing order and structures, and it also, prophetically, announces a different order of things, a new society. Indeed, it functions like a utopian vision that produces revolutions because human beings are dissatisfied with things as they are now, things that must be repudiated in the name of what is still to come, which is the best.[7]

Related to the *telos* toward which the creative process moves is the whole question of the content of the divine command. We stated several times that God's creative activity through the command has as its content the divine creative will of love which, because it is characterized by a willingness to give and sustain life, is found expressed in creative works. These works give both life and being to finite creatures who are the objects of this divine love. Also, creatures become agents in a continuing creativity, so that God's love, goodness, mercy and justice may be channeled to other creatures.

It is important to note that what connects the goals in this world and the victory to come with the Kingdom is their content, namely, justice, righteousness and love. In this world, they are attained in limited and penultimate forms while their absolute attainment comes with the Kingdom. Love is, however, the soul and impulse of the other two. For righteousness remains what it is because it is done in God's sovereign love. The same is true of justice; it is done for the sake of and in God's love. The core of both justice and righteousness is love. Victories that are won in this world, as limited justice and righteousness are attained, and those in the next world when ultimate victory is achieved, are all intended to let God's sovereign love permeate all, surround all, embrace all, dwell in all and be incarnated in all of finite reality. For it was for God's creative will of love and for life that finite creatures were created.

However, to define the command in terms of its content, as God's creative will of love, is to raise the question of the criterion and, therefore, the standard of creative acting. Indeed, it is to demand that the divine agents, who are partners in the creative dynamics with God, should act as God does, and thereby embody or incarnate God's own love which must be allowed to flow through them to others. This means that, unlike Elert, who defines the law negatively as retribution, our thesis is that there is a positive criterion and content by which actions can be judged with regard to their functional role, namely, whether they serve God's love. But, unlike Barth, who identifies the content of the law with the person of Jesus Christ, or the second person of the Trinity, as the form and content of God's command with the resultant problems that arise as to how any connection can be made between this command and other human laws, our thesis is that love as the criterion and content of the command is not identical with God as such. Rather, it is a quality or an attribute in the being of God that expresses itself in creative acts. And love is nothing else but the will of God expressed in this creative and loving manner.

As an attribute or quality of the power and activity of God, directed outside the divine self through the creative commanding, and thereby giving being to creatures who are also empowered to become channels of God's love, this creative love is embodied in those who are its repositories. Through them and through what they create, as the medium of channeling this love, God's creative love can be viewed as taking historical, particular, relative and cultural forms. Indeed, God's love does not exist for us outside the human capacities to love and be channels of divine love. It is found incarnated, as Gutierrez rightly points out, in the love of parents, spouses, children, friends, neighbours and community;[8] for their services, their creative activities through socio-political, economic and legal, administrative and other cultural undertakings, should aim no further than to be channels of justice, righteousness and, ultimately, of the love of God in which the divine will is expressed. To refuse to serve God's love is to refuse to embody God's own way of relating to finite beings.

When the totality of the creative process that the divine command brings forth is seen as historical creativity, through which laws and other structures are created so that they may become instruments to serve God's Sovereign love, the need to eternalize laws and structures is removed. They have to be seen for what they are, as human constructions *par excellence* that have to be judged by love as both the criterion and the content of the divine command or will. All structures, customs, mores, values, norms, laws, and all kinds of institutional structuring of interpersonal relationships should be evaluated and accepted on the basis of their functional usefulness, on the basis, that is, of God's love, which is active and must be experienced in its temporal, historical and social forms. And the need to accept them on the basis of their functional usefulness arises out of the fact that all structures and institutions, all laws and social mores — all of which aim at promoting life — are as imperfect, relative, limited and culturally conditioned in their attempt to apprehend and bring the divine creative and self-giving love to expression as those who create them.

Our previous discussion of the victory that comes with the Kingdom has made it painfully clear that these human, historical and imperfect incarnate forms, through which human beings experience love, are able neither to apprehend nor to exhaust God's love fully by means of any existing conceptual, linguistic and institutional structures. For this reason, love is not only the criterion by which these historical vehicles of God's creative love must be judged as to their usefulness, but also it remains forever an ideal, goal and victory to be sought after and approximated, as the existing laws and structures are evaluated, relativized, humanized, revised, improved, replaced, rejected and pulled down because of inadequacy or obsolescence.

Because God involves us in the dynamics of creative activity so that divine love may finally be realized, it remains always our task to bring about, construct, design and create or will the very best, just, righteous laws or structures possible. Indeed, because God's love has not been fully incarnated, the existing conditions should not be idolized, deified or always defended because none of them is divine, for they are all human creations. This means that freedom must be exercised in relation to them. We must control them and, where love requires it, these laws and structures must be overruled, changed, dismantled and replaced, so that they may serve their purpose. This freedom is necessary because, without it, we might become subservient to these historical vehicles even though they have not fully embodied God's creative will of love.

In the meantime, however, we must strive for the best within the limits of the possible structuralizations and innovative constructions of laws, because the *really best,* the ultimate and absolute victory, is still ahead and is still to be realized in the history yet to be made with God. Consequently, iconoclastic and innovative activities are inevitable until the best has been achieved.

The preceding observations lead us to the final prospect, one which is perhaps the most important discovery in this investigation, namely, that the command of God or Law (spelled with the initial capital letter 'L' in contradistinction to laws spelled with the initial lower case 'I') must be understood as a "limiting concept." This follows from several considerations: (a) The command of God in its expression of the divine creative will of love embraces the totality of the creative process. Not only does the Creator usher in history by creating *ex nihilo,* but also, in sustaining and transformative creativity, the divine creative power and activity of the command becomes historicized by empowering and involving finite creatures to be its agents and repositories in a continuing creation. The aim of this creation is to channel God's love through historical media in which God's love assumes constitutional and concrete form, thereby being experienced in a human, finite, and relative justice and righteousness that may be attained in society.

(b) Even though God's command (Law) is the power behind the totality of the creative process, it cannot be asserted that this creative power has been fully exhausted, encapsulated and realized in partial and limited victories often won in historical development. God's creative power is present there, but it also transcends present achievements. Like the Kingdom of God, which Christ proclaimed, the dynamics of God's creativity has present and outstanding (future) aspects. That is, the command of God, which constitutes the totality of the creative process, is both a present and a future victory. There are productions yet to be made in which the world and humanity will be completed and will become what the Creator wants them to be. This work is somehow a hidden production *(creatio abscondita, fabricatio abscondita)* from the viewpoint of the present. And, as we have observed elsewhere above, present structures, laws and orderings of the world are only a part of the whole structure of the world the completion of which shall be a future victory or goal yet to be attained in the unfolding of historical creativity.

(c) Because this whole structure (consisting of achieved creation and its outstanding part) is one which, when it is achieved after the totality of the divine creative process has run its course in history, shall be filled with justice, righteousness and ultimate sovereign love, the command of God (Law) should be understood as co-extensive with the fullness of God's love. The divine love, as it has been argued already, is the content of the command of God, or will, which is essentially creative, a command which both now and in the future seeks to be realized and consummated, so that God's fatherly heart may at last become transparent in all things. However, because it is a goal that has not been fully realized in the historical structures and institutionalizations, and because malice, injustice, unrighteousness, sufferings, oppressions, hatred and lovelessness must still be overcome by the content of the coming Kingdom, God's command (Law) should be seen as co-extensive with love; for both the command and love imply an eschatological dimension in which God's justice and righteousness in divine love will dwell and rule over all in their absoluteness.

As a motivation and power, involving us in its dynamics so that its future vision, goal, and victory can be fully embodied (when creativity is completed), the command of God is not only co-extensive with God's creative love but is also, as we have already pointed out, a limiting concept; for it is greater than the sum total of all human or historical laws, socio-political, economic-judicial, administrative-educational and other cultural creativities and institutionalizations in its eschatological and cosmic scope.

Barth, who appears to be aware that the command of God is a limiting concept, had a correct instinct when he tried to distinguish God's command from all other commands, thereby refusing to identify God's Law directly with the sum total of historical laws. However, he was wrong to think that the transcendence of Law, as a limiting concept, lies in some abstract law-in-itself, namely, the eternal Law of the Kingdom, Jesus Christ, whom human construction must reflect, mirror, listen to, exemplify, and reproduce in imperfect human form.[9] He did not realize that the uniqueness of transcendence of the command of God lies not in abstractions from the historical reality but, rather, in its futurity in which the totality of the creative process will have reached its *telos.* In this *telos,* the command of God, to be sure, will be co-extensive with God's love, but it is a *telos* that is a historical victory won by the creative God who struggles against all odds to bring the world to its completion in the coming Kingdom.

There is no suprahistorical law that must be reproduced. All laws are historical, just as creation is a historical activity and the production of God in mutual concert with human agents. And all historical laws and structures are human constructions, as we have already observed, that are but building blocks in a continuing creativity. But, in themselves, they do not exhaust the breadth and comprehensive nature of the command (Law) of God as revealed in its outstanding futurity and creativity, both of which transcend finite comprehension (Is. 9:2–7; 11:2–9; 35:5–10; Rev. 11:15–18; 21:1–7, 22–27; 22:3–5). Even if human beings must and can aspire after the vision of the victory of the coming Kingdom and its ideal, only God can bring about this outstanding actualization of the divine creative love. For, indeed, what the totality of the creative process (which constitutes God's command) brings about is a city of the future that cannot be identified with what has been achieved thus far.

The analogy that comes to mind is the Gospel, which can also be construed as a "limiting concept." It embraces the entirety of the redemptive process, beginning with the death and resurrection of Jesus Christ, the news about forgiveness which is proclaimed, conversions that take place, sermons, liturgies, theological reflections, baptisms, and the Holy Supper, and the promise of comprehensive future salvation that is partly being experienced. There is a sense in which the Gospel is a present but also a future reality, and it cannot be fully exhausted either in sermons, or in one's experience or in theological reflections. Because of its transcendence and futurity, the Gospel is able to call into question present formulations or expressions of it and to urge for revisions and corrections which remain as a continuous and incomplete activity.

Günter Krusche's discussion of "human rights" comes closest to our position here. He argues that "human rights," as a limiting value (we would prefer "limiting concept."), always points beyond the existing empirical realities because there is always a need for "more humanity" than is presently available. This means that the present achievements of some "human rights" in their particularity, limitation, and imperfect forms will always call for conditions in which the existing achievements are called into question. As needs are met by what is achieved, they awaken new needs that must also be met because they are an incomplete provision of "human rights." Therefore, we must forever continue to seek for ways toward a "fuller humanity" within the limits of the possible, knowing full well that "more humanity"can only be realized in the actualization of a future vision beyond these present particular, limited, and inadequate rights, that is, in the universal, all-embracing "human rights" which come with the Kingdom and its outstanding promises.[10]

These two examples should suffice with regard to the way in which Law as a limiting concept is used in this study. Because it is a limiting concept, Law remains an ideal, a victory, which is still to be won when the totality of the creative process has run its course. When this victory is finally won in the coming Kingdom, the Law will be co-extensive with God's love in its absolute and ultimate fullness. This victory is much greater and comes only after all penultimate and relative achievements through cultural creative activities have expressed themselves. Consequently, the command (Law) has to be understood in a dialectical sense. On the one hand, God's Law is transcendent of all historical conceptualizations and structuralizations by virtue of its future eschatological and cosmic dimensions. On the other hand, it is a historical reality that is found embodied in human, particular, penultimate, cultural and institutional forms in society because God involves humanity and stands behind its creative works.

However, because the Law remains an ideal, goal, vision and ultimate expression of divine love in its fullness which must be sought after, it is also something that both calls existing achievements into question and inspires, urges and motivates. It is a power that invites even greater creativities to approximate the content of the victory still outstanding. As such, the Law (command) of God, like creation, remains a promise. Because creativity must go on, and because Law is a promise and not a finished task, these observations constitute the basis for the preaching of the proper use of laws by the Church, so that what is achieved or produced may not be divinized or absolutized as if it were identical with the over-all embracing creative process that makes up for the command of God. Indeed, because all productions are human works in an incomplete world, human beings should be constantly reminded of the future and outstanding victories that must be won so that they may struggle for more creativity. Only in this way will the world and "more humanity" be at last what their Creator had intended for them.

It is to be regretted that theologians have not fully appreciated the fact that the command of God or Law is as much the definitive Word of the creative speaking of God as the Gospel with which it is often contrasted. Like the Gospel, Law is much more comprehensive than the sum total of the empirical laws in the legislative books; for it involves the totality of God's creative process. What is more, it is to be regretted that the participatory motif of God's involvement of us in the ongoing creative dynamics has not been given the same emphasis as God's involvement of the human effort in the redemptive process. Had theologians appreciated this, they might also have regarded participation in the continuing creativity in which God involves us as something that remains a task not yet complete, in the same way as the spreading of the Gospel.

Creation through the command of God is a promise rather than a complete and finished reality, as much as the final salvation through the redemptive Word is a promise. It is, therefore, time that theology addresses itself to the need for the involvement of foot-soldiers and missionaries in the divine creative dynamics and thus in the creative changes and social transformations of the world and existing social structures (embodied in laws and institutions), in addition to the involvement of missionaries in the redemptive dynamics of God and thus in the healing and salvific work through the gospel. In this way, the Church would move from being a rear-guard manager of "crisis" situations through relief work to an institution that equips men and women so that they might become creative innovators and initiators within the all-embracing context of God's creative activity through the law (creative *logos).*

Notes

1 Cf. note 4 of chapter seven.

2 Some theologians seem to forget that there is a sense in which there is a not-yet in the creative sphere just as it is in the redemptive sphere. As much as salvation is not fully realized but Christians do participate in the foretaste and hope of its coming, so the creative process and activity is born out of our anticipation and hope of the world which is yet to come.

3 The totality of the creative process in its originating and sustaining creativity should here be born in mind when Law with a capital letter is used. The significance of this will be clarified later.

4 Ragnar Bring, "The Gospel of the New Creation," in *Dialog* (Vol. 3, Autumn 1964), p. 278.

5 Klaus Nürnberger, *Dogmatics* (unpublished lectures, Mapumulo, Natal, 1971–72), pp. 92, 110, 127. The need to connect the old and new is clearly indicated by Paul who argues that the resurrection of the body was truly new but is related to the old and that were the two not connected, resurrection would not make sense because without bodies human beings would not be whole. Indeed, it is this creation which is groaning in trail but when the completion comes the old is not left behind but is made free for incorruption. Cf. Bring, "The Gospel of the New Creation," in *Dialog,* p. 278; Norman Geisler, *Ethics: Alternatives and Issues* (Grand Rapids: Zondervan Publishing House, 1971), pp. 179ff.

6 Cf. Is. 9:1–7; 11:1–9; 35:1–10; 51:11; I Cor. 15:26, 54; Rev. 21:1–6.

7 Gutierrez, in his *A Theology of Liberation* (New York: Orbis Books, 1973), pp. 233f, discusses the function of utopia in a manner that is very illuminating. It is clear that it approximates the prophetic vision of the Old Testament which denounces evil so as to mobilize people to action in the name of the maximum justice, righteousness and love they can attain for the benefit of the defenseless and the poor in society.

8 Gutierrez, *A Theology of Liberation* (New York : Orbis Books, 1973), p. 199.

9 Barth, *Church Dogmatics* IV/2, pp. 680–682, 711ff, 720–724.

10 Günter Krusche, "Human Rights in a Theological Perspective: A Contribution from the GDR," in *Lutheran World* (Vol. 24, 1977, No. 1), pp. 61–64.

Chapter ten

Epilogue: Barth and Elert revisited

The issues and concerns Barth and Elert raised in their debate are important. Therefore, it is proper that we should close this study by quickly returning to them. The main objective here is to state how the alternative understanding of law (creative *logos),* as expounded here, relates to theirs, and in what way their concerns have not been unfairly disposed of in a heavy-handed manner without also addressing them.

Barth's main thesis is that theological conception of the law must be grounded Christologically because there God's will has been indubitably disclosed and proclaimed. Consequently, Jesus Christ is the basis, the ground, the form and content of God's law. Any law that does not come from or point to Jesus Christ, who is the grace and eternal Word of God, has another source and must be rejected. Against Barth's position, we contended that no mileage is gained by suggesting that law be grounded in Christology because Christians have no special epistemological advantage over the rest of humankind. Further, we argued that Barth's claim that the command of God is given for the sanctification of man is unpersuasive because it is not the purpose of the law to save. Against Barth, we argued that law does not save but involves us in the dynamics of ordering, structuring and transforming the world. Moreover, to correlate law with justification and sanctification is to confuse the question of ethics with that of salvation. For here two kinds of righteousness are involved. The law involves us in the world for the production of penultimate or relative social righteousness in interpersonal relations. The gospel has to do with the vertical dimensions of human standing before God. The two need not be confused.

Despite these differences, we had to applaud Barth's insistence that any theological discussion about the law of God would have to deal with the question of both the content and the criterion of law. It is when the content is known that God's law can be distinguished from distortions of the law in various historical forms. However, Barth made a serious blunder by identifying the command of God with the second Person of the Trinity, Jesus Christ, who is understood as the eternal Law of the Kingdom. All other laws were simply human attempts to *reproduce* this immutable and eternal law by the Church and finally by the civil community, as the latter reflects on the Church's exemplification of God's law. The consequence of identifying law with Jesus Christ not only leads Barth to talk about the law in abstractions but also to create an unbridgeable gulf between God's law and historical laws. For it now requires miracles to enable historical laws to serve as garments or veils of the divine law, a law incapable of conceptualizations.

In other words, Barth is a victim of his own definition, a definition that lifts the law out of the immanental to the transcendental sphere, the result of which is that there are no continuities between God's law (which hovers above the historical and concrete law) and human laws. Yet in reality, no such suprahistorical law exists. That is, any concrete law is a human construction and is never a reproduction of immutable law. Barth has, therefore, failed to conceive of the transcendence or uniqueness of the divine law in terms of its futurity rather than in its abstractions. For God's law is transcendent of the existing ones because of its outstanding futurity and completeness which comes at the end of history.

The alternative construction advocated here addresses the question of the content and criterion of God's law in a different way from that of Barth. The burden of this study was to argue that God's command has a positive content, namely, the creative divine will of love. Law expresses God's inner nature, that is, a willingness to give abundantly. But the command should not be identified with any person of the Trinity as such. Rather, the command of God is that distinctive divine creative attribute with the power both to create and sustain creatures. When this power was translated into realities or actions, creation began, and with it history. God's command, therefore, is capable of being historicized when it assumes historical forms. The command of God not only ushers in history but also is the context and basis of all historical and cultural creativities in the temporal process.

Because God's creative word stands behind all human historical creativities, it is not possible to draw sharp distinctions as Barth does. For God's activity is continuous with the on-going cultural creativities but it is not imprisoned in them. Therefore, the divine law is transcendent of all historical constructions. It can call their imperfections and inadequacies into question and thereby call for changes. But this transcendence does not lie in its abstractions but in the outstanding historical victory yet to be won – a victory toward which the totality of creative dynamics move. Until we reach this final goal, humanity has to be reminded that its creative achievements (laws and structures) are still imperfect. They are tools and instruments to order the world in a long historical struggle; therefore, these tools should not be idolized because the best are still to come.

The position taken here is much more complex in its relation to that of Elert. His main thesis is that the law should be grounded in the "orders of creation" and in the gubernatorial activity of God. Of course, we rejected his static conception of creation and his correlation of the law with the Fall. This brings us to his basic contention: the law of God is the law of retribution in the strictest sense of the word. This declaration follows his contention that God uses the law to pass judgment of guilt. For, according to Elert, in the use of the law, God presupposes human sinfulness and thus law administers punishment.

By contrast, our exposition of the command of God not only questions the assumption that law is a means of salvation but also raises objections to Elert's thesis that God's law is retributive because we have not fulfilled its demands. Because we reject his promise, we have largely discussed the command of God in its first use, that is, the political or social uses of law. Consequently, the position taken in this study understands the command in the exclusively positive sense of an activity of God that is creatively life-giving. Law is thus correlated with the dynamics of God's creativity and is not based on the fact of sin or fall.

The question which immediately arises is this: Does the law of God still "convict of sin" in the position here advocated? If the answer is yes, in what sense does it differ from that of Elert? First of all, we wish to draw the attention of the reader to the fact that the law in our position has not been construed entirely within the framework of justification, because we do not believe that it is the purpose of the law to save or justify humankind before God. Therefore, we argued consistently that the content of human obedience to God's law has to be specified with reference to social justice and righteousness. It is in the horizontal plane rather than on the vertical that law has its place. It is limited to the ethical questions and productions of penultimate good, as humans order their world for the benefit of one another. But it does not follow that a discussion of law within the context of social righteousness necessarily implies that we dismiss as unwarranted Elert's claim that law may be seen as a threat or an accuser. There is no way that the command of God can truly function in the social sphere without some implications for human responsibility before God. For the social sphere is the realm in which God is actively creative and sustaining life.

So the first use of the law has its echo in the second use, namely, the theological use in which human standing before God is called into question. Because we act as those who must embody God's own way of dealing with the neighbour, our actions must of necessity be justifiable before God to whom we are ultimately responsible (as repositories of the divine creative power and therefore God's trustees) chapter eight of the constructive chapter tries to make it abundantly clear that creative responsibility before God carries with it moral implications. We are forever expected to justify our actions before the Creator who has entrusted us with some creative ability. The existence of sin and the continuation of oppressive and destructive structures, we argued, suggest that we have not lived up to stature of those whom God has appointed as divine masks or representatives in the world. The failure to live up to expectations means that in a sense we are being convicted of sin.[1]

While it is conceded that law exposes sin, we disagree fundamentally with Elert that God's law accuses because it is intrinsically retributive. His conception of the law of God which does not have love as its content, in our opinion, has no support from biblical testimony. Neither is it illumined by the message of God's redemption in Christ where God's willingness to give life was clearly demonstrated. The biblical God is far less demonic than Elert is willing to admit. God's use of the law there is expressly for the purpose of serving love because the biblical God is merciful. The divine command, to be sure, when understood in a strictly moralistic sense, does accuse because it reveals our ethical wrong-doing. It exposes our destructive acts in relation to others, thereby revealing that we are not what we ought to be, or what the Creator intended us to be.

When it shows that we are not agents of divine love and goodness, that we hurt, destroy and obstruct creative acts and, therefore, do evil, the law accuses. But this accusation does not come about because the law is inherently retributive, as Elert believes. Rather, the self-accusation, which results from the effect of the law, occurs when we realize that we are responsible before God for our actions toward other finite creatures. That is, our realization of sinfullness that comes about through the law carries with it a self-accusation (a self-accusation unknown outside the sphere of human experience). This accusation comes to an end when God forgives our sins. But to attribute retribution to law *per se* is untenable because the content of law is love.

In bringing the discussion to a conclusion, it seems appropriate that something briefly be said about the methodologies that were operative in the theological positions of Barth, Elert, and the one advocated here. This is necessary because the sharp disagreements that have surfaced here may be attributable to approaches that are essentially different. Without going into details about the methodologies used by Barth and Elert and, at the risk of oversimplification, a claim can be made that these two theologians, coming as they do from a deep-rooted German idealism (informed largely by Kantian-Hegelian traditions), are victims of methodological idealism. Put differently, their theologies are defective because they used defective methods that had strong leaning toward idealism that is incapable of becoming historically realistic. Consequently, the questions they asked, and answers given about humans, do not arise from their concrete encounter with humans being in the socio-political, psycho-historical cultural context. Rather these questions and answers spring from a human reality that is highly idealized.

It naturally follows that when they talk about the "new man" who is the addressee of God through the law or the gospel, Barth and Elert never think about a particular person who is rooted in a concrete particularity of an actual group or culture to which such a person belongs and is nourished by its language, values, biases, cultural norms (general ethics) and other social aids. By contrast, they usually miss the concrete, the particular and therefore the real person in their concentration on the "man" in general, indeed, some abstract species of Platonic idealism, who may be said to be beyond biological and cultural influences (Elert) and who is said to be able to bracket everything he knows about right and wrong in ethical decisions and thus has no need for social aids (Barth).

We have protested vigorously in the critique about this abstract portrayal of humans, humans who are idealistically believed to be products of no cultural influences, and who make ethical decisions "purely" at the instigation of the Spirit with no use of cultural aids and, indeed, who thus acting at direct guidance of the Spirit may reach ethical decisions that are solely, "unpollutedly" Christian, because these decisions have been arrived at intuitively without guidance whatsoever from a particular cultural ethos. It was argued that for those who take the insights of social sciences seriously find social life in its givenness more complex than methological approaches of Barth and Elert are willing to concede. We pointed out again and again about how frequently these two theologians ignore the analysis of the essential nature of human behaviour and its complexity of its motivation, for their thoughts were largely removed from the actual and empirical realities of human situation.

It seems reasonable to suggest that pre-occupation with the unhistorical and *a*social human beings in the theologies of Barth and Elert is not purely accidental. Rather it has to do with methodological claims of German idealism that has prevented them from a real encounter with real human beings who, in their concrete and actual existence, cannot be separated from a participation in socio-political history of a people. This encounter with real and historical humans would have been possible, had their methodologies allowed them to focus on the historical reality of human actions, the historical reality which has been brought to light by studies of sociologists, psychologists, social philosophers, and political scientists, etc. Unfortunately, however, Barth simply ignores the empirical data provided by these social sciences in preference of insights that are directly given by God.[2] Similarly, Elert would rather declare a war against the insights of all social sciences than enter into a meaningful dialogue with their analysis of the nature of human behaviour and psychology.[3]

As it should be clear in the critique and elsewhere, the position advocated in this study takes the view that theology should enter into a meaningful dialogue with all social sciences, because it is as it encounters their insights that socio-political naiveté that characterizes much of theological discourse in its discussion of the socio-historical dynamics of human actions in society might be corrected. Indeed, there is no substitute for a real encounter with socio-political analysis of human situation if theology is to talk realistically about human situation and what is possible in human actions aimed at embodying and manifesting divine love through concrete social structures (however imperfect and limited the achievement). Therefore, the methodology that we adopt in doing theology must be such that a fruitful encounter with secular sciences is facilitated rather than hindered if the results of our theological reflections are to be historically realistic and illuminating to the complexity of human situation. We are afraid that Barth and Elert were not careful in their choice of methodology and therefore allowed idealism to obscure their vision about what is constitutive of humans in society by looking past what is concretely human action and thus human reality.

To sum up, the position taken in this study shows that it is possible to construct a positive understanding of the law while, at the same time, addressing the concerns of both Barth and Elert without paying the heavy price they paid both theologically and methodologically.

Finally, it is hoped that the questions raised by this study will provide a starting point in the direction of a theology of social transformation, a theology whose primary purpose will be to clarify the role of humans in the dynamics of God's ongoing creative activity so that men and women might be motivated to become willing participants in the creative process for the realization of a future but historical victory which awaits humanity and the world. Also, it is hoped that others more able than myself will expound or express the issues and concerns that have been raised here in better ways.

Notes

1 See extended comments in subsection 8.2 of chapter eight. Law there accuses but for different reasons than those that Elert gives.

2 Cf. chapter five above.

3 Cf. subsections 5.1, 5.2, 5.3 of chapter five above.

Bibliography

PRIMARY SOURCES

Barth, Karl, *Church Dogmatics,* ed. Geoffrey Bromiley and Thomas Torrance, 4 vols. in 12, Edinburgh: T. & T. Clark, 1936–1961.

Barth, Karl, *Community, State, and Church,* New York: Double-day and Company, 1960.

Barth, Karl, *The Humanity of God,* Richmond: John Knox Press, 1960.

Barth, Karl, *How I Changed My Mind,* Richmond: John Knox Press, 1966.

Barth, Karl, *Eine Schweizer Stimme,* Zollikon/Zürich: Evangelischer Verlag A.G., 1945.

Elert, Werner, *Law and Gospel,* "Social Ethics Series," Philadelphia: Fortress Press, 1967.

Elert, Werner, *The Christian Ethos,* Philadelphia: Muhlenberg Press, 1957.

Elert, Werner, *The Structure of Lutheranism,* St. Louis: Concordia Publishing House, 1962.

D. Martin Luthers Werke, Kritische Gesamtausgabe, Weimar, 1883–

Luther's Works, American Edition, ed. Jaroslav J. Pelikan and Helmut T. Lehmann, St. Louis and Philadelphia, 1955–

SECONDARY SOURCES

Althaus, Paul, *The Divine Command : A New Perspective on Law and Gospel,* "Social Ethics Series," Philadelphia: Fortress Press, 1966.

Althaus, Paul, *The Ethics of Martin Luther,* Philadelphia: Fortress Press, 1972.

Aulen, Gustaf, *The Faith of the Christian Church,* Philadelphia: Muhlenberg Press, 1960.

Aulen, Gustaf, *Christus Victor,* New York: Macmillan Company, 1951.

Baillie, D.M., *God Was in Christ,* New York: Charles Scribner's Sons, 1948.

Bainton, Quanbeck & Rupp, *Luther Today,* Iowa: Luther College Press, 1957.

Von Balthasar, Hans Urs, *The Theology of Karl Barth,* New York: A Doubleday Anchor Book, 1972.

Bennett, John C., *Christian Ethics and Social Policy,* New York: Charles Scribner's Sons, 1946.

Bennett, John C., ed., *Christian Social Ethics in a Changing World: An Ecumenical Theological Inquiry,* New York: Association Press, 1966.

Blayney, Ida W., *The Age of Luther,* New York: Vantage Press, 1957.

Billing, Einar, *Our Calling,* "Social Ethics Series," Philadelphia: Fortress Press, 1964.

Bornkamm, Heinrich, *Luther's Doctrine of the Two Kingdoms,* "Social Ethics Series," Philadelphia: Fortress Press, 1964.

Bornkamm, Heinrich, *Luther's World of Thought,* St. Louis: Concordia Publishing House, 1958.

Braaten, Carl E., *The Future of God,* New York: Harper & Row, 1969.

Brueggemann, Walter, *In Man We Trust: The Neglected Side of Biblical Faith,* Richmond: John Knox Press, 1972.

Brunner, Emil, *The Christian Doctrine of Creation and Redemption,* Vol. II, Philadelphia: The Westminster Press, 1952.

Brunner, Emil, *Man in Revolt,* Philadelphia: The Westminster Press, 1947.

Bultmann, Rudolf, "Adam and Christ According to Romans 5," in *Current Issues in New Testament Interpretation,* eds. Snyder and Klassen, New York: Harper and Brothers, 1962.

Butlmann, Rudolf, *Existence and Faith,* New York: The World Publishing Company, 1968.

Bultmann, Rudolf, *Jesus Christ and Mythology,* New York: Charles Scribner's Sons, 1958.

Calvin, John, *Institutes of the Christian Religion,* Philadelphia: The Westminster Press, 1960.

Carlson, Edgar, *The Reinterpretation of Luther,* Philadelphia: The Westminster Press, 1948.

Cone, James H., *God of the Oppressed,* New York: The Seabury Press, 1975.

Cone, James H., *The Spirituals and the Blues,* New York: The Seabury Press, 1972.

Cox, Harvey, *God's Revolution and Man's Responsibility,* Valley Forge: The Judson Press, 1965.

Cox, Harvey, ed., *The Situation Ethics Debate,* Philadelphia: The Westminster Press, 1968.

Cranz, Edward F., *An Essay on the Development of Luther's Thought on Justice, Law, and Society,* Harvard Theological Studies XIX, Cambridge, Massachusetts: Harvard University Press, 1959.

Demant, V.A., *The Idea of a Natural Order,* "Social Ethics Series," Philadelphia: Fortress Press, 1966.

Dillenberger, John, *God Hidden and Revealed,* Philadelphia: Muhlenberg Press, 1953.

Dodd, C.D., *Christ and the New Humanity,* "Social Ethics Series," Philadelphia: Fortress Press, 1965.

Dodd, C.D., *Gospel and Law,* New York: Columbia University Press, 1951.

Ebeling, Gerhard, *Luther: An Introduction to His Thought,* Philadelphia: Fortress Press, 1972.

Ebeling, Gerhard, *The Nature of Faith,* Philadelphia: Fortress Press, 1961.

Ebeling, Gerhard, *Word and Faith,* Philadelphia: Fortress Press, 1963.

Ebeling, Gerhard, *The Word of God and Tradition,* Philadelphia: Fortress Press, 1968.

Ellul, Jacques, *The Ethics of Freedom,* Grand Rapids, Mich.: Wm. B. Eerdmans Publishing Company, 1976.

Friederich, Carl Joachim, *The Philosophy of Law in Historical Perspective,* Chicago: The University of Chicago Press, 1963.

Forde, Gerhard, *The Law-Gospel Debate,* Minneapolis: Augsburg Publishing House, 1969.

Forde, Gerhard, *Where God Meets Man,* Minneapolis: Augsburg Publishing House, 1972.

Forell, George W., *Faith Active in Love: An Investigation of the Principles Underlying Luther's Social Ethics,* New York: American Press, 1954.

Gardner, Clinton E., *Biblical Faith and Social Ethics,* New York: Harper and Brothers, Publishers, 1960.

Geisler, Norman, *Ethics: Alternatives and Issues,* Grand Rapids: Zondervan Publishing House, 1971.

Gustafson, James M., *Can Ethics Be Christian?,* Chicago: The University of Chicago Press, 1975.

Gustafson, James M., *The Church as Moral Decision-Maker,* Boston: Pilgrim Pres, 1970.

Gustafson, James M., *Christ and the Moral Life,* New York: Harper & Row, 1968.

Gutierrez, Gustavo, *A Theology of Liberation,* New York: Orbis, 1973.

Heinecken, Martin J., ed., *Christian Hope and the Lordship of Christ,* Minneapolis: Augsburg Publishing House, 1969.

Hertz, Karl H., ed., *Two Kingdoms and One World,* Minneapolis: Augsburg Publishing House, 1976.

Kadai, Heino O., ed., *Accents in Luther's Theology,* St. Louis: Concordia Publishing House, 1967.

Kaufman, Gordon D., *An Essay on Theological Method,* Missoula, Montana: Scholars Press, 1975.

Kaufman, Gordon D., *God the Problem,* Cambridge: Harvard University Press, 1973.

Kaufman, Gordon D., *Systematic Theology: A Historicist Perspective,* New York: Charles Scribner's Sons, 1963.

Knight, G.A., *Law and Grace: Must Christians Keep the Law of Moses?,* Philadelphia: The Westminster Press, 1962.

Lazareth, William H., ed., *The Left Hand of God,* Philadelphia: Fortress Press, 1976.

Lazareth, William H., *Luther on Christian Home,* Philadelphia: Fortress Press, 1961.

Von Loewenich, Walther, *Luther's Theology of the Cross,* Minneapolis: Augsburg Publishing House, 1976.

Løgstrup, Knud E., *The Ethical Demand,* Philadelphia: Fortress Press, 1971.

Moltmann, Jürgen, *The Theology of Hope,* New York: Harper & Row, 1967.

Muelder, Walter G., *Moral Law in Christian Social Ethics,* Richmond: John Knox Press, 1966.

Mueller, William A., *Church and State in Luther and Calvin: A Comparative Study,* Nashville: Broadman Press, 1954.

Niebuhr, Reinhold, *Christian Realism and Political Problems,* New York: Charles Scribner's Sons, 1953.

Niebuhr, Reinhold, *Moral Man and Immoral Soceity,* New York: Charles Scribner's Sons, 1960.

Niebuhr, Richard H., *Christ and Culture,* New York: Harper Torchbooks, 1956.

Niebuhr, Richard H., *The Responsible Self,* New York: Harper & Row, 1963.

Nürnberger, Klaus, *Dogmatics* I, Natal: Lutheran Theological Seminary, 1971f.

Pelikan, Jaroslav, *Luther the Expositor: Introduction to the Reformer's Exegetical Writings* (companion volume to *Luther's Works, American Edition),* St. Louis: Concordia Publishing House, 1959.

Pinomaa, Lennart, *Faith Victorious,* Philadelphia: Fortress Press, 1963.

Prenter, Regin, *Creation and Redemption,* Philadelphia: Fortress Press, 1967.

Preus, Samuel James, *From Shadow To Promise: Old Testament Interpretation from Augustine to the Young Luther,* Cambridge: Harvard University Press, 1969.

Saarnivaara, Uuras, *Luther Discovers the Gospel,* St. Louis: Concordia Publishing House, 1951.

Schilling, Paul S., *God in an Age of Atheism,* New York: Abingdon Press, 1969.

Schleiermacher, Friedrich D., *The Christian Faith,* Edinburgh: T. & T. Clark, 1968.

Siggins, Ian D. Kingston, ed., *Luther,* New York: Barnes & Noble Books, 1972.

Siggins, Ian D. Kingston, *Martin Luther's Doctrine of Christ,* New Haven: Yale University Press, 1970.

Tappert, Theodore G., *The Book of Concord,* Philadelphia: Fortress Press, 1959.

Temple, William, *What Christians Stand for in the Secular World,* "Social Ethics Series," Philadelphia: Fortress Press, 1965.

Tiel, Rudolf, *Luther,* Philadelphia: Fortress Press, 1955.

Tillich, Paul, *Love, Power, and Justice,* London: Oxford University Press, 1976.

Tillich, Paul, *Morality and Beyond,* New York: Harper Torchbooks, 1963.

Tillich, Paul, *Political Expectation,* New York: Harper & Row, 1971.

Tillich, Paul, *Systematic Theology,* 3 vols., Chicago: The University of Chicago Press, 1971.

Troeltsch, Ernst, *The Social Teachings of the Christian Churches,* 2 vols., New York: Harper Torchbooks, 1960.

Vajta, Vilmos, *Luther and Melanchthon,* Philadelphia: Muhlenberg Press, 1961.

Vidler, Alex R., *Christ's Strange Work,* London: SCM Press, 1963.

Watson, Philip S., *Let God Be God!,* London: The Epworth Press, 1947.

Willis, Robert E., *The Ethics of Karl Barth,* Leiden: E.J. Brill, 1971.

Wingren, Gustaf, *Creation and Law,* Philadelphia: Muhlenberg Press, 1961.

Wingren, Gustaf, *The Flight From Creation,* Minneapolis: Augsburg Publishing House, 1971.

Wingren, Gustaf, *Gospel and Church,* Philadelphia: Fortress Press, 1964.

Wingren, Gustaf, *The Living Word,* Philadelphia: Fortress Press, 1960.

Wingren, Gustaf, *Luther on Vocation,* Philadelphia: Muhlenberg Press, 1957.

Wingren, Gustaf, *Theology in Conflict,* Philadelphia: Muhlenberg Press, 1958.

Wright, Ernest G., *God Who Acts,* London: SCM Press, 1952.

Yoder, John H., *Karl Barth and the Problem of War,* New York: Abingdon Press, 1970.

Zahrnt, Heinz, *The Question of God: Protestant Theology in the Twentieth Century,* New York: Harcourt, Brace & World Inc., 1969.

Ziemke, Donald C., *Love for the Neighbor in Luther's Theology,* Minneapolis: Augsburg Publishing House, 1963.

OTHER SOURCES: ARTICLES AND ESSAYS

Braaten, Carl, "Reflexions on the Lutheran Doctrine of Law," in *The Lutheran Quarterly,* Vol. XVIII, February 1966, No. 1.

Bring, Ragnar, "The Gospel of the New Creation," in *Dialog,* No. 3, Autumn 1964.

Brueggeman,, Walter, "King in the Kingdom of Things," in *Christian Century,* September 1969.

Burtness, James H., "Life-Style and Law: Reflections on Matt. 5:17," in *Dialog,* Vol. 14, Winter 1975.

Carlson, Oscar, "Luther's Conception of Government," in *Church History,* December 1946.

Ditmanson, Harold, "The Call for a Theology of Creation," in *Dialog,* Vol. 3, Autumn 1964.

Forde, Gerhard O., "Lex Semper Accusat?: Nienteenth Century Roots of Our Current Dilemma," in *Dialog,* Vol. 9, Autumn 1970.

Forell, George W., "Can We Endorse the Barthian Ethics?," in *Dialog,* Vol. 3, Winter 1964.

Heinecken, Martin J., "Luther and 'the Orders of Creation' in Relation to the Doctrine of Work and Vocation," in *The Lutheran Quarterly,* Vol. IV, November 1952, No. 4.

Krusche, Günther, "Human Rights in a Theological Perspective: A Contribution from the GDR," in *Lutheran World,* Vol. 24, 1977, No. 1.

Lazareth, William H., "Luther's Two Kingdom Ethic Revisited," in *Dialog,* Vol. 1, Autumn 1962.

Mbiti, John S., "Christianity and African Culture," in *Journal of Theology for Southern Africa,* No. 20, September 1977.

Nygren, Anders, "Christianity and Law," in *Dialog,* Vol. 1, Autumn 1962.

Rieke, LuVern V., "The Comfort of Law," in *Dialog,* Vol. 9, Autumn 1970.

Scharlemann, Robert P., "Christian Theology and Law," in *The Lutheran Quarterly,* Vol. XIII, August 1971.

Sherman, Franklin, "God as Creative Artist," in *Dialog,* Vol. 3, Autumn 1964.